"Miracle of Words and Sight"

by Mr. Bibiyan

Secrets of the Iranian Revolution

JAAM-E-JAM Television's Open Forum

Manouchehr Bibiyan

Compiled and Translated by Dokhi Bibiyan, Ph.D.
Sponsored by Mona Tabib, M.D.

Library of Congress Control Number: 2010903293
ISBN: Hardcover   978-1-4500-6052-3
               Softcover   978-1-4500-6051-6
               Ebook   978-1-4500-6053-0

1.Iran—History—Revolution, 1979. 2.Iran—Politics and Government 1941-1979. 3. Iran—History—1941-1979. 4.Iran—Politics and Government—1979-2004. 5.Iran—History—1979-2004. 6.Iran—Monarchy. 7.Iran—Foreign Relations—1941-1979

This book was printed in the United States of America.

To order additional copies of this book, contact:
Xlibris Corporation
1-888-795-4274
www.Xlibris.com
Orders@Xlibris.com
73446

About the English version of the Book

This book has been translated from the Persian language into English so the people of the world and the Iranian youth of today who left Iran since childhood and or who were born outside of Iran and are not fluent in the Persian language, and the many bilingual marriages which have occurred whose spouses also are not fluent in the Persian language, are able to utilize these historical documents.

The translation is verbatim utilizing exactly the same words. The reading might not be very fluent in some segments in order to preserve the meaning of the issues discussed in the interviews to preserve the authenticity of the documents. This is the only book in the Persian language that, for the first time, its video, i.e. sound and sight, exists and in the very near future, they will be accessible at reliable research universities throughout the world, including Library of Congress of the United States. The text is verbatim from the videos.

About the Table of Contents

The list at the beginning of the book contains interviews with key figures who have been interviewed by JAAM-E-JAM many times, including the interviews contained in this book. The remainder of the interviews have been included chronologically to facilitate search functions.

Table of Contents

About the Interviewees:

Ali Amini, In the Shah's regime: Prime Minister (1961-1962); Minister of Finance; Parliament Deputy; After the Iranian Revolution: the first Opposition Leader against the Islamic Republic Abroad, Leader of the Iran Liberation Front.

Menashe Amir, Middle East Affairs Analyst; Chief Editor of Israel Foreign Ministry Website in Persian; Ex Head of Persian Services of the Voice of Israel.

Kourosh Aryamanesh (Reza Mazluman), Professor of Criminology, Tehran University Law School (in the Shah's regime); Deputy Minister of Education in the Shah's regime. Reza Mazluman (Kourosh Aryamanesh) was assassinated in Paris in 1996.

Shapour Bakhtiar, the last Prime Minister of Iran in the Shah's regime (Bakhtiar Administration was 37 days), Active member of the National Front; Opposition Leader Against the Islamic Republic Abroad, Leader of National Resistance Movement of Iran. Shapour Bakhtiar was assassinated in Paris in 1991.

Abul Hassan Banisadr, the first President of the Islamic Republic

Abdulrahman Boroumand, active member, National Front of Iran; Deputy Secretary-General, National Resistance Movement of Iran. Shapour Bakhtiar's deputy in the National Resistance Movement of Iran. Abdulrahman Boroumand was assassinated in Paris in 1991.

Shahin Fatemi, Secretary-General, Iran Liberation Front; Chair & Professor, International Business Administration, the American University of Paris

Daryoush Homayoun, Journalist; Minister of Information (1977-1978) during the Iranian Revolution; Deputy Secretary-General, the Rastakhiz Party (in the Shah's regime); Editor-in-Chief, Ayandegaan (in the Shah's regime)

Moshe Katsav, the Iranian-born President, the State of Israel (2000-2007); Deputy Prime Minister; Minister of Labor; Minister of Transportation; Minister of Tourism; Knesset Member

Ahmad Madani, Commander of the Navy and Governor of Khuzestan after the revolution

Reza Pahlavi, Heir to the Iranian Throne

Sir Anthony Parsons, the last British Ambassador to Iran in the Shah's regime; In the 1960's he was Ambassador and had many political missions in Khartum, Oman, Ankara, Cairo, Baghdad, and ultimately Tehran.

Amir Taheri, Journalist and Scholar; Author of several books on the Middle East, Contributor to many newspapers and magazines,

Editor-In-Chief, Kayhan International prior to the Iranian Revolution.

Abdul Azim Valian, Minister of Land Reform (1967-1974); Governor of Khorasan (1970's) in the Shah's regime.

Ardeshir Zahedi, Iran's Last Ambassador to the United States; son-in-law and Adviser to Mohammad Reza Shah Pahlavi; Foreign Minister; Ambassador to England; Deputy Director of the Point Four Program in Iran prior to the Iranian Revolution.

Marvin Zonis, Professor, University of Chicago; consultant to the various administrations, United States; former Director, Center for Middle Eastern Studies, University of Chicago; and American Institute of Iranian Studies (president, 1969-1971).

I dedicate this book to the pure spirit of my mother and father

Nosrat and Morad Bibiyan

The Miracle of Words and Sight

When first stepping onto the land of America, like thousands of other Iranians, my feeling resembled those of the first immigrants who after worriedly passing through the mountains, deserts, and high seas, could feel some degree of security and comfort. Nevertheless, the crushing blow that shook our country and suddenly disintegrated the foundation of its several-thousand-year history was too horrible for any man of heart and feeling to bear and overcome so easily.

In the beginning, when I reflected on the past, I saw that what I had achieved in the course of those long years had suddenly collapsed like sandcastles—my life's hard won achievements in ruin. And, from my achievements throughout all those years, through much endeavor and over many years of hard work, only my valuable experience remained that in this new era can also be successful.

Years before, in Iran, I thought of creating a path for a new music with young, new and different singers and presenting it to the people whom I knew wanted such change in music. For this reason, I established Apollon Music Company, which became a center for producing, recording, and presenting music and songs in Iran. This time also in a new land and in the beginning of the path which I had to commence, it came to my mind that I had to continue with words in a different form, and in a different way so that I could present my message more powerfully and more effectively—words strengthened by sight. Therefore, JAAM-E-JAM Television replaced the vast activities that, in those days, entitled Apollon, was the arena of the flourishing new music of Iran.

JAAM-E-JAM was established outside of Iran and for the people who wanted to struggle against the regime, the Islamic Republic, which had made them wanderers. They wanted to remember their country and its culture in exile; they wanted their children not to forget the Persian language and Iran; they wanted to have an important share in the political and cultural development of Iran, at least beyond its borders.

I did not consider a simple television network that would just fill the leisure time of people. We were not living or working in an ordinary situation and in those extraordinary times I set out the following goals for the new network:

1. Helping Iranians organize in Los Angeles; and later wherever the words and sight of JAAM-E-JAM Television reached them.

2. Establishing a Tribun-e-Azaad (Open Forum) for the exchange of various ideas and developing the spirit and culture of democracy among Iranians.

3. Preserving Persian language in a community whose youth is rapidly absorbed by American culture.

4. Strengthening Persian cultural activities outside of Iran, especially in the fields of theatre and music.

5. Aiding in the establishment of Iranian businesses and introducing business owners and institutes to the Iranian people in order that they could provide the public needs while at the same time stand on their feet.

6. Charitable and humanitarian activities, such as: the gathering of donations—and encouraging people to assist—for the treatment of patients whose treatment was not and is not possible in Iran, or those who did not have the resources for treatment, or those who escaped from the Islamic Republic—to the extent possible.

JAAM-E-JAM furthered all these goals in the course of time to the utmost extent of its ability. And we did not resort to any religious organization (i.e. church, temple, or mosque), and we did not resort to any country or organization. Only commercial advertisements have made possible the continuation of our work. We are proud of what we have done for the Iranian community and culture, but consider Tribun-e-Azaad (Open Forum) program that was started by JAAM-E-JAM as one of the most important services of JAAM-E-JAM.

In this program, political leaders and activists, and people of ideas and those key players who were present in the historic days of the year 1979, who had escaped from such a dangerous situation of riots and turmoil, were able to freely and without censorship analyze the past hundred-year history and the political events of our homeland from their perspectives. Also they were able to propose solutions to problems for millions of their compatriots who in any way had directed their hopes to these men who had made history, or who had escaped from a historic time or had crossed a direction of historic crisis.

This was how the dialogues with different political figures were broadcast by JAAM-E-JAM Television entitled Tribun-e-Azaad (Open Forum). These dialogues that in their own time caused anxieties are now regarded as historical documents.

Now that those waves, anxieties, rumors and controversies have largely receded, and many of those images have faded and vanished and are pictures on the frame of history, we see that only the words remain—the words that make history. The history whose pages have been turned with these very words until today, and whether willingly or unwillingly, is the political culture of a nation that in order to renew the past glory and find the path of civilization and progress has to place this light for the enlightenment of its future path.

On this route I had the valuable cooperation of so many political and cultural figures; I am thankful to them. But more grateful than all are the researchers who would benefit from this unique collection in the future, would know the value of the hard work that have been conducted for these interviews, as well as compiling, and editing them. It would be a long list to mention all those who in the service of culture and history of Iran who have collaborated with me, but I want to remind of the resolute share of my dear daughter, Dr. Dokhi Bibiyan. If she had not made the effort to compile these documents, the publication of this book would not have been possible.

I am certain that the contents of this collection which will be published in several volumes and its existing videos will be among the sources in writing regarding the past hundred-year history of Iran, and it will be considered as a reliable source by researchers and historians.

If these interviews were conducted and broadcast and if now are published in the same manner, with no interference whatsoever, it is because we are living in a free, democratic country that declared its independence by proclaiming and adhering to Human Rights and in which the First Amendment to the Constitution is freedom of speech. Everybody has given a name to America. I name America the refuge for wanderers and those who have suffered from disaster. Living in America is the dream of most people in the world, but even living in America has not been able to prevent the Islamic Republic from violating my rights even in this country. For several years, the Islamic Republic, realizing the popularity of JAAM-E-JAM, has been broadcasting its television programs outside the country by falsely using the JAAM-E-JAM name in the hopes of benefiting from its credibility, but, of course, people know better.

Manouchehr Bibiyan

from left:

Sitting: Manouchehr Bibiyan
Standing: Ramesh (Artist)

At Apollon office in Tehran a few years prior to the revolution

from left: Manouchehr Bibiyan, Executive-Producer of JAAM-E-JAM Television; Sassan Kamali (the Opener of the first JAAM-E-JAM Television program in Los Angeles in 1981)

Text of the Tribun-e-Azaad

(Open Forum)

Introduction

At the beginning of JAAM-E-JAM Television's Tribun-e-Azaad (Open Forum) programs, the following announcement was broadcast prior to the interview with every figure who was interviewed by JAAM-E-JAM Television:

Text of the Open Forum announcement:

Dear viewers, as we have stated many times, JAAM-E-JAM Television, in accordance with the pursuit of its own nationalistic goals, as a Tribune Azaad (Open Forum), is at the disposal of all compatriots. Considering this and to more politically inform all compatriots, we make efforts to make available this Open Microphone at the disposal of all people who have words to state. Again, we reiterate that the expressions contained herein are solely the views, political thoughts and opinions of the individuals who express them. JAAM-E-JAM Television's Open Forum serves as a medium for the communication and presentation of such views within the public at large.

About the Number of Interviews Published in this Book

The interviews published in this book are less than 10 percent of the interviews conducted in the JAAM-E-JAM Television's Open Forum—regarding both the figures who have been interviewed in this program which we could not include in this book due to page limits, and also the figures whose interviews have been included in this book have had other interviews and revealed other issues which exist in JAAM-E-JAM Television USA's archives. These interviews may be published in the future.

Ali Amini

In the Shah's regime: Prime Minister (1961-1962); Minister of Finance; Parliament Deputy; after the Iranian Revolution: the first Opposition Leader against the Islamic Republic Abroad, Leader of the Iran Liberation Front.

Ali Amini

January 24, 1982

JAAM-E-JAM: Before contacting Paris, we are going to review the Charter of the Liberation Front of Iran outlined in 7 articles.

Charter of the Liberation Front of Iran

1. Political campaigning for the use of all national resources to overthrow the rule of cruelty, corruption, and violence.

2. The urgent dissolution of all institutions of the Islamic Republic, and the abolishment of laws and regulations unilaterally made by the current government, i.e. the Islamic Republic. The restoration of law and order, and the rule of law; efforts to provide judicial

security; the restoration of prestige for judges through provisionary execution of the laws that are regulated on the basis of the Constitution [1906] until the current situation of anarchy is over. And, creating a secure environment that will enable the people of Iran to make decisions regarding their lives without any threat or corruption.

3. Restoration of the loss of the basic rights; respect for the Iranian people along with rights for various ethnic and religious elements. Preservation of the ancient Iranian culture and the replacement of imposed alien ideologies by the principle of freedom of choice.

4. Respect for the religion of Islam and the elimination of despotism of some groups which have imposed their own authority in the name of God, and have separated God and people.

5. Establishment of territorial integrity, independence, and national sovereignty. Avoiding the current political deadlock and isolation from other nations worldwide; adhering to international laws and regulations; and observing the principle of non-commitment in foreign policy.

6. Campaign against corruption and the misuse of authority in spiritual or material arenas.

7. Making urgent decisions on [the] rights [of the people of Iran]; using all opportunities for creating the best atmosphere for improving the poor economic conditions of Iran. Encouraging people to cooperate and express creativity; and Encouraging educated people who had escaped from Iran, to return.

The measures mentioned above will continue for a short time until the people will be called to approve the formation of a government. During this period the country will be run by a High Council including well-known, experienced, patriotic, and honest people—some of them from outside of the country and some from within the country. A strong government will run the country under the supervision of the council mentioned above.

JAAM-E-JAM: Dr. Amini, Iranians are impressed by the Charter of Liberation Front of Iran. Our question is whether your call is an invitation or you have been in touch with different Iranian political groups planning for unity and cooperation?

Ali Amini: As you know, last February [1981] I invited the different groups of opposition to the Islamic Republic to converge for a National Reconciliation in order to form a single group for saving Iran. Obviously, since that time my friends and I have been talking to different groups of opposition to the Islamic Republic explaining that the current regime of Iran, the Islamic Republic, is still in power due to the conflicts among different groups of opposition against the Islamic Republic outside of Iran. And, if they remember, I have told them that opposition against the Islamic Republic does not exist—as organized as it should be—outside of Iran. And, without unity of groups it would be impossible to do anything to overthrow the evil regime, the Islamic Republic. After negotiating with our friends, we decided to formulate a charter in order to gather different groups and persons under a common umbrella and at the same time to preserve their own political identity. In a united group no one is above the others and all the groups try to save Iran from the rule of the current regime, i.e. the Islamic Republic. It is obvious that after the country is liberated, and freedom and democracy prevail, the groups would be able to express their ideas inside the country and adjust their ideas to the needs of the people. This group, truly a wide-ranging group, will be a source of hope for people inside of Iran too.

Serious efforts must be made to attract the attention of the free world—to draw their attention to the cruel and continuous killings and executions inside Iran—and to indicate that Iranians have decided to move towards the liberation of their country, and as a result the name of Iran would not be forgotten.

Since this is our country, we should be the first to strive towards this goal. Of course, we have the expectation that they help us morally in order to be able to achieve success in this goal.

JAAM-E-JAM: Which political figures or which political organizations have joined you or this movement? And who do you expect to join you?

Amini: First, I should mention the name of Major-General Jam who has greatly contributed to editing the Charter and has promised to continue to cooperate with us in the future. Major-General Aryana[1] also announced his wish to join us last Tuesday, and we hope that Mr. Oveissi will do the same.

I do not wish to mention names of people [here] to avoid creating problems for them. A person who has courageously joined us was Mr. Nasser Qashqayi residing in London, and his son who lives in Paris. I really admire the courage of the representatives of Baluchis, the Kurds, the Bakhtiaris, and the tribes of Iran who play an effective

---

[1] General Aryana was one of the leaders of the Shah's military.

role in the collapse of the current regime, i.e. the Islamic Republic. They are looking forward to a movement from abroad. We hope they cooperate with the people inside Iran with whom we are in touch, to announce their policies.

Of course, the Iranians inside the country, according to the contacts that we have with them, they are preparing for the time when the political activities from abroad begin, in order that they too could publicly present their ideas.

And, meanwhile, I am sure that you have been informed that [Ayatollah] Shariatmadari has also announced his opposition to the acts of the current regime, the Islamic Republic, stating that these acts are against the Islamic laws, but to also show his definite support. But regarding the last stage and the final political activities to overthrow the Islamic Republic, he expects that this stage begin when serious support exists. And, I hope that gradually if we can truly strengthen our relations with the people inside the country, they will also join us.

JAAM-E-JAM: The question I am about to ask could be the same one that many patriotic Iranians, living around the world, have on their minds i.e. how they could participate in these movements?

Amini: I think we must establish a coordination center in order to make it possible for these people to send their representatives or to contact us in any way to exchange information and ideas. Since they are scattered around Europe and America, I think we should have representatives there or they should have representatives here so that we can contact them for further cooperation and activities. I hope we will, in any case, attract the attention of everybody by holding demonstrations and conferences.

JAAM-E-JAM: Would you please explain briefly the type of future government in Iran which you have endorsed, and whether it is compatible with the will of the nation of Iran? And, what is the plan of the Liberation Front of Iran regarding how the future government will be transitioned?

Amini: As it is mentioned in one of the articles, if the regime, the Islamic Republic, collapses, all its institutions and laws will go with it. During the interval, after the fall of the government of the Islamic Republic, the laws legislated on basis of the Constitution [1906] should be put into practice. What people want is important to us, and therefore the type of regime in the future—republic or monarchy—will be defined by people.

JAAM-E-JAM: Thank you for your kindness to give your time to JAAM-E-JAM. I hope we will be able to have more interviews with you.

Amini: Thank you very much for your kindness. I wish you success. The success of this movement and Front belongs to all Iranians. I hope that everybody will be involved in saving Iran. As I have mentioned before, my motivation in doing such political activities is not due to personal ambition, but to contribute a small part in this effort.

JAAM-E-JAM: Thank you. Together with Dr. Amini we say good-bye to our viewers.

Ali Amini

April 4, 1982

JAAM-E-JAM: Dr. Amini, considering that Iranians consider you as a powerful political figure of Iran who has maintained his status since the beginning of the contemporary political processes of Iran, and consider you as the pioneer of the Liberation Front of Iran, the first question is this: what positive results your plan has had up to today inside and outside of Iran? And, to what extent do you believe in the success of the plan of the Liberation Front of Iran?

Ali Amini: Thank you very much. I thank the gentlemen who have provided a means that once again I can talk with my own voice to the gentlemen who reside in that area [Los Angeles].

Regarding the question which you raised, the answer is that the principles written in the Charter of the Liberation Front of Iran—which encompasses the wishes of the majority of the Iranian political groups and figures outside [of Iran] and the supporters of democracy and freedom in the moderate and progressive elements inside of the country—has from the beginning been approved by a large number of moderate groups outside [of Iran and], well received by the very strata inside the country who have been addressed by the Liberation Front of Iran.

If some Iranian political leaders have basically agreed with the principles written in the Charter, but they have not officially approved it, [to reach a consensus] however, there are negotiations in process regarding the method of implementing it and coordinating the [political] activities in a unitary direction to overthrow the current regime in Iran, the Islamic Republic. This is a special priority. I personally hope that considering the speedy changes which has occurred in Iran, and pressure against the opponents of the regime of the Islamic Republic intensifies day after day, the time has arrived that agreement on general principles among all the political groups opposed to the Islamic Republic be implemented regardless and despite the personal differences which up till now has caused the delay of this undertaking. And, that discussion regarding secondary issues be placed aside so that disappointment among Iranians inside and outside the country does not intensify.

In any case, my friends and I have achieved progress in the direction that we have presented, and up until now despite the existence of limited material means, we have achieved progress. And, with reliance on more material and moral assistance from compatriots, we will utilize all of what we have in our power in order to achieve our goal, i.e. the goal of the liberation of Iran. And we are always ready to collaborate with all Iranians who think about Iran and the liberation of Iran.

JAAM-E-JAM: Dr. Amini, there are numerous plans, as you said yourself, put forth by the opposition leaders against the Islamic Republic. But in fact none of these gentlemen have expressed how they want to overthrow the current regime in Iran, i.e. the Islamic Republic. Please state your view regarding this issue.

Amini: None of these leaders can be solely the adequate means to overthrow the regime, the Islamic Republic. In my view, the establishment of the Liberation Front of Iran was for the purpose that there be established a political nucleus in the preparation of public opinion, and according to this measure the military plan and overthrow be organized with the necessary exactness and implemented in time considering the favorable [political] environment.

JAAM-E-JAM: How do you foresee the future of Iran and the situation of the Islamic government of Iran considering the current upheavals in Iran? Don't you think that if the current regime of Iran, i.e. the Islamic Republic, is overthrown there would occur the danger of civil war?

Amini: The current government, the Islamic Republic, with the loss of popular base, and its terror and daily killing of the opposition to the Islamic Republic, does not have legitimacy. It is not able to resolve the economic and social problems of the people. And, the continuation of the war with Iraq has become an excuse for the continuation of the government. Therefore, with the end of the war or the removal of Mr. Khomeini, if the moderate elements—with the assistance of the moderate clerics and troops—would not be able to re-take the government, the country would be faced with an extremist left or right government that at that time the possibility of the occurrence of civil war increases.

JAAM-E-JAM: You referred to a leftist government. Do you mean the Soviet Union? With the continuation of the current government and chaos which exist inside Iran, would not the direct or indirect intervention of the superpowers occur in Iran? Especially the very communist superpower?

Amini: It is natural that [in] the government of chaos, the possibility that the superpower which is closer to the country and has also proponents inside the country would benefit more [from the situation]. But the geopolitical issue of Iran, and the significance of Iran's independence and its territorial integrity for the stability of the region, results in no superpower intervening directly or indirectly and results in Iranians themselves considering their own national interests finding a solution to prevent crisis.

JAAM-E-JAM: Dr. Amini, please state as an Iranian opposition leader whether you endorse a regime of monarchy for the future government of Iran or a Republic?

Amini: You know, in my opinion if you believe that ultimately people must be involved in the decision regarding the type of regime which is appropriate for the future of Iran, and this to be implemented by the vote of the people, referendum now that Iran has not been liberated from the current regime, i.e. the Islamic Republic, is not right.

If I, who am the speaker of the Front, express my own personal vote, the slogans of the Front would loose its structure, and the Front would be directed in one direction—while we have wanted to plant the seeds of democracy and tolerance in the slogans of the Front.

JAAM-E-JAM: Considering the current political situation of Iran, especially the situation in Kurdistan and of other ethnic groups, also the news of the detainment of Ayatollah Shariatmadari which we heard and certainly you have much more information regarding this issue—considering these crises and upheavals and arrests of significant religious and political figures, what measures would guarantee the independence and territorial integrity of Iran?

Amini: Well, in my opinion the preservation of independence [and] territorial integrity of Iran is possible with the restoration of order and calm by the establishment of a democratic government that would be supported by the people.

I have no doubt, that the compatriot Kurds, Baluchies, Qashghayi, and other tribes, while seeking self-rule for their district—which is a legitimate demand and was also predicted in the 1906 Constitution, but unfortunately not implemented in practice and in time—are in total agreement with other compatriots in preserving the territorial integrity [and] independence of Iran. Ultimately, the will of the people of Iran will be the biggest factor [in] preserving the independence and the territorial integrity of the country.

JAAM-E-JAM: Dr. Amini, we congratulate you—while the political figures and political elite of Iran who are of your age are dispersed in the world and continue their usual and convenient lives, a political figure like you has created legend that for his nation, for the independence of his homeland, and for the restoration of his national flag which proves the Iranian identity, engages in political struggle and inspires the young Iranian forces to rise in the political struggle with him. We sincerely send our praise to you, and not only you, but those who have joined you, and have been influenced by your views and are in harmony with you for the liberation of Iran.

The last question: please state your views regarding what we at JAAM-E-JAM perform—considering that this is the second interview that JAAM-E-JAM is conducting with you, your views regarding this media and its impact in Europe, and generally outside of Iran. What is your view regarding the path and direction that we have embarked on?

Amini: First, I want to thank you for the good thoughts that JAAM-E-JAM expresses towards me. I think that anyone at any age, today when the country is in danger and has duty not only to him/herself but toward the next generation in this country, ought to truly with all power capability take measures for the liberation of the country. And, I truly appreciate and have admiration for those running JAAM-E-JAM that I am certain with very limited material means have taken this responsibility to guide the gentlemen outside of the country, but also to an extent inside the country in order that these people take measures to the extent possible for the liberation of the country with unity and solidarity among themselves.

Therefore, I have resolute faith and I truly hope that the gentlemen, with the help of God and the efforts which you have, succeed in Iran and God willing this sacrifice which I feel in you gentlemen spreads to other levels of Iranians outside Iran. And, indifference, which unfortunately in recent years prior to the revolution was pursued in Iran regarding the events of the country; let this be a lesson for Iranians outside the country that they forget this indifference and lack of attention to the future of the country, and think that life is not solely limited to an individual and it does not end with an individual.

The country must remain not for us who are embarking on the path of the end of our lives, but exist for our children and the children of our compatriots, and all the people who were proud of their Iranian identity, and I hope that you will continue your success and I wish the success of you gentlemen sincerely from my heart.

Ali Amini

September 19, 1982

JAAM-E-JAM: Dr. Amini, thank you for the message that you sent regarding the second anniversary of the establishment of JAAM-E-JAM Television. The first question is regarding the recent changes in international politics that have caused hope among Iranians afar from homeland. Do you also consider these changes as hopeful signs? And, what message do you have regarding this issue for the viewers of JAAM-E-JAM Television?

Ali Amini: Thank you very much for giving me this opportunity to have correspondence again with JAAM-E-JAM Television. I want to first renew my congratulations regarding the success of JAAM-E-JAM Institute and ask God that God willing there would be more success for this Institute.

JAAM-E-JAM: Thank you.

Amini: And regarding the question that you asked, because you know that the current regime, the Islamic Republic, has not in any way succeeded to solve any of the problems of the people inside Iran up till now, but rather day after day these problems have increased; and in order to cover its incompetence this regime, the Islamic Republic, has tried to create terror inside Iran, create the war with Iraq, and incitements in Islamic countries of the Persian Gulf.

Because today the Islamic Arab countries have established closer ties with each other, especially Syria and Iraq, there are hopes that there would be calm in this region. Of course, this calm would not be without impact on the future situation of Iran. Therefore, [with] this common factor that is the current circumstances such as war with incitements, I am hopeful that it would be neutralized, and this causes hopefulness. But on the condition that the Iranian opposition to the Islamic Republic outside the country would become more organized and unify some of their lines and set aside small differences in order to created more hopefulness for the people inside Iran.

But, the message that I have for the Iranian compatriots whether inside or outside the country, is that we are truly situated in a very difficult situation. And, I was hopeful, and I still am hopeful that we learn from the bitter experiences of the past, from the divisiveness which caused the misery of the country, and try ever more to set aside these small differences which in my view is truly small—and this is the only way that—with all the problems ahead of us—increases hope for success. I personally have always been hopeful and I am also now and, truly, the continuation of life for me is also hopefulness.

JAAM-E-JAM: Dr. Amini, we heard that your last statements have been regarding armed struggle. Please elaborate on this issue.

Amini: Armed struggle; which I confirm that for the overthrow of the regime, the Islamic Republic in Iran, which is governing with terror, it cannot be overthrown solely via propaganda. And since the first day of the struggle against the Islamic Republic, both my views and others' has been that we ought to create preparedness inside Iran in order that it will lead to uprising inside Iran. And, of course, it requires military assistance in order to restore order in the country—and, this uprising of the people of Iran support it. Therefore, I mean this armed [struggle] in this meaning, but I have always been against increased bloodshed and we are trying to ever more forge closer ties among individuals to prevent bloodshed.

Ali Amini

Location of the Interview: JAAM-E-JAM Studios, Los Angeles, California

June 27, 1984

JAAM-E-JAM: We have had several telephone interviews regarding different issues with Dr. Ali Amini, the former Prime Minister of Iran and one of the opposition leaders against the Islamic Republic. This time during his short visit to America we have interviewed him here at the Jaam-e-Jam Studios. In this interview, which lasted about 50 minutes, Dr. Amini answered our questions about the contemporary history of Iran including the causes of the revolution, the rumor of his differences with the Shah, and many other issues.

JAAM-E-JAM: Dr. Amini. Thank you very much for accepting our invitation and being present in our studios. We are living during a critical moment in the history of our country; surely what has happened since the beginning of the changes in Iran, i.e. the Iranian Revolution, has greatly affected the destiny of this country. Therefore, with your permission, I will begin our interview with questions about a subject of great importance to the people. Dr. Amini, it is said that in the final days of his reign, the late Shah offered you the position of prime minister, and that you did not accept his proposal—although people believed you to be a solution for the problems. Why didn't you agree to be Prime Minister and a member of the Regency Council?

Ali Amini: I am thankful to God for the opportunity to be present at the Jaam-E-Jam Studios for an interview. As you know, I have been interviewed long distance many times by Jaam-e-Jam, and I really appreciate you for that.

About the late Shah's proposal that I accept the post of prime minister, I must say that after 15 years distance from politics, I went to him [the Shah] and I talked to him for more than an hour about the country's past and then extant situation. Early in our meeting, I remarked that contrary to rumors, I did not intend to be prime minister. I said during the early stages of the meeting: "You have tested me and you know that I really am not eager to hold a political position. My only motivation in coming here despite differences and disagreements is saving the country and the regime." Of course, we talked about the past and I repeated the points I had told him when I was a prime minister [in the 1960s].

I said to him [the Shah]: "while I was a prime minister, you believed that you should govern, otherwise you would be deposed, and my answer to you was that if you governed, you would be deposed, and the regime will be gone with you. The situation now is similar to that time", I added.

I stated to the Shah: "I have come here and I am prepared to help in any way in order to render help to save the country from the extant anarchy and that I would not agree to be the prime minister under any condition." Of course, his offer that I accept the post of premiership was not proper, and because I had stated my disagreement at the beginning, he did not pursue the subject until the time that he appointed Bakhtiar.

The late Entezam was also present, and the Shah said that "because some people had demurred, we have no other choice but to proceed."

I said that "if the reference is to me, I had mentioned my opposition to accepting the role [of premiership] on the first day."

Concerning the Regency Council, I should mention that we had differences regarding this issue. I believed that, considering the fact that according to Article 40 of the Constitution [of 1906], the Shah has the authority to assign the members of the Council, my suggestion to the Shah was: "you should choose members who would be acceptable to the people." At that time there were some people, such as Sadighi, such as Bazargan, and other such people. "In that case people may endorse it", I said [to the Shah]. At first, he [the Shah] said: "these people are all my enemies." I said: "They are not your enemies, enmity is different from disagreement."

There were two theses: one was my thesis which was in the majority, and the other was the thesis of some other individuals including the Prime Minister, who believed that the same people, such as the Chairman of Majlis (parliament), the Chairman of the Senate, and others should take part in the Regency Council. I told him that "regardless of whether my thesis or the opposing one was approved, I would not be taking part in the Council. Considering that he is the Prime Minister and responsible for managing the country, we should approve his proposal."

Well, he [the Shah] approved his thesis then and asked: "why don't you participate in the Council?"

I said, "first of all, it is not among the political endeavors in which I would participate because if I want to continue my political activities, I cannot be in the Regency Council."

Dr. Sadighi also said that: "I also would have accepted if the Shah would stay in Iran and would not leave the country and, since the Shah had indicated that he would leave the country, I will not accept it." Therefore, we didn't accept it. And, other people were there too. Any time I recall this memory, I feel very sad; he accompanied Dr. Sadighi and I while we were leaving him. When we kissed his hands he [the Shah] said: "I hope we'll see each other somewhere in the world." I said: "No! I hope to see you soon in this country, with God's help." And, we said good-bye.

Thus, the matter was not one of offering me the role of Prime Minister, and such. I stayed there, of course this is not a claim, but I lost everything as a result. Once the Shah asked me, "will you go earlier than I?" I said: "well, would you want that I leave after you, but I essentially have nothing to do." In fact I had nothing to do, and of course, I am not sorry for what I did. I stayed there, all my life remained there, in order to try until the last minute to save the Shah's regime and unfortunately it was impossible.

JAAM-E-JAM: Dr. Amini, What is your purpose in traveling to the United States? Have you met American officials while staying in Washington? What was the result?

Amini: Well my main purpose, in fact, in the first stage, was to visit my compatriots residing in this region, about whom I have spoken many times with Mr. Bibiyan. I was really interested to let the ladies and gentlemen who live here know about our political activities—not only through papers, writings, and so on, but to let them see me. Suppose some of them did not have any idea whether Dr. Amini is alive or not; it is a good opportunity to show that I am alive although I am old. Well it is natural that on these kinds of journeys, some meetings may also occur, but allow me not to say about what and with whom.

JAAM-E-JAM: Dr. Amini, You have refrained from revealing some issues, including the issues that were discussed between you and the late Shah in the final stages of the Shah's regime.

Some people have said that the Shah discussed all the secrets of his regime with you, and others believe that there was discord between you and the Shah. Did you have complete information regarding what was occurring in Iran?

Amini: First, it is a big mistake that the Shah would tell me his secrets, because often he did not. Thus, I do not have any secret to reveal or try to refrain from revealing. Regarding your question about the discord between the Shah and I, of course, even if I were upset with the Shah, I never attempted to take revenge. And, the reason was that I always placed the interests of the country ahead of my own personal issues, and I had the same attitude towards people from those even much further down the hierarchy than him. So really there were not any differences except in the case of the Shah's main illness, cancer, which is a point to which many people may not pay attention that this illness had made him very tired and exhausted.

He [the Shah] once said to me, "I cannot sleep at night; I don't have any appetite. What kind of sleeping pills do you take?"

I mentioned a kind of sleeping pill.

He said: "I take various kinds of pills, but cannot sleep."

I said, "It shows that you are ill, but a person like you, who is at the highest level of decision making for the country, should be able to concentrate on his daily work. If I do not sleep one night, then the next day I have to make a greater effort to do my work, even ordinary work. Your work is more important at this critical juncture." So I suggested [to the Shah]: "you should appoint a Regency Council in accordance with the Constitution that you have initiated and amended. Thus, Her Majesty, the Queen, would be Regent. Your young son is also in his teens. You could bring him to the center of power and you would then be able to rest a little. In the meantime, you could be inside the country and not go abroad." The Shah said: "Won't it be bad for me?"

There are many things I would like to say, but omit because they are in the distant past and two to three months before the Revolution, I found him to be not his usual self. In fact, the events were unexpected to him.

"I never thought that that person, the people would be like this", he [the Shah] said.

I said: "Well, of course they are like this, because people have found an occasion; there has been discontent which has caused an explosion."

The Shah was confused due to his main illness—about which we did not know. This factor plus his anxieties, sleeplessness and other problems were obstacles to his making decisions.

JAAM-E-JAM: Was he informed of the dissatisfactions?

Amini: Well, I can say yes and no. Yes, because I frequently used to warn the late Alam, who was the Court Minister and was close to me.

I told him, "the situation is not good and the reports you receive are incorrect or inexact. Besides, you do not try to be among people to see what is going on. Although I am on the sidelines, I am in contact with people from the middle class." And, I even provided an example: "Do you know how much, for example, I, a former Prime Minister, receive per month [salary]? Eight thousand Toumans. You do not pay attention to inflation [not audible] so you are not informed of how the people live and this will finally lead to an explosion and revolution. And, you and I are in the same situation, and we will suffer the same consequences. They may hang me once, but they will hang you twice. But it makes no difference; we will all be ruined. That is the issue that we should take into consideration."

He said: "Yes, that's correct." And I said to him [Alam]: "so please tell the Shah about these problems on my behalf."

He [Alam] said: "At the current time, he will be upset."

I said: "Well then set a time for me to see him."

He [Alam] said: "It won't have an effect on him."

I said: "At least I will state it. Then I'll ask permission and leave." Of course, these issues go back several years. I continued: "Then I will leave like a refugee, but I cannot leave before I tell the Shah"

Well, you know of these issues that I sometimes mention in the interviews, and negotiations, i.e, unfortunately, we are all guilty and we are all responsible. That is why I said to Mr. Alam: "you are from a respected family and I am from a respected family too. We have a greater responsibility. People's expectations of us are greater than from others. So, we [not audible] responsibility. Well, I have been sidelined and, in fact, he [the Shah] has not been kind to me, but I am brave enough to go and state my views. Surely he will not insult me. Well, he is a good person, but you are mistaken, and later people will consider me to be self-interested and may assume that I am upset because I am not a prime minister any more."

In fact, some people thought that I would like to come back to the country and live there without doing anything. Well, my life is important, but I found that the country was being destroyed from the economic and social perspectives. The country was like a house being gradually ruined by termites and which would collapse, and it is not surprising, but unfortunately they did not deal [with these problems].

JAAM-E-JAM: Dr. Amini, It has been stated that the late Shah had been under the strong influence of Washington and did not undertake any initiative without informing Washington, and that his departure from Iran was a decision made in Washington. How did America suddenly turn its back on the Shah? What is the truth about what occurred? It is said that you are better informed of this issue than others and for this reason you never traveled to America after the changes in Iran.

Amini: Well, I cannot confirm one hundred percent that everything he said was by order of Washington, but it happened several times when the late Entezam and I were there with him that he answered the phone and then he himself said that it was Berzezinski. It was Carter . . . those who called.

I remember that one day, due to his respect for me, he told me that Carter had told him to "tighten power." In the meantime, he looked at me, expecting me to explain Carter's meaning. I said: "in my opinion he means that you are the King, you are the chief of state, now fortunately or unfortunately, every authority is at your disposal—do something. They cannot do anything; you should do the work. I think this is what he means."

I can honestly say I believe that he was against bloodshed, and he emphasized this in his commands. I even suggested to him: "I have seen great demonstrations in India. Well, they gather some of the leaders of the opposition in India and put them in prison, and they release them after fifteen days." I said to the Shah: "Your intelligence service is active in a way that people think if they are there, they may never be released, thus I suggest arresting some of their leaders and you will see that the uprising will subside to some extent."

The situation had not gone too far at that time. The Shah was not able to decide. He was really against bloodshed. He thought that if his successor attained power through bloodshed, his reign would not last long. To be just, it was a logical opinion, but I said to him: "in exceptional situations, one should take exceptional measures. You should immediately announce to the people on television that [Prime Minister] Hoveida has been lying to you and that he carried out such and such policies, and you have fired them and really do this. Then we will arrange a trial and instruct them to try them in some way. In this way, you may enable people to calm down. Otherwise, just changing people's posts will not be of help."

In such a situation, i.e., when one is depressed, one is not able to make decisions. All these are caused by a lack of decisiveness. Yet, if I say that America and others are not at fault, nobody will accept the idea. America, which is a superpower, like the Soviet Union, and others, cannot tolerate political vacuums. Well, they have interests in the world as a whole and we are one of them. As Iranians we have the right to say they carried out such and such policies, but to tell the truth, the blame is ours. All these intellectuals and others first came out in the streets. Different people joined them including government employees, the Bazaar merchants. Wealthy people joined after the workers and farmers. Anyway, I do not deny that—as I have said many times and still believe—we should forget the past. Well, if there were no faults, the Shah's regime would not have been destroyed.

Of course, there were many positive points, but even a small fault could have been crucial in causing the fall of the Shah's regime. Now, what happened belongs to the past, but I think that we must really confess that the blame is ours, and if he was at fault, still we are guilty to some extent because we did not clarify things to him. We should forget about it. Looking back may be useful to learn lessons, but if it is stated for the sake of criticism, it is not a good idea. These are best to be forgotten. Regarding dependence, it may be said in our defense that today not only small countries in the world, but even France and England depend on America. The point is that we should not be too strongly dependent, to the point that we ourselves become nothing.

At present, those who should save the country are we, the Iranians. Of course, we need the help of the foreigners in terms of political, economic, and future recognition. We need their help, and do not need to be dependent on them. Well, we ask what should we do? I believe asking such a question is wrong as it implies that the country is yours and you know it better than we. The mistake made in the past was that we waited to listen to them. During my political career as Prime Minister, neither the American Ambassador nor any other American talked to me or sent me a message about Land Reform. Not at all. It just occurred once, in connection with the Point Four Plan when they suggested that they assist with the Land Reform. They asked us how long it would take to implement the Land Reform. I answered that if we would have salary and work, it would take 30 years [not audible]. This reform should be carried out gradually because Iran has different climates in the north and south and in some areas we have water [shortage] problems.

The rumor that President Kennedy had insisted on assigning Dr. Amini as prime minister or the executive in charge of the Land Reform program as a condition for receiving financial help is not true.

JAAM-E-JAM: Dr. Amini, You have been on good and friendly terms with the religious leaders of Iran. Considering the fact the you stated that you were aware of what would happen to the Iranian people under Khomeini's rule, why didn't you take any measures to prevent this misfortune which was clear to you prior to its occurrence, and if you did take any measures would you please explain.

Amini: I had always had contacts with religious leaders of Iran, but after having differences with His Majesty, the Secret Intelligence Service began to report about my visits to the Qom's Scholarly Assembly. Thus,

I was even deprived of pilgrimage. By chance, a week after talking to His Majesty, I traveled to Qom to visit Ayatollah Shariatmadari and talked to him for some time. Ayatollah Shariatmadari and many others in Iran insisted on implementing the Constitution [of 1906]. The overthrow of the Royal Government, i.e. the Shah's regime was not mentioned. I told Shariatmadari to support this idea of implementing the Constitution and he said that he was under severe pressure and could not support this idea. I then went to visit Marashi. There was a misunderstanding. A group of young Mullas at the gate of Marashi's residence told me that he was not home. Of course this was not relevant to me.

He said: "Well, Dr. Amini, You stated in your interview with Kayhan Newspaper that you have resolved your difficulties with the Shah. What kind of differences?"

"Are you authorized to ask me such a question?" I answered.

"No. We do not accept the Constitution at all", he said. "Come into the residence and explain to us", he said.

"No, you come to Tehran and I will provide you a detailed explanation", I said.

I went to visit [Ayatollah] Golpaygani to express my condolences over the death of his son. I suppose it was his other son who came downstairs—he owns a hospital. He said that his father was sick and he spoke the truth. I asked him to send my regards and tell him that I had been here to express my sympathy on the fortieth day of his son's death. I returned.

Montazeri was supposed to come to Qom also, and at that time I took the measure and [not audible] Sharif Imami to free Montazeeri and Ayatollah Taleghani. I tried very hard to encourage other people to help me regarding this policy. In fact, I did not pursue these negotiations to derive any benefits for myself. I thought we all ought to reach a consensus and implement a policy. In this way my contacts with the religious leaders was interrupted and this continued until Arbaeen Day [a religious commemoration in Iran]. I was preparing to leave Iran. I went to meet Ayatollah Taleghani whom I had not seen very often.

After some discussions, I said, "Sir, if you don't try to solve the economic problems such as [inaudible], you will fall and be ruined."

"Dear Sir You have a doctorate in economics; economics is bread and cheese", he replied.

I said, "Mr. Taleghani, what you have in your house and in Mr. Sadr's house, [such as] eggs and so on—this is not my house—tomorrow you won't have even what you have now. If you don't implement this policy, then tomorrow what you eat today would be finished."

He said: "Well, why are you leaving?

"I want nothing to do with you. I am not going to collaborate with you. I have come here because I believe [not audible]", I said.

When I found out that they would like to misconstrue; in fact the Shah should have paid attention to the problem even long before Entezam and I and others pointed it out to him.

The conflict started after June [1963], when Entezam said that Alam's cabinet has shed blood and ought to be replaced. The Shah was upset and dismissed Alam, Entezam and others. Well, it would have been good if [the Shah] had paid attention. Even after June 1963, when I wanted to leave, I went to the Shah. I had issued an announcement signed by Farivar, Alamouti, Derakhshesh and I. It was against the actions of the Alam's cabinet in dealing with the religious elements and the people. Well, afterwards we spoke to the Shah about Entezam. I do not know what he said but surely he did not speak against [not audible] His Majesty. At the end of the meeting, I found out that His Majesty had been upset.

I want to say that in this case—while it was not necessary that I be the Minority Leader—many problems could have been resolved if I had been, because if the Opposition Leader in the government in the Shah's regime was somebody else, he might have followed royal ceremony in working with the Shah, but I wasn't like that. While I never used to be tough while I was working as a cabinet minister or prime minister, I always used to state my purpose frankly and directly. In fact, once Sadighi, after a session in which we were in the presence of the Shah, later had said to Entezam that "Dr. Amini speaks to the Shah in a such and such manner although he was a polite man." Even though Sadighi was tested at the time of Qavam, he thought that what I stated was impolite, while in fact I had stated to the Shah himself that I talk frankly and directly. In any case, what have been said to the extent that I spoke impolitely, whereas I said to the Shah himself that I am a straightforward man and state my purpose frankly. I told the Shah that I disagree with some of his ideas or actions, but my statement was interpreted as malicious. Well, in that country I was the Prime Minister. I was the Prime Minister working with the Shah.

JAAM-E-JAM: Dr. Amini, to reach your aims, do you still believe in the principle of national reconciliation and the cooperation of the opposition leaders to the Islamic Republic and the groups who oppose the regime, i.e. the Islamic Republic? Are you regularly in touch with Reza Pahlvi and Shahpour Bakhtiar?

Amini: Yes, I cannot say that I am in touch with them regularly, but even at Mr. Bakhtiar's house we had a lengthy discussion with a few of our colleagues and a few of his colleagues. There were disagreements—of course, I cannot say disagreements, it is better to say there were differences of taste—but in general, we agreed on five main articles. We agreed to cooperate and act in the same direction.

Of course, I am in touch with the young Shah. I called him before traveling and said I wanted to travel to America. I didn't tell him about my intentions and programs, but I promised to let him know about my political activities. We are in touch and I think that this is necessary. About Mr. Bakhtiar, I must say that we have different tastes and we must try to moderate these differences in order not to face difficulties.

JAAM-E-JAM: But is the relationship good?

Amini: Yes, very good. He trusts me. I said it is not enough to trust me, you should trust everybody. I mean we should try not to be an obstacle in each other's way. If you remember, some people opposed the idea of National Reconciliation. I still believe that without the help of the people and elements inside the country, it is impossible to liberate Iran. We believe that there must be national reconciliation; a transitional cabinet must be established and include both those who are inside and outside Iran. If you consider only internal elements, well they cooperated with Khomeini, and these people also accuse those in exile of having cooperated with the Shah. If this situation continues, and there is no national reconciliation, then the reconstruction of Iran will be impossible. Reaching this aim necessitates a generous reconciliation from all sides in order to reconstruct Iran, otherwise revenge and condemnation would lead to bloodshed. There are some events we are not able to prevent. We cannot expect that one who has lost his father or mother will not seek personal revenge, but in our government program or in the effort we intend to make, we should really try to attract the confidence of people who live inside the country. Some people know the Mullahs as a factor in the differences between Dr. Bakhtiar and I and they think that the Mullahs won't compromise. I tell these people to let me deal with the Mullahs and you do the rest.

JAAM-E-JAM: Excuse me for interrupting you. We have heard that Dr. Froughi has come to Paris on behalf of Reza Pahlavi in order to arrange negotiations between you and Shahpour Bakhtiar, yet you say that there are no differences.

Amini: No. Mr. Froughi came to Paris but [not audible] because I had not seen him for a long time. I called him to come in order to know what he has done during this period and he came. But the claim that Mr. Froughi came to make peace between us is not true.

JAAM-E-JAM: Dr. Amini, You have repeatedly announced your views and your ideas. This time there is also an opportunity that our viewers be informed of your views about the future of Iran, the Islamic Republic, and the monarchy.

Amini: I take coming and speaking here as a good omen, because the situation in Iran has changed a lot, and with God's help, if we try we will be close to attaining good results. Well, you see the situation in Iran. I am not talking about the internal situation. The airplanes that escape and leave or youth who escape and leave and what they say; they do not come to just say to Bakhtiar or myself and others statements that we like to hear. Nowadays there are many people expressing a favorable opinion regarding the Monarchy and the reason is very clear; it is a reflection of a situation in which there is not any choice. It is either this regime i.e. the Islamic Republic, or the Monarchy. One must take into account that, for a country in this situation, if you want to elect the president and also the parliament, you need a calm environment. These people need at least one year to be psychologically calm because the problem is not only addiction to alcohol and opium, but suffocation, and the psychological atmosphere which exists there is terrible. How can you establish a republic in such a situation? If we remember, you are surely too young for that, Reza Shah also wanted to establish a republic; at that time, Modarres and some others disagreed and said: Monarchy. Thus, Monarchy in Iran is a matter of tradition and choosing to be a republic, regardless of whether it is called a People's or Islamic Republic—to the people it is the same regime that they have now.

JAAM-E-JAM: A monarchy as it was before?

Amini: Not at all. Even the king himself, Reza Pahlavi, has mentioned many times and has truly emphasized that government must be the representative of the people. There must be king and monarchy. In my opinion, there must be a Constitutional Monarchy. Fortunately, Reza Shah II has a suitable character. He is frank and not timid and shy. His father was so shy, and to some extent, his disaster was created by his shyness, but this young man is not like him. In fact, we are lucky to be able to coordinate our political activities with him. You know that Monarchy [not audible]. I do not love the idea of Monarchy, but if we think deeply, we will find that this system is the best way of saving and stabilizing the country.

We need Iran to be stable. For Iranian people, it would not be easy to elect a president every two or four years while lacking political parties and political education. Some people insist on the point that monarchy will lead to dictatorship. Well, look at all the presidents in the third world. Which one is not a dictator? Most of them are military people and then become civilians. Thus, if Iranians think realistically about politics, the problem will be fully solved.

JAAM-E-JAM: Dr. Amini, you mentioned in your speech that the current regime in Iran, the Islamic Republic, will be overthrown, but when? Many people are waiting. You have said that you will enter Iran—in an area of Iran—with Reza Pahlavi to overthrow the Islamic Republic. If this issue is not a secret, would you please elaborate how this plan will be carried out?

Amini: Excuse me. My view is that this thesis was actually initiated in my name. I believe that a person engaged in political struggle to overthrow the Islamic Republic must be present at the scene of battle, otherwise, the campaign will be meaningless. With respect to the king, I, like some other people, believe that there must be a safe place for this young man to go, otherwise he will be killed. We must publicize in such a way that people will believe there is no alternative except Monarchy. That means if a military man will govern—no doubt military people should take part—he should not act as a claimer to the throne but rather work for the Monarchy, even in the absence of the King. We must strengthen this phenomenon so much that people would not accept rival claimants to power.

I said to the Shah: "they say that they even prefer "Shemr" rather than this regime, the Islamic Republic. Therefore, they prefer you to Shemr; that there must be someone there." They have called me and written to me several times.

I told Bakhtiar also that if you do not invite anybody to the opposition movement against the Islamic Republic, somebody will come and say: "I am here" [to join the opposition movement]. I mentioned to the young King, by way of example, that his grandfather [Reza Shah], while talking to my mother, stated that he had not removed the crown from the head of the Qajar Dynasty to put on his own head. He swore. It is a long story [not audible]. He [Reza Shah] had stated that: "I placed the crown on my head." I said to the King that the power is waiting for somebody to possess it; whoever takes it he would become Shah.

At the present time, if the people are separate and dispersed, where can they find refuge; to whom can they refer? There ought to be individuals—and I hope that there are—who are monarchists. And, if they want to come to power, they rule in a monarchy not for the Shah as an individual. We believe that the Monarchy suits the traditions and customs of the country. It is a stable form of government and from this perspective we can be assured that well, he would someday be able to go there. And, I told him [Reza Pahlavi] that "from the perspective of the law, you are not king, but you ought to carry the flag of Iran."

JAAM-E-JAM: What are his own thoughts on the matter?

Amini: He agrees with me. I said to him that he should make clear to them that he does not want to go and seize power, but if the people rise up on his behalf, he would go to Iran. "People should know that you would go and you should be determined", I said to him.

Of course, arrangements need to be made and we know that there would be, little by little. Our external influence is altogether good and we are trying to increase our influence as much as we can. And, at the least, the groups who are monarchists here and love the Shah, these people must pay attention that what harms the Shah is a return to the past, as it had been. This is impossible, and it will result in nothing but an extreme reaction. Therefore, in my opinion, these people ought to pay attention that if they want to [liberate] their country, and they surely want their country [to survive], if they truly consider monarchy as an urgent call for the [liberation] of the country, well, they should know how to create a monarchy.

I believe that if these people love their country—and no doubt, they do—and think that a monarchy is necessary for the country, I hope that they have gone through a great change in comparison to the past two years.

JAAM-E-JAM: Dr. Amini, I would like to mention that, from the perspective of the people, the activities of the Opposition Leaders against the Islamic Republic are currently too slow and ineffective.

The events which occur were they to be published would shake the world, yet the Opposition to the Islamic Republic, which should utilize these aspects, indifferently ignores them. And, the Mullahs' regime interprets these events to the advantage of the regime, the

Islamic Republic's. And, the issues are simply forgotten, including: hangings, killings of children, problems caused by war with Iraq, and the people who are escaping the country, the embassy employees who seek asylum, escaping in airplanes, and thousand of other problems that demonstrate the oppression that is taking place in Iran. These are signs to which no attention is paid. What is your opinion?

Amini: It is not that we are not paying attention. We are utilizing all means. I don't know if you listen to our radio or not, but besides radio, there are people who come and go. They frequently come to me here. The solution is arrangement. To hurry, especially in such a crucial matter, could—God forbid—lead to our failure. In this case, not only we, but also the country will be ruined. In such a critical situation, if people keep talking all day about their plan, it may cause the plan to be revealed. We try our best to gain publicity. Two or three Iranian officers came to Niece. Our friends there announced that they were 300 persons. A lot of noise was made; television reporters gathered, students went there and the police officers did not want to allow them to disembark. Anyway, I was busy up to midnight or maybe dawn to arrange food and a hotel for them. I paid for their hotel and expenses in Niece. I called a gentleman in Paris—whose name I don't want to mention. He answered that he was ready to meet their expenses relating to traveling and staying in Paris if a political group would write to him requesting it. Well, after I stayed there, wrote up the event, and submitted it to him, he undertook to pay the expenses and, as a result, the police permitted them to stay there. This is an example of the work we do. It is not easy, but if we had more possibilities, we would be able to work better and probably much better. I believe that for an Iranian exiled from Iran, 5 years is not so easy, but as far as international politics is concerned, I surely know that everywhere in the world is unstable. I truly believe that human rights what they do not believe in is human being.

JAAM-E-JAM: Thank you very much for accepting the invitation of JAAM—E-JAM Television and coming to our studio. Do you have any message for the JAAM-E-JAM Television viewers?

Amini: Thank you, it was an honor for me to come. You do not owe me, rather I owe you. My message has always been the same. I would like to say that we enjoy the greatest opportunity to do something; reaching this aim necessitates unity and harmony. I mean, as you know well, they curse each other all the time; they speak ill to each other; they speak ill in the presence of foreigners. I think that lessons should be learned from history in order to avoid repeating past faults and mistakes. Thank you very much.

Manouchehr Bibiyan's Interview with Ali Amini

Broadcast in Part: 1987

Manouchehr Bibiyan: Dr. Amini, the question that everyone is thinking about is, with the removal of Ayatollah Khomeini from the political arena of Iran, what will be the future of the country of Iran? Do you think that the Islamic Republic will continue?

Amini: In my opinion, until a successor in government is not found in Iran, or until an alternative is found, the death of Khomeini will be very dangerous for us. Because, currently, Khomeini is ill and his son, Ahmad Khomeini, to some extent facilitates this endeavor. But the existence of Khomeini himself has resulted in these government officials to avoid turmoil with one another. And we hope that while Khomeini is alive, an alternative will be created. After Khomeini's death, these conflicts will intensify. And no one can mediate between these two different factions. Because each of these two groups have power and this struggle to increase their power, they will eventually reach a dangerous point for the regime. For this very reason, I do not pray that Khomeini dies. But, if he does not die, while the current government is in power, a group of people believe that after Khomeini's death the Islamic Regime will cease to exist. I believe this to be a mistake.

After a period of time, maybe little by little, this issue—the separation of politics from clergy—will be created. But, currently, in the current state of affairs, it seems to me to be very difficult that after eight years that this Khomeinism has been in the minds of the people—not only in Iran, but also has influenced people in Lebanon and many other places. More than in Iran itself. This can not be extinguished soon.

Manouchehr Bibiyan: Dr. Amini, do you think that in the past nine or ten years the opposition's activities outside of the country has had an effect that will have a place in Iran's future?

Amini: I very much regret that I myself was part of the opposition. But what we were able to do is, to some extent, we identified the nature of the regime, i.e. the Islamic Republic, abroad; who they are, what they stand for, and what type of individuals they are, and that they are fanatics and fundamentalists and these are dangerous for the country's citizens. To this extent, we had success. But, in my opinion, our friends in the international community did not take adequate notice. Meaning that, instead of empowering individuals who are truly experienced and educated, they went after—I don't want name any names—people that were unwanted in Iran. [The Iranian] people do not believe in them.

Now whether right or wrong, this is the situation. But, of course, the opposition could have facilitated more activities, but it didn't. And the cause of it was this conflict between the differing groups of opposition outside of the country. All of them want to be chiefs, but first Iran has to be liberated, and a relatively stable regime must come to power. Of course, Iran belongs to all Iranians. They can go . . .

The opposition has not succeeded to inform the foreigners that they are truly effective or beneficial.

Manouchehr Bibiyan: Dr. Amini, if you remember, an agreement was signed between you, Reza Pahlavi, and Bakhtiar. But you did not follow up on this agreement.

Amini: There was no agreement between the Shah, Bakhtiar and I. But, between Bakhtiar and I, there was an agreement. We considered five principles and, unfortunately, despite my efforts that this be published, and Mr. Bakhtiar and I would present ourselves to the people, by television or by press conference, so that it would be presented to the public. Unfortunately, this was not the case, and I told him that a "Triangle Alliance" would be established first with the Shah, then him Bakhtiar, and then myself. Many Iranians truly believed. I don't want to say that this will 100% liberate Iran, but it certainly will encourage the opposition inside the country. For example, we performed such a test on the Anniversary of the Constitutional Revolution. When the people of Iran saw that Bakhtiar and I and the King of Iran ultimately agreed, the people in Iran demonstrated in the streets in our support and they gave a positive response to our call. But, as I said, because of the motives, it was to no avail.

I still have respect for Mr. Bakhtiar but, unfortunately, during this time, instead of sincerely cooperating with the Shah and I, he did not. And, in truth, I am not in a position to defend the young Shah. But I believe that he made every sort of concession so that this "Triangle Alliance" would reach results. Unfortunately, this did not occur and you know the reason why better than I. And you know better than I that in this part no success was reached. And, in my opinion, this was the only way that, little by little, the "Triangle Alliance" would have gained more support from many groups.

You remember that at the beginning of the establishment of the Liberation Front of Iran, many groups of people joined us. Our internal conflicts, which were again the result of not knowing what to do and ambition, paralyzed us. And I don't want to say that they had been destroyed, but we no longer had the power and the strength to perform positive tasks unless we review and we have the correct agenda. But, considering unforeseen events that occur, I don't foresee success.

Manouchehr Bibiyan: Again I will ask my question regarding the death of Khomeini and Iran post-Khomeini. Do you think that, after Khomeini, if an impacting event occurs in Iran, there is a powerful successor outside the country that can replace him?

Amini: We know no such power in Iran. But, with the new set of events that have occurred, it is possible that a group of government officials will reach consensus, although temporarily, because all of them are in a dangerous situation. Therefore, it is possible that they will reach a consensus regarding an individual who can preserve this system and prevent it from disintegration. Because if this system disintegrates, there is no telling what would happen. In my opinion, eventually, such an event will come to occur.

Manouchehr Bibiyan: Dr. Amini, there has been discussion that the people who worked in the Shah's regime, there is a group of people that believe that all of the orders and instructions were given and implemented by the Shah. There is another group that believes that the King gave no instructions and that the prime minister and ministers of the Cabinet made these decisions and it was the Parliament that approved the laws to be implemented. Which of these two is true?

Amini: The Shah himself had repeatedly said—and the late Hoveida also had approved—that we only implement the policies of the Shah. And even I, when I was prime minister, recollect that the Shah said, "I either have to rule or I will have to go." I told him, "If you rule, not only will you go, but you will take the regime with you." Because you are a king without responsibility. Officials like me, we report on the country's situation. If people are not satisfied with us, others replace our positions. For a hundred years, Iran has been administered like this. And the meaning of constitutional monarchy is this: that the king be without responsibility. Therefore, if something occurs, and they blame on the Shah, it is, in my opinion, the largest of betrayals. Unfortunately, the Shah believed that I have to rule, not reign. In my own time, whether I was a Cabinet minister or prime minister, I did my own work. And, sometimes, he was upset with me, and he would say, "Dr. Amini refuses to accept my words." I told him, "No. You have intruded in the day-to-day affairs of the regime, You have demoted yourself to prime minister, and even to the level of a common Administrator."

In my opinion, of course, the past is the past. The Shah had some positive attributes: he was a benevolent person, but from the perspective of monarchy, it would have been ideal had the Shah remained a constitutional monarch. But a king that has to govern, there was a particular pre-condition that in critical situations, as it happened in Iran, that he would be able to make a decision. I, myself, was a witness at the beginning of the riots of the revolution. When the Iranian military leaders and others would call asking what to do. The Shah would answer that, to the extent possible, they not shoot at the people. If they had to shoot, he told them to shoot in the leg. Therefore, these government officials awaited instructions on what to do. This time of uncertainty caused what occurred and now everyone can have his or her own interpretation.

But I, myself, was an eye-witness. What I am explaining and writing in my memoirs is what I have witnessed. Foreign countries are of no use to Iran; even Russia steals Iran's gas. Russia was upset that the Shah favored the United States and American military in Iran.

Manouchehr Bibiyan: Dr. Amini, during your premiership, did the Shah's family interfere with your policies?

Ali Amini: Absolutely not. I did not allow them, and I accepted this political position on the condition that they would not interfere in my policies. Mr. Bibiyan, I believe that truly, if everyone would have stated in one voice that a particular policy was wrong, then everyone would have said that it was wrong. It was that simple. Truly, then I would have been able to convince the Shah that [certain policies were wrong]. But it required a precondition that others would have also endorsed and approved that this statement was correct, and then he [the Shah] would have accepted it. But, unfortunately, there were a group of people in the government, in order to keep their positions in the government and due to their ambitions, did not say it [to the Shah].

I have never forgotten the day that, in a meeting that the Shah and I had, the Shah turned to me and said: "None of these people in the government resigned so that at the least we would know that the situation is bad."

Regarding my refusal to accept the post of prime minister, I told the Shah: "Two heads of my family, one of them Ghavam, and the other, Mossadegh. I am not willing to refrain from utilizing the experiences of these two heads of state. I will not wait until the day that they kick me out. For the first time in the government of Iran, a prime minister, i.e. I have come to thank you that you have trusted me, I have performed my work, and now I leave. I do not accept the post of premiership."

Manouchehr Bibiyan: There was a rumor that your meeting with Kennedy in America resulted in your becoming prime minister. And, in case that you become prime minister, there would be provided assistance to Iran.

Amini: There was absolutely no statement by the United States and Kennedy regarding providing funds and assistance on the condition that Dr. Ali Amini would become prime minister. It is impossible that a president would suggest—directly or indirectly—who would become prime minister, but he [Kennedy] had said that the prime minister should be an individual who is righteous—[did not] name names, particularly Dr. Amini—

When Kennedy was a senator, he and Mrs. Kennedy invited me to a meeting. At the meeting, my wife and I were there and a journalist at the meeting consulted with me regarding President Eisenhower. This was all. We did not have a meeting with Kennedy.

If you remember, this issue was raised during the revolution, this was said, when Carter came to power. And in my opinion, it meant that he [Carter] warned that he [Carter] would accept anyone to be the premier except Dr. Amini and to tell the Americans that he does not accept Dr. Amini.

Manouchehr Bibiyan: Now that Iran is in a war with Iraq and Iraq is occupying part of Iranian soil, is this correct that parts of the Iranian opposition to the Islamic Republic obtain funding from Iraq and use Iraq's media against the regime in Iran?

Ali Amini: Absolutely not. When I saw the Iraqi Ambassador, he complained to me that Khomeini incites opposition. I told him:

"incitement is different from attacking a country. You engaged in a dramatic war; now, whether a group encouraged you, I do not want to discuss it. But your country's intelligence service is so wrong that you believed you would attack and capture Khuzistan. In addition, the issue that you raised as the second Qadesiye[2] which you yourselves mentioned—was a mistake. Khuzistan does not belong to Arabs. Iranians will not accept that foreigners occupy Khuzistan."

---

[2]   Qadessiye War: the Arab attack on Iran, 1,400 years ago.

Manouchehr Bibiyan's interview with Ali Amini

Location of the Interview: Dr. Ali Amini's residence in Paris

Broadcast: October 1989

Manouchehr Bibiyan: It is a good situation to be in Paris and talk to Dr. Ali Amini, since he has had a major role in the politics of Iran for more than half a century. Therefore, at the beginning of our conversation, we asked him to tell us what should be done to bring Iranians living inside the country and those living abroad closer to one another, to build a bridge between the Iranians abroad and Iranians inside the country.

Ali Amini: Mr. Bibiyan, Thank you for visiting me on your way crossing Paris. This shows your sincere kindness towards me. Our relationship has lasted for the past ten years and it is as close as a family relationship.

Even though I was ill for over a year, I was aware of what is going on in Iran, as it is the duty of any Iranian to keep in touch with Iran. Today, there is a power struggle in Iran. The extremists try to prevent a stable government from being established. It is not the duty of people living abroad as we do, to focus on the details of the government—deciding whether it has been good or not or comparing it to the past. The present is what should be important to us since it is a matter of Iran's survival. Obviously, the reconstruction of Iran will not be simple, and it cannot be achieved by one person only. It requires the sincere cooperation and unity of those who really care about Iran and its future. In America, some people have gathered young Iranians, trying to convince them to go back to Iran in order to start the reconstruction of Iran, and [I believe] this is what should be done. The opposition to the Islamic Republic exists outside the country, but even though it exists, I believe it is not at all effective because the more pressure we create directing world public opinion against them, the more will they [the Islamic Republic] tend towards being hardliners having a platform aimed at preventing the establishment of a stable government. In order to reconstruct Iran, the brains outside the country should go back to Iran, and in order to do that, people should feel safe going back to their country. People in Iran holding high-level positions should prepare this kind of [secure] environment in their country. I think that the utmost goal of every Iranian patriot is to go back to his country and live there until he dies. Well, there are some good people who should relinquish their [high] positions and benefits. The young should be supported, encouraged, and given the opportunity to bring about change. They must learn a lesson from what they see so that they would not be involved with dictatorship, tyranny, and injustice.

People living inside Iran should know that the most important task is unity and cooperation. People who are not on friendly terms with one another, or those ambitious about obtaining high positions and so on should be willing to relinquish their own interests for the sake of Iran—even though all people have their own ambitions.

Right now, what is important is the survival of Iran. This is possible only through unity, cooperation, and forgiveness which unfortunately do not exist among we, Iranians. We should try to be united and cooperate, even for a short time, so that the government would be more or less stable. Foreign countries will help us only if there is stability in the country.

This is my personal opinion. Even though I am ill, I think about Iran just like anybody else, but without criticism about the present or the past. I would rather disregard all that. Whatever happened already did, but it should not be repeated. It is correct that there is an increase in the rate of crime, murder, and robbery, but all of that has happened in the past as well. However, the past should not be compared to the present. Each period has its own necessities. We should see today's reality.

In my opinion, by putting pressure on the regime, the Islamic Republic reinforces the extremist groups and as a result it would neutralize the activities of people like Rafsanjani. I do not mean to make a judgment regarding Rafsanjani saying whether he is good or not. In the meantime, he is a person who has made a commitment and his success depends on the help of others. I am referring to those living in Iran. And, since we live abroad, we cannot really do anything special except to refrain from blocking activities, so at least we should not disrupt his attempts to lead.

We should not turn world public opinion against him describing them as criminals, terrorists and so on. I think Rafsanjani was brave enough to reveal the real nature of Mohtashami and persons like him. He let people know that they were the ones who established terrorism in Syria. I am personally hopeful and pray that all Iranians could go back to our homeland, and regardless of what they would do, at least they would [let us] die and be buried there near our relatives.

Manouchehr Bibiyan: Dr. Amini, Some people would like to go back to Iran, but there is no guarantee that the regime, the Islamic Republic, would not cause them difficulties. There have been talks about general amnesty, but it has never been implemented. Many people are afraid to go back to Iran because they do not have any reassurance at all that they will be safe in Iran. What is your opinion regarding this issue?

Ali Amini: You are right in saying that for people who would like to go back to Iran, there is a need for reassurance that they would be safe. The solution for that is to unify the different authorities still existing in Iran so that people would know where to turn—the court or the president. I have a few examples regarding this point. Some good persons [who had positions] in the previous regime, i.e. the Shah's regime, left for Iran without experiencing any difficulties. They may be prohibited from leaving the county, but they are in Iran and nobody bothers them, or . . . [inaudible].

I believe that the authorities [in Iran] are gradually trying to prepare the path for a general amnesty to be announced. I believe it will happen after a referendum. Even following a public amnesty, it would still not be safe to go back to Iran. There must be a definite body that would make decisions in Iran so that Iranians can go back. Otherwise, someone like Mr. Lajevardi would imprison them at the Evin Prison, and later on, there would not be a trace. In the meantime, they have eradicated all the leftists, thus there is no issue of leftists now; they do not exist at all in Iran. There are no communists and no Mujahedin-i-Khalgh—none exists. What has remained is the distribution of authority among them in order to be more established, and as a result, maintain stability in the country. The stability of Iran not only encourages Iranians living abroad to go back home—it also provides foreigners with a sense of security to invest and help. They [usually] help and invest in a country with a well-organized judicial authority that could make their investments safe. They would like to be sure that their money would be returned to them rather than be wasted. Thus, we should be hopeful and encourage people to . . . I am not referring to cooperation with the regime, the Islamic Republic. We have nothing to do with the regime, the Islamic Republic, but [not audible] just to save the country from destruction. Anarchy will lead to the destruction of the country. No doubt, no one would benefit from destruction. I believe that the Soviet Union, the United States, and England do not like it either. I think we should be hopeful. Iranians living abroad should wait to some extent until they are sure that there is a central authority in Iran and then travel to [the country] without having to worry about their safety.

Manouchehr Bibiyan: I would like to ask another question. It is about the Persian language. Children who were 7 or 8 at the time the revolution occurred in Iran, are now young men and women outside the country. What means is effective in preserving our language outside of Iran?

Ali Amini: Mr. Bibiyan, I believe that language is very important, because if the language of a country is forgotten, it will lead to the end of that country. Those who live abroad should teach the Persian language to young people so that they would not forget the language. It is certainly not easy, but I believe [not audible]. If the country's language is forgotten, that country itself will be gone. Currently, there are language schools for young children in different places including in Los Angles where you live. In Paris, Mr. Seyyed Nia and Mr. Kaldani and others have established language classes. The Paris municipality has placed the school at their disposal for one or two days [a week] and the [students] study there when schools are closed. This may not be considered an achievement either in Los Angeles or in Paris, but since you have always been pioneer in great activities and really have done many excellent deeds, also in this part, in helping in saving the language, and you encourage them to do something that the language of the country would not be forgotten. I know that it is a hard work, but they should know that if the language is forgotten, the country will be gone. I am sure that since you contributed your deeds during this long period, you will continue your good deeds and undertake this one too. No doubt, it will be effective.

I hope that with the help of God, this current administration in the Islamic Republic will be established very soon regardless whether it is good or bad. This regime, the Islamic Republic, needs 5-6 months to be established. If so, it is possible to undertake many tasks. Our duty abroad is to help the country survive, and language is one of its principles. We should prepare the children born here and have not been absorbed—and will not be absorbed either—to go back to their country [not audible]. It makes no difference whether they go there to work or study. They would learn the language. They definitely need teachers, but the teachers here are not suitable for teaching there. Considering the fact that they have some knowledge, they can go there and adjust themselves to the environment in Iran in order to improve the cultural situation of the country.

Money can always be found. It could be borrowed [not audible]. The main point is that there [Iran] would be a country which would be useful to Iranians and be the country of Iran.

Manouchehr Bibiyan: Don't you think that in areas abroad where the Iranian mass media such as newspapers, magazines, radio, and television are active—more attention has been paid to the Persian language and even children speak Persian too?

Ali Amini: Mr. Bibiyan, I sincerely tell you that the Mass Media has done great service during the past 10 years. Because, in critical situations, it has always been they who have elected to really shed light for the people there.

Of course, there are some groups who are not very literate to be able to read newspapers and magazines or other things, but ultimately they listen to the words by ear. Therefore, the service that you and your friends have done is very important. It helps young children who are unable to read and write—to listen to the Persian language and via this method ultimately they learn Persian and try to speak Persian. I really appreciate and hope that you will continue to dedicate yourself to society as you always have, and this service, will God willing achieve positive results.

Manouchehr Bibiyan: Thank you Dr. Amini, it was a pleasure for me to come and talk to you. I hope that our viewers will get the benefit of your ideas and opinions. I wish you a long life and hope to have more conversations with you.

Ali Amini: Thank you very much Mr. Bibiyan. It was really a pleasure for me to meet you on your short trip to Paris. We have been talking to each other repeatedly for ten years and our family relations have been such that I can say that you have truly been regarded as a member of our family. My picture is still in your daughter's room.

I really think highly of you and appreciate what you have done for our fellow compatriots who live outside of Iran, especially in Los Angeles. I know you did it with great suffering and campaigns.

Of course, no action is without problems and without facing the problems created by jealousy and attack of some people, but you managed to overcome everything through your perseverance and stability. I hope you will continue your good work, and the good name you have always had will remain alive for us.

Be certain that there are fair and just people who are aware of what you have done and what you are still doing there [in America].

I wish you success in the future and hope you will continue your good work.

Manouchehr Bibiyan: Thank you.

Declaration of Joint Statement by Ali Amini and Shapour Bakhtiar

Broadcast July 24, 1983

JAAM-E-JAM: Dear viewers, in the last meeting of Dr. Ali Amini and Dr. Shapour Bakhtiar, a declaration of joint statement was published which caused hope for the majority of Iranians inside and outside the country. JAAM-E-JAM values any type of national solidarity in the direction of the liberation of Iran. And now, we draw your attention to the text of this joint statement.

Text of the Statement:

Whereas our dear homeland has been placed at the crossroads of destruction under the totalitarian control of a group of ignorant and unpatriotic people; and whereas the uncivilized actions of the current regime, the Islamic Republic, has reached to the degree that they are imprisoning and torturing and illegally executing women and men, old and young, on the charges of freedom of thought and to have rights and individual freedoms and social freedoms, and are convicted without defense.

Whereas the regime's, Islamic Republic, initiation of useless internal and external wars, the youth of the country are being killed, and the national wealth of the country are unilaterally being destroyed, and from another direction with the destruction of cities and industrial centers, millions of our compatriots have remained displaced and unemployed.

Whereas the continuation of the totalitarian control of the current regime, the Islamic Republic, in addition to the disaster which it has caused for the nation of Iran, it has seriously threatened the peace and security of the region and the world, we, the signatories of this statement, announce our understanding and agreement on the basis of the following principles:

1. Recognition and endorsement of the Constitution of Iran [1906], and the indisputable rejection of what has been imposed on the nation of Iran by the Islamic Republic via fear and dictatorship under the name of constitution.

2. Endorsement of constitutional regime with emphasis on the undeniable principle of national sovereignty and following the popular vote of the people.

3. Emphasis on the necessity of separation of religion and government, and respect for all religions.

4. Emphasis and Respect for the ethnic characteristics of the people of Iran without causing damage to the integrity and independence of the country.

5. Recognition and respect for the rights and freedoms written in the Universal Declaration of Human Rights.

WE invite all the people of the nation of Iran to unification and solidarity, side by side, in order to liberate our country from the disaster which it has faced, to absolutely expand the ultimate struggle against the regime, i.e. against the Islamic Republic the foundation of which is shaking.

Long live Iran and the people of Iran . . . Iran will never die.

JAAM-E-JAM: Dear viewers, after the publication of the joint statement which was signed in Paris between Mr. Ali Amini and Mr. Shapour Bakhtiar, the leaders of Iran Liberation Front, and the National Resistance Movement of Iran, it was necessary that the perspectives of the political organizations of these leaders also be explicitly clear for the information of the people of Iran. Therefore, regarding this issue, we had brief telephone interviews with Dr. Ali Amini, the leader of Iran Liberation Front, and Dr. Abdulrahman Boroumand, the Secretary-General of the National Resistance Movement of Iran, which will be broadcast in today's program.

Interview with Ali Amini

July 24, 1983

JAAM-E-JAM: Dr. Amini, I have two questions: Our first question is whether the joint statement dated 28 of Tir which was announced by you and Dr. Bakhtiar, is endorsed by the Iran Liberation Front? And whether this is a declaration of understanding or whether this is an agreement which will be implemented by the executives of both organizations?

Ali Amini: As you are informed, from the beginning of the establishment of the Iran Liberation Front, we tried to gather all the individuals and political groups who are against the Islamic Republic around a program in order to have an organized opposition against the Islamic Republic in order to have a better chance of success. And, I am happy that at last, after all our efforts, there was an agreement with Mr. Bakhtair, but of course, this is an agreement between him and I.

In fact between the same group of the National Resistance Movement of Iran and Liberation Front of Iran. And, I repeat that we must follow-up on this issue in order to render it a serious coordination, otherwise this joint statement in itself is not sufficient for the next [stage of] struggle. And, I hope that following this we will establish a coordination committee between these two groups, and I am hopeful that others will announce that they will join. And after these few years of hard work, a truly organized opposition to the Islamic Republic be created outside and to create hope inside the country.

JAAM-E-JAM: To what extent are you hopeful in achieving success regarding the overthrow of the Islamic Republic by the oppositional leaders abroad against the Islamic Republic?

Amini: In my opinion, this period of hard-work, has not been without result. Of course, on one political issue, and with a government inside the country which has resorted to terror, it has prevented all the people from engaging in association and protest. This was not a very simple work, and I think that one must congratulate all the groups which have participated in this struggle, and now the situation which has been created inside the country—and this uprising which is nearly reaching a general uprising—is the resultant of these struggles which have been taking place in these years. And, I think that rather than been unhopeful, and rather than hesitate in the future result of struggle, they must continue and follow-up in order to reach a positive result. And, this is the same policy which I have had since the first day—that is, that a national and popular uprising be created inside the country and overthrow this regime, i.e. the Islamic Republic. And, we are reaching closer to that goal.

Abdulrahman Boroumand

Active member, National Front of Iran; Deputy Secretary-General, National Resistance Movement of Iran. Shapour Bakhtiar's deputy in the National Resistance Movement of Iran. Abdulrahman Boroumand was assassinated in Paris in 1991.

Interview with Abdul Rahman Boroumand

July 24, 1983

JAAM-E-JAM: Mr. Boroumand, we are contacting you from JAAM-E-JAM's headquarters in Los Angeles. The reason for the call is to inquire about several issues including the publication of a joint statement dated 28 of Tir which was signed between Mr. Amini and Mr. Bakhtiar in five clauses regarding which they reached an agreement which has had a wide impact, and some of our compatriots who are interested in the future of Iran have been in contact with JAAM-E-JAM and are interested in the perspective of the National Resistance Movement of Iran regarding this agreement. In order to shed light on this perspective, we tried to contact Dr. Bakhtiar, but we were informed that he is recuperating from a surgery and unfortunately we were unable to reach him,

and for this reason we are contacting you. Considering that you are the Secretary-General of the National Resistance Movement of Iran, please tell our viewers your opinion regarding this jointly agreed statement.

Abdul Rahman Boroumand: Regarding the issue that you mentioned, that Dr. Bakhtiar is recuperating from surgery, I must say that Dr. Bakhtair has recuperated; he is well, and he will only be outside Paris for a few days for rest.

The other issue regarding your question regarding what was signed between Mr. Bakhtiar and Mr. Amini, it is a joint statement—and not an agreement—and Dr. Bakhtiar had an interview with Iran Radio this afternoon Paris-time the text of which will be provided to the media.

What I could add now, as the Director of the Executive Board of the National Resistance Movement of Iran, is that the statement under discussion is the result of a number of responsible discussions between Mr. Bakhtiar and Mr. Amini and indicative of a constructive effort and struggle in the direction of enlightening the points of agreement among the opposition to the current regime of Iran, i.e. opposition against the Islamic Republic.

The National Resistance Movement of Iran has always announced that it is prepared to talk, and possibly reach agreement, with all the forces which endorse the element of popular sovereignty—that is, the will of the people in determining the destiny of the country.

JAAM-E-JAM: Mr. Boroumand, I have another question and that is with the expert knowledge which you have regarding the struggle to overthrow the current regime of Iran, i.e. to overthrow the Islamic

Republic, in the past four years, would you briefly tell our viewers your perspective regarding this issue?

Boroumand: The struggle to overthrow the current regime, the Islamic Republic, in the past and in the future is comprised of two stages: 1) political struggles, and 2) armed struggles.

Because it is improbable that success would be achievable only via peaceful struggle with the Khomeini regime, therefore, the National Resistance Movement of Iran has never set aside armed struggle to overthrow the Khomeini regime, and towards this aim, it has engaged in many efforts, which I hope that at the appropriate time, successful results will be reached and reported, and you agree that more than this regarding this issue and [inaudible].

JAAM-E-JAM: Therefore, your statement indicates that we should be very hopeful.

Boroumand: I have never been disappointed even for one second, and I have always been hopeful, and a nation which struggles to remain alive, has to be hopeful, and it will surely succeed.

JAAM-E-JAM: Mr. Boroumand, many thanks for your time to JAAM-E-JAM.

Boroumand: I want to add another issue for you, and that is, in the current situation of our country, more than any other occasion, we believe that the dialogue among the forces sympathetic regarding the situation of the country must expand in order to reach the absolute unity of the nationalist forces.

Shapour Bakhtiar

The last Prime Minister of Iran in the Shah's regime (Bakhtiar Administration was 37 days), Active member of the National Front; Opposition Leader Against the Islamic Republic Abroad, Leader of National Resistance Movement of Iran. Shapour Bakhtiar was assassinated in Paris in 1991.

Shapour Bakhtiar

May 2 & 9, 1982

JAAM-E-JAM: Dear viewers, Dr. Shapour Bakhtiar has been one of the political figures and news-makers of our country in the course of the past four years. In continuing the series of interviews with Iran's political figures, JAAM-E-JAM has conducted an interview with Dr. Bakhtair in Paris.

JAAM-E-JAM Television: Dr. Bakhtiar, in this critical time, considering the current difficult situation in Iran, how do you foresee the future of our country? And, principally, what are your views regarding the future government of Iran and how to elect the future government?

Shapour Bakhtiar: I do not believe in a type of fatalism, that is, I do not believe that the future of our country and our destiny is pre-determined. Destiny must be determined and therefore Iran will be a country that the people of Iran desire. But, regarding my personal perspective and what I have said and written, I think I have repeated many times that after the overthrow, that is after the end of the Khomeini's conspiracy, which must be conducted and followed with all means, and until the restoration of a permanent, democratic and nationalist government, Iran has no choice but to have a provisional government which I hope would be for a very brief period.

Two years ago I expressed the principles of this united government. I am very glad to see that recently some individuals who are opposition leaders against the Islamic Republic have considered this issue, and now have noticed that those statements of two years ago have been true.

The future regime of Iran must be determined by the people, and I have agreed that until that time the Constitution of 1906 be the foundation of government in that provisional government. The principles of the Constitution are sufficient for a democratic and nationalist government, unfortunately these principles have not been observed in its entirety, if not to say, it was never implemented. Therefore, what I am considering, I said before, a provisional government: I have placed the [text] at the disposal of the public and whoever wants to read it, it is approximately two pages containing the principal system of this government and the views which I have regarding government. But, as I said, the future regime of Iran is dependent on the will of the nation of Iran, and it must be planned and approved in an informed and stable environment considering the interests of the country.

JAAM-E-JAM: Dr. Bakhtiar, there are talks everywhere of invitation for reconciliation, solidarity, and coalition for the liberation of Iran, while it appears that there are deep gaps between the opposition leaders against the Islamic Republic. How, do you believe, these gaps could be filled, and principally, please state with which political groups are you willing to form a coalition?

Bakhtair: The fact is that these groups or individuals who consider themselves opposition leaders against the Islamic Republic are three groups: 1) a limited group of Iranians outside and inside the country who have predicted what Khomeini stands for and the disasters which he caused the country, and [this group] had expressed their opposition to the government of the mullahs since the first day. 2) the second group were those Iranians who, with whatever reason or logic which they express, believed in the Imam and considered him the saviour of the nation of Iran. These gentlemen, one by one, for whatever reason and ultimately separated from Khomeini—including the person who was their president in the Islamic Republic, including the person who was their cabinet minister, and the person who held other positions—and later on, now, they have come and express their opposition with Khomeini's regime. This second group, as I said, entered the opposition movement against the Islamic Republic gradually, one after another. But, they were themselves part of the founders of Khomeini's Islamic Republic. 3) the third group are Iranian people who had lived outside Iran for many years prior for different reasons, and when Khomeini came to power they did not protest the least. And, they did not dare to speak despite the fact that they had absolute security. They lived in the free world. But gradually, when they saw the Khomeini's situation worsening, these gentlemen also slowly found courage and power and entered [the opposition movement against the Islamic Republic] and said: "why should we not be part of it". For example, the former

Imperial Iranian military leaders in Los Angeles had come outside of Iran many years prior with sufficient wealth and were not willing to return to Iran in anyway. After they saw that, well, everyone says "we are opposed" [to the Islamic Republic], slowly they also entered the arena of opposition to Khomeini as national heroes.

Therefore, here is the issue of authenticity and unauthenticity, and I want to state an issue. Some were waiting for [the time] when Khomeini's situation reached this point, and when as they refer to it, receive the green light, and then express their nationalist feelings.

A number of people believe in a principle that [states] Iran belongs to Iranians and our destiny must solely be determined by we Iranians. Now, there is another world, there is the East, there is the West; we must, I do not say agree with, but to an extent we must hold their status as reality.

The responsible political people could not disregard reality. All of these groups, each of them agrees regarding Khomeini and his overthrow, in the current situation, and due to different reasons. However, the differences begin at [the stage of] what Iran must be in the future and how.

Some, in the old fashion way, and according to old schools, and Taarof, and such, are saying that when Khomeini is overthrown, when his regime is overthrown, any person can go and whatever one wants to . . . Theoretically, saying this is accurate; however, in practical terms we know it is not as such.

One of my criticism of all Akhunds and supporters of Khomeini whether those Moa'mam [a cleric wearing a turban] or Mokala [a cleric who removes his turban, wears a hat, and might also wear a tie] was and has been this: when a bunch said that "the Shah must go", and he should have gone, for instance they did not tell me and they did not tell the nation of Iran "what regime do you want?". Neither exactly, nor approximately, none of them could really imagine the Islamic Republic. Now, saying that now Khomeini must go, and later we will see what would happen, this is one of those dangerous statements. We could not disregard freedom, independence, social justice, and technological progress for Iran, and for this reason a regime must be developed that would rely on these principles that I stated.

Therefore, the convergence of these gentlemen, had they been fair, would have been a little easier, but unfortunately we Iranians are not essentially fair persons, and especially when we think of the fact that [they] all have interests but they seldom have political beliefs and an ideology—I am saying this generally—therefore, differences occur, and these differences are sometimes intensified by foreigners, because they each negotiate with one of these gentlemen and they also talk to the last individual who has come from Iran.

That Mr. is a person in the opposition movement against the Islamic Republic, and God knows what is his background. His background is shameful. But they say "you are included". And the [political situation] has reached a point that each of them is under the impression that without any real political support or a distinguished background in the struggle for the liberation and independence of their country, and with the deep corruption that they had, and now once again they have come and say that "I am include, just as you are". Therefore, the foreigners also develop these differences. The foreigners do this in a very wise way, and the gentlemen who have long been in the habit of being in contact with foreigners agree.

JAAM-E-JAM: Dr. Bakhtair, the oppositional leaders against the Islamic Republic and the leaders of opposition groups against the Islamic Republic, have called for political struggle, but no one has a clear plan or program regarding the how of this political struggle for conducting it. Are you also waiting for a designated time, or as some say, waiting for the green light?

Bakhtair: I presume that one of the criticisms that I have regarding the gentlemen of the opposition against the Islamic Republic is this, "why did you wait or are waiting or will wait for the green light?" In any case, I believe that all of us outside of Iran could be the voice of the people inside the country, and it is necessary to draw the attention of public opinion and world public opinion, essentially, to the catastrophes occurring in Iran and those disjunctions which are in no way comparable to the old regime, i.e. the Shah's regime.

This is what every Iranian to the extent of his/her possibilities, has the duty to carry out, but we are in part a speaker and in part an antenna for the expression of the situation in Iran. But it is neither sufficient—and I think it is far from reality—that we would think that 35 million Iranians or 36 million Iranians inside the country would be comparable to a group of hundred-thousand outside the country.

The problems of Iran must be resolved inside the country, but we can keep them hopeful, and it is not as such possible without contact and communication with nationalist elements inside the country. When I talk about live, nationalist elements, I do not mean a group of Akhunds, nor a group of corrupt Iranian military officers, or a group of people who surrounded Khomeini until yesterday.

The nation of Iran, the masses of the Iranian people, have noticed that this solution is worse than what existed in Iran before, therefore one can not call this a revolution, nor can it be acknowledged as a type of progress for the country. According to these considerations I state that I have never waited for a green light, and I have never waited and I am not waiting for it. Khomeini himself knows this very well, and perhaps the fairness of Khomeini and his group is more than—considering these incitements which have been conducted against me personally—some of friends, and even some of those who represent themselves as friends. Regarding this issue, they might perhaps judge more fairly.

I believe that we must increase our communication with all means—without further explanation—with the forces that are inside Iran, and with the means that we place at their disposal conduct a national uprising that is entirely Iranian and nationalistic for the overthrow of the Islamic Republic.

JAAM-E-JAM: My next question was exactly regarding the same issue which you answered in part. In order to overthrow the Islamic Republic do you solely rely on issuing announcements, interviews, and solidarity with the Iranians outside the country? Which you answered above.

Bakhtair: Not at all.

JAAM-E-JAM: Do you have any forces inside Iran to carry out your plans and programs?

Bakhtiar: I can not speak on this issue openly. When one of my cassette tapes reaches Iran, or an announcement, the person in possession of the cassette or announcement is executed. How do you want that I state further explanation regarding what occurs in Iran.

JAAM-E-JAM: Dr Bakhtiar, there are a few questions regarding the past. Your opponents claim that your acceptance of the post of premiership in that specific situation was due to your ambitions, and also that your request to meet Khomeini in that crisis situation again was due to maintaining the post of premiership.

Bakhtair: I am very glad that you stated this because it is necessary for the hundredth time I repeat, although this repetition and shedding light on it would not be considered a response by those who spread repeated false accusations.

I want to state to you just this issue that after the fall of Dr. Mossadegh, all the possibilities existed for me to reach all the positions which I was willing to reach: I was young, I was active, I was educated, and I had an influential family. But, I rejected.

If after twenty-five years, after very dark days, I accepted the post of premiership it was to save the country, not solely for the destruction of that regime ruling the country. On the contrary, it was to prevent [the coming to power] of a regime which I had predicted and stated in a timely manner. However, when they invited me [to join the government as the] premier, I can only say that one should refer to the forces of history, and not the willingness of anyone. If there was calm in Iran, if there were wealth, if there had not been any news on the international arena, there had been again the continuation of Eghbal, Hoveida or Assadollah Alam, and any one of them. No, I was not a regular prime minister, meaning that I was a responsible prime minister and I had accepted responsibility according to the constitution. Now, the measures which I initiated were not similar to any of the gentlemen who called themselves prime ministers, but were in fact office managers. Every Iranian has the right to reach high positions in the country. If you are a democrat, you must accept this. I do not know why I was deprived of this right, while those who were before me what additional advantageous did they have? I want to state that my acceptance of responsibility was for saving Iran so that Iran would not be transformed into this situation. Had I been appointed three months earlier in the Shah's regime—that is instead of Sharif-Emami—these opposition gentlemen against the Islamic Republic had been in Iran today, and Khomeini would not have been in Iran. [Adequate] time was not given to me, but what was given to me, and what I did is evidence and witness.

Regarding the last part of your question: meeting with Khomeini—I have said it many times, and I have written in the Ghiyam newspaper, and in my own words it has been recorded on cassette tapes and has been stated on radio, I accepted this meeting for the reason that, and I accepted the responsibility myself. None of my colleagues encouraged me. I proposed to Khomeni that as two Iranians, without my resignation, to consult in Paris and to make decisions regarding the future of Iran that would be in the interests of the country. It can not be disputed that Khomeini at that time, either due to incitement of foreigners or due to all the miseries that we suffered, had the [support] of a force of regressive people of the country, and [also] the intellectuals of the country, university professors, the elite of the country. This issue was a reality, and I had to talk about this problem with Mr. Khomeini. And, I initiated the planning for negotiations for the coming generations. If during this time, that is, when after my death and that of Khomeini, and others, the history of Iran is one day written, it might be written: "why did not Bakhtiar himself try to talk to this stubborn man? What would have happened? Then, this person was selfish. Then, this individual did not acknowledge anyone." To reject this criticism and I know that if I reject this criticism, I would face a subsequent one, and another one, the gentlemen criticized me saying why did I accept. I accepted because either Khomeini would have accepted—and if I had come here, he would have lost half of his power, that is, he had no choice but to recognize me and talk—or he would not have accepted, and I would have been acquitted by history and I would have said: "I tried my best to go and talk to this man, but he was ignorant. He absolutely does not believe in Iran and Iranian culture and heritage, and so on." Despite this fact, I initiated the planning of negotiations. Well, the individuals who blocked this move, one of them was the former president of Iran, Mr. Bani Sadr who there is no need to state his background, another one was Mr. Sanjabi and his entourage, and other individuals, and a number of other Mullahs. But, of course, there were one, two, or three individuals who agreed with this issue, there is no doubt, that is, they were supporters of Khomeini at that time.

This meeting was for two reasons: one, to break the spell of Khomeini—and if he had rejected, which he rejected in the last minute, after agreeing, then people would have said "poor Bakhtiar, he tried to see him, to talk, but Khomeini did not accept. Then, this seyyed is rebellious", then, this was a credit to me and I won in that regard.

JAAM-E-JAM: Dr. Bakhtiar, a group of people have the opinion that, you ought not have permitted Khomeini to enter Iran in those days that destiny was being made, and not to leave the arena with his arrival. They say that you caused the disintegration of the Imperial Iranian military due to your conservatism.

Bakhtair: I want to say that this issue is very interesting, and recently a number of corrupt individuals and mercenaries of the old regime i.e. the Shah's regime, with their rudeness, are engaged in these types of propaganda. And, I personally want to tell you that Mr. Khomeini—first I want to tell you from the perspective of the law, and prior to my becoming prime minister I had stated in interviews—is an Iranian, unfortunately, are all the 36 million Iranian individuals are all nationalists?

No. There were too many people like Ghotbzadeh, but that is not a reason to say that these individuals are not Iranian—to prevent him from coming was contrary to rights and to the principles of my beliefs. For this reason, I had previously stated to the Shah that: "if I become the prime minister, he would come. If he came and behaved, then he behaved, if not I am not going to exile him; I would take him to court."

I believe that this is what the Shah should have done, with the situation that he had. Mr. Khomeini entered Iran; but had he not come, we would have had much worse problems.

I put all these aside. At that time, I expressed that Khomeni is like the planet mercury from a distance; but when he comes to Iran, you would see that he is a stupid and unknowledgeable man.

I do not know whether an individual who described Khomeini in such terms at that situation could be called conservative or not. Conservatives were those who escaped prior to the arrival of Khomeini; with the situation and the wealth in the old regime, i.e. in the Shah's regime, and with the background that they had, they escaped, and they left the Shah—who was their benefactor—alone. They were the conservatives. In the good day, they were there; in the difficult days, they escaped. I worked for the country of Iran, and nothing else.

When Mr. Khomeini came, I ordered all the instructions to the leaders of the Imperial Iranian military; and all of my aim was this: if time passes, again two three weeks, then day by day, the forces of Khomeini—whom then I told him that he has no right to appoint a government, and that it would be a joke, and I ordered to stop and detain each government Minister who would be appointed at the Ministry's Office.

This is not called conservatism at that situation; people are forgetful. When he came, as I have stated in detail with the newspaper Ghiam-e-Iran, everyday I and the Iranian National Security Council were in contact with the Imperial Iranian military leaders. And, I had stated to these gentlemen that you must perform your duties with coolness but seriously. Now, if the leaders of the Imperial Iranian military were of no use to Reza Shah on the 20th of Shahrivar, and this time they were of no use to the country, the Shah, and I, and the prime minister, this is because our military was not a nationalistic military, our heads of the military 90 percent of them were puppets of foreigners. They took their orders from others, and they took their salary from us, and the result is that people like Gharabaghi and Fardust—themselves either directly or indirectly—with Beheshti, with Bazargan, via Huyser or without Huyser, I don't' know, they would convene and ultimately declare the neutrality of the Imperial Iranian military.

What does this mean? Principally, what does the neutrality of the military mean? If the Imperial Iranian military is at the service of the government of Iran, declaring the neutrality of the military is meaningless, this is a rebel army. If it is not at the service of the Iranian people, why does it take its salary from the people of Iran? Why does it impose on the budget of the country of Iran? For this reason, I presume that not only did I not weaken the Imperial Iranian military in any way, to the contrary, I utilized all my power to ensure that the Imperial Iranian military perform its duties exactly—i.e. to stand against the Akhunds, and had this process continued for another two three weeks, then Mr. Khomeini would have been forced to negotiate, and then at that time, he would have been defeated again.

JAAM-E-JAM: Dr. Bakhtiar, it has been stated many times that you encouraged the Shah to leave Iran—at the same time it appears from all the published documents and the writings of the Shah himself that the Carter Administration forced the Shah to leave the country. Which one is correct? Was your demand that the Shah leave the country related to the mission of General Huyser to Iran regarding this issue?

Bakhtair: I was informed of the presence of General Huyser in Iran days after his arrival and I never even had telephone contacts with him. I neither saw him, nor did I have a telephone conversation with him, and nor did I understand for what reason he has come. This is regarding General Huyser in general.

I believed that the Shah—because the fever of the people had reached a point that they did not tolerate the Shah—had this happened three months earlier, that is, three months earlier a government had come to power that listened to the people, and did not have the background of the former prime ministers, it would have been unnecessary that the Shah leave the country.

What the United States, and the American Ambassador and the British Ambassador said and done was undisclosed to me. My suggestion was he leave on a trip so that I could decrease this uneasiness, and so that perhaps—and in my opinion the Shah, after 37 years of rule now that it had reached this point, was best to resign in favor of his son, because regarding this young man, regarding the Crown Prince, no one could have enmity unless they have perspectives of Khomeini on humanity. But I considered that the best strategy was that the Shah leave Iran for a trip, this was what I requested from him, and he also accepted. Now, the issue of the Shah writing later in his writings that "the American Ambassador or the British Ambassador told me and I accepted", this is a separate issue.

The American and the British Ambassador did not tell me such things—and it is regrettable that a king that must rely on his own people, and the Iranian nation must prevent the Shah from leaving, the types of governments were in power in this period that the people welcomed his departure. Now, a year after his departure, the fact that what Khomeini did caused the people to regret, this is the sign of the fact that those administrations caused the dissatisfaction of the people, and this regime, i.e. the Islamic Republic is worse than them.

JAAM-E-JAM: Dr. Bakhtiar, in most of your interviews, you refer to documents and evidence, for example regarding the neutrality of the Imperial Iranian military, and the opposition of the United States to the Shah's regime. Don't you think that it is best to publish these documents for the enlightenment of the general public?

Bakhtiar: Firstly, whatever documents are at my disposal, it is not best to publish after a year or two, because we have to learn from others. The problem of the Shah and the Shah's regime—we wrote to him officially, a year and a half prior to his departure—was the lack of implementing the Constitution. These people who come to me and tell me that "these administrations, the young king, or that time if Iran would have a regime of constitutional monarchy, you can be certain that it would no longer be authoritarian, and it is a nationalist government". I hope that this is true, but I can not guarantee in this regard.

Had the Shah respected the constitution, you can be certain that the nation, the parliament, the government of the prime minister had been opposed to the departure of the Shah. Unfortunately, the Shah did not respect the constitution, and the warnings which we gave, in exchange we received harsh words: "they are negative; they are spies of foreigners". And, the Shah himself, later in his last days of life, writes that the American and the British Ambassadors looked at their watch and said: "when are you leaving? What time are you leaving? Are you going to leave in this manner?" This is what I was not informed of, but had our government been a real constitutional government, and the Shah had not been permanently under pressure, and had he not overtaken all the powers of government, what has occurred now would have never happened.

Shapour Bakhtiar

Broadcast Date: December 26, 1982; January 3, 1983

JAAM-E-JAM: Dr. Bakhtiar, with our thanks for your second interview with Jaam-e-Jam Television. Considering the fact that you have been interviewed many times, however, it seems that many facts remain concealed, or perhaps due to political considerations, you do not reveal them. Don't you think that the time has arrived to set forth for discussion some of the facts including whether foreign countries were involved in the process of the revolution or the conspiracy, and also in the past events in Iran?

Shapour Bakhtiar: I think more than anybody in the field of politics, I am bold and frank enough to state my views. I have both stated and written whatever is relevant to the destiny and future of Iran. I have spoken of these subjects many times and left nothing unsaid. Anyway, about the disaster of Khomeini and changes, disorder and disasters that Iran and Iranians have been suffering from, I have repeated many times that to some extent, they were caused by lack of implementing the Constitution[3] [of 1906] and not being attentive to the wishes of the Iranian people, otherwise Khomeini would not have found any supporters. So, as I mentioned on the anniversary of the Constitutional Revolution, the blame is ours. The mistakes were made by Iran itself and the cabinets governing it. When the great powers found out that they can not permit that situation and they should do something there,

---

[3]   Shapour Bakhtiar believed in the implementation of the Iranian Constitution of 1906 which in the Pahlavi regime also was to some extent implemented, and he believed in the restoration of the same Law after the overthrow of the regime of the Islamic Republic in Iran.

they tried to do something, of course not for the people of Iran, but for their own interest in the region. To achieve this aim, they tried to find a specific element whose power was based on ignorance, lack of political growth, lack of knowledge of the political outlook of the country and world problems and to exploit it to the fullest. This element was a "seyyed" [Khomeini] whose name I first heard in 1963 and didn't hear about him later, but he took advantage of the dissatisfaction, class differences and so on, created by the governments, especially among the youth. Well, the powerful countries or better said those who have interests in the Persian Gulf and the Middle East, found out that the situation was getting out of control of the Shah's regime, and decided to pressure the late Shah and ask him to grant more freedom to the people. In fact the freedom was not granted in time. I think the worst thing is not to do these things at the right time. If freedom were given six months or a year earlier, and if there had been a real change in government and the same elements would not have come back with different slogans, the Khomeini disaster would not have grown so much so rapidly.

Of course at the last stage Khomeini was supported by all countries specially the Great Powers, he was supported morally; he was supported financially by some Arab countries.

The ignorance, foolishness, and hypocrisy of Khomeini himself attracted many wealthy people. Besides those, there were some dissatisfied people who followed him.

At this stage, the foreigners thought that whatever kind of government comes, it would surely be better than a communist one, which would cause the country to leave the West, and thus they helped those elements. Even President Carter, in his recent book, writes of this help and I myself have fully explained it in my book called Yekrangi [Ma Fidalite in French version, Yek Rangi in Persian version].

Some of the media, including radio stations of so called "Leftist Progressive Intellectuals" in the West, recognized Ayatollah Khomeini as a symbol of humanity and justice and so on, and the result is clear to everybody.

JAAM-E-JAM: What was the role of the National Front of Iran and its schism and the split of the National Democratic Front of Iran as well as your separation from the National Front of Iran? In fact what was the role of the National Front of Iran in the revolution? In your interviews you have said that you knew Karim Sanjabi to be a coward, if it is true how was he chosen as the leader of the National Front of Iran? You also voted for him and as some of your colleagues have said that you insisted on this issue.

Bakhtiar: I should say that after the fall of the late Dr. Mossadegh, we wanted to continue, with the help of some people who believed in his way towards Nationalism and Liberalism. Iranians suffered a lot in order to achieve this aim. However, during the last 25 years the National Front of Iran, contrary to other organizations, has never been free to continue the way of Mossadegh. Every now and then when we found a small opportunity for freedom, we started to organize the Front, but I tell you blocking the activities of the National Front of Iran caused the increase of the [activities] of the democratic and progressive movements, and thus encouraged the rise of leftists who sometimes were pro-Russia, sometimes Maoists and sometimes they were so-called independent. The above mentioned phenomena caused flourishing Marxists ideas under the cover of a religious layer. About

Mr. Sanjabi, as I said many times, he has proven a few times to be weak, and this is his big negative point.

For a leader it is the most dangerous thing to be lacking of strong will and the power of making decisions. He tried to satisfy everybody, both the Shah and Khomeini. He agreed to become president and also a prime minister of the Constitutional Monarchy! He was ready to conclude a treaty with insurgents of Azerbaijan and at the same time to issue pronouncements against them! Such a person is too dangerous for a position of leadership. As an answer to your question why I voted for him and how he came to power after Mossadegh, don't be surprised. As you can see even in a developed and democratic country like America, after Roosevelt persons like Johnson and Nixon were elected, and likewise, after Kennedy came leaders who could not be compared to him. In other countries we see that after a strong person like Stalin came Malinkov. It goes to show that it sometimes happens in other countries. I did not recommend the election of Mr. Sanjabi; I was not a dictator. He used to try to collect votes for himself and I believe such persons are not leaders, just followers. I do not remember anyone insisting or requesting anybody to vote for him or to strengthen him. I think the answer should be given by those who took part in the Khomeini's conspiracy and the demonstrations against me.

I do not know such miserable persons like Sanjabi and others of our fellow countrymen who showed such a characteristic in politics; in what a shameful condition they are living. I have always respected Dr. Mossadegh and so will I in the future, for his policy, nationalism, and respect for the Constitution in which he always believed but it was never implemented.

JAAM-E-JAM: Don't you think that decision that was made during the time of your Administration; in fact slowly you withdrew, and provided the opportunity for the rioters to reach their goals sooner, including: the issue of Martial Law, showing an interest in meeting with Khomeini, making contact with the religious leaders, and open printed press and radio and television in that situation, and other similar measures, don't you think that all of these issues and measures helped Khomeini to achieve his goal?

Bakhtiar: You should pay attention that I did not come to continue the policies of Sharif-Emami and Azhari.[4] I came to bring something new; something that every liberal Iranian wished to enjoy. We had never had a Constitution and democracy as we used to claim. We made the freedom of the press possible. In this case, I was like a doctor who has been called to a dying patient and it was too late. It was so easy for me to hide myself behind the slogans of the National Front of Iran and to decide not to interfere in the affairs of the country, and then I would be free of the charges made by my opponents. It was very easy to take that stance, but I am proud I didn't take that stance. I decided to risk my political capital and to maintain the interests of the nation of Iran. I was a man who was opposed to Khomeini's entrance into Iran even a year prior to his arrival in Iran, and if you read the English and French newspapers, you will know that there, I introduced myself as secular, supporter of the Constitution [of 1906] who was against the participation of Mullahs in the cabinet. Khomeini had weapons in hand given to him by the Shah's regime. He could claim that there was no freedom; he could claim that the constitution had not been

---

4   Jaffar Sharif-Emami and Gholam-Reza Azhari were the last two Prime Ministers in the Shah's regime prior to Shapour Bakhtiar's premiership.

followed, that the Security Service used torture, and that the press is such and such.

Well, these weapons should have either remained in his hands or should have been taken by us. I planned to disarm them, and as the people of Iran wanted, perform according to the Constitution, before forming my cabinet. Not what some people intermittently wish.

When I started to form my cabinet, I planned an emergency program including freedom of the press, cancellation of martial law, gradually after achieving calm in every region, respect for every Iranian, guarantee of human rights for every Iranian, which could have disarmed Khomeini.

He was dealing with a prime minister with 30 years of political activities, who did not care for his own promotion; a prime minister who didn't want to be involved with non-democratic and non-nationalistic activities that were against his ideals.

I decided that the plan had to be implemented for two reasons, and the first one was to fulfill what I had promised.

I am not and have never been a kind of politician to change my words. For me, the flag of Iran is an Iranian flag[5] without any sickle and hammer, and without verses of the Koran or a Kalashnikov. I have my own principles in life. I can not follow the policy that these gentlemen suggest, for example, to say "in the name of God" before

---

[5]   In the video of the interview, Shapour Bakhtiar points to the flag next to him, the flag of Iran with the Lion and the Sun.

making a speech, or like Sharif-Emami who expresses his opposition to Mossadegh and the nationalists.

Sharif-Emami has said "the divine light which has lighted Iran comes from the activist religious leaders"! I have never seen an activist religious leader! If I had, I would let you know. The misery of Iran started when the Mullahs and Zoroastrian religious leaders started to interfere in daily politics. I had never been in contact with Mullahs, only when Ayatollah Taleghani was released from prison—considering the fact that I was in prison with him two—three times—I visited him in his house for ten minutes to congratulate him for being released—as was customary. Since then I have never seen him again. I spoke on the phone to Beheshti once; He was with Montazeri and both tried to dissuade me regarding an issue, and I told them that [I will] never [be dissuaded regarding that issue].

On the point of my offer to meet with Khomeini, as I mentioned in my talks last year on Iran Radio[6] which is really the voice of the Iranian people, if I had not done this, your children would only know me as a selfish man who was not able to believe anybody and was not ready for negotiations. I, myself, without any pressure or suggestion by my colleagues, decided to offer to meet with Khomeini in Paris as two Iranians. I believe it was a good answer to future criticisms. Khomeini had two options, either he would agree to meet me, and then he would not be the same Khomeini who used to speak from the moon[7] and if not, he might say to me that I should resign, and that

---

[6]   An opposition radio abroad which beamed into Iran.

[7]   During the Iranian Revolution, as part of their propaganda, the opposition against the Shah's regime and opponents of the Shah's regime said that they had "observed" Khomeini's face in the moon.

was what happened. I told him I would not resign because I did not see any reason to resign.

I said: "Why don't you resign from being an Ayatollah? I don't agree with your view that 'being an Ayatollah is more important than being a prime minister' and that you have more knowledge than I". "No, I will not resign. We can talk as two Iranians." He did not agree, so I didn't go there and thus my conscience is clear.

JAAM-E-JAM: Some of the leaders of the opposition to the Islamic Republic say that you oppose unification of the groups and convening of opponents into a single entity. What is your view regarding the unification of different groups, regardless of their ideology, in the struggle against the regime currently ruling Iran, i.e. the Islamic Republic? And, why are you opposed to some of those groups during this critical situation?

Bakhtiar: I have mentioned many times that except for those who receive orders or ask for a green light from foreigners, I have never had nor do I have any opposition to any group which struggles against the current regime of Iran, i.e. the Islamic Republic. But, in order to clarify, let us see what opposition means? By opposition we mean those people or groups who opposed Khomeini from the beginning. The understanding of opposing Khomeini among the Iranian people should have been made by the clear-minded and not by someone who has not had time for studying and thinking. I have always been against forwarding the government to people like Khomeini. At the time I followed this policy, the majority of people, majority in numbers, supported Khomeini for the reason you certainly know. Those people who currently consider themselves the leaders of opposition groups against the Islamic Republic, cooperated with Khomeini at that time.

How do you expect me to treat such a people who performed such crimes and brought Iran to the current situation—to accept them warmly and ask them to join the struggle against Khomeini? While it is not clear if, had Khomeini not thrown them out, they would still be in their positions. Thus such people are not opposition; they are opportunists, selfish, inconsistent and egoists who change their minds every day to achieve their aims. I mean that they renounce their ideology, if they ever had any.

In order to reject such accusation, I repeat here for the 100th time that the basis for me is Iran, the Constitution [of 1906], social development and, in short, whatever is compatible with ideals of a healthy minded Iranian. This is, in fact, different from the ideas of the current regime, i.e. the Islamic Republic.

What I can suggest is, to put aside those groups that take orders from abroad, the groups which have or have had ties with Khomeini.

I am ready to cooperate with everyone, but I am sorry to say that when I was in the opposition to Khomeini and his regime, none of them were present. Some of these gentlemen were comfortable and silent in Europe and they would have kept silent if their properties had not been taken from them. Then one day, they said we should fight the struggle against Khomeini. I do not take orders from anybody; this is my personal conviction to fight or not. As a member of the opposition to the Islamic Republic, I am ready to cooperate with every group that wants to overthrow Khomeini except for those groups who do not have ideas of their own, but I am not ready to cooperate with Mr. Banisadr and people like him, and for example say that well sir, you made a mistake, there is no problem. No, I believe that these [issues] must be dealt with in a court of law, but not in Khomeini's Islamic court. Rather, a national court with the right of defense with the utilization of [the services] of an attorney, and even under international supervision.

JAAM-E-JAM: In most of your interviews, especially with the press organizations of the National Resistance Movement of Iran (Nehzat-I Moghavemat-I Melli Iran), you have mentioned the betrayal of the Shah's regime's military generals, but in your recent book which contains your interview with the Radio Iran research team, you have mentioned the names of Imperial Iranian military generals like Brigadier General Badre-yi, Brigadier General Mehdi Rahimi, Brigadier General Yazdegerdi, Brigadier General Pakravan and Brigadier General Bid Abadi, the commanders of divisions in the provinces, and praised them for their nationalistic attitude. If you accept the fact that the announcement of neutrality of the Imperial Iranian military during the revolution was prepared and signed due to the threats of the American General Robert Huyser[8], and the pressure of General Hossein Fardoust [of the Imperial Iranian military] and General Gharabaghi, the chief of staff [of the Imperial Iranian military], despite this the numbers of signatures were not enough to blame the entire Imperial Iranian military leaders. Would you please express your views regarding this issue?

Bakhtiar: With your permission, let us divide your question into two parts: the question of the Imperial Iranian military and the question of the Imperial Iranian military generals. The Iranian military is an

---

[8] General Robert Huyser, an American General and Deputy Commander of the North Atlantic Treaty Organization [NATO] was sent to Iran approximately a month prior to the revolution on a mission to Iran by the Carter Administration.

inseparable part of Iran; that means every Iranian, whether he is a colonel or an executive or a farmer, is Iranian and should perform his duty for his nation. Unfortunately, the Iranian military, due to various reasons, did not give a chance to the nationalist patriots and deserving officers. By chance, besides the officers you mentioned, whom I respect, if the opportunity were given to the deserving people, and they would progress according to their abilities, we would have other generals. This is also true for other societies.

The Iranian military, which for two years has been without arms and staff, and without respect from people in the Khomeini regime, which experienced mass killings in it and is still defending the territory of Iran for 2 years, deserves admiration. As I said if we had a nationalistic military and nationalist officers had the possibility of promotion, they could not have been among those generals in the Imperial Iranian military who signed the announcement of betrayal of the Imperial Military.

As you see, most of them were commanders like Rahimi who until the last minute and the last stage in Tehran, Biglari, Badreyi, Bid Abadi, Yazdegerdi and others including Shams Tabrizi, one of our best officers, in the provinces.[9] I was in touch with them because of their duties in relation to the Ministry of the Interior; they worked mostly as governors. I really respect them.

---

[9] Some of the Shah's military officials declared their neutrality in the Iranian Revolution. But, General Rahimi and tens of other high ranking officials of the Imperial Iranian military conducted resistance, and later they were executed by the succeeding regime that came to power, i.e. the Islamic Republic.

There were also Iranian generals who, being excessively wealthy, had escaped from Iran before Khomeini came. Of course all of them were not like [General] Fardoust and [General] Ghrabaghi. We thought they would at least choose to be silent and would not have claims, but we see that they claim to be pioneers for saving Iran! They say, "we want to save Iran". If they can save Iran! it means that if the same regime should return, what would we obtain? We lost hundreds of thousands of our people, that is enough! I don't know who causes discord between me and the army? Why they are trying to show that I have discontent toward the military?

I ask you to please read the speech I made in the Senate on February 10th, 24 hours before the betrayal of Mr. Fardoust and Mr. Gharabaghi and others, and see what I said about the Iranian military, and the flag of Iran. Concerning the recently acquired documents, I think [General Robert] Huyser had told them to do such although it is not known whether he told them to do so in this manner. They [the Imperial Iranian military] obtained their salary from us and our nation; they ought not have followed the orders of foreigners. I would like a kind of Iranian military and a kind of Iranian generals, who would support Iran, would serve Iran, and take orders from Iran and not from foreigners, no matter who they are.

JAAM-E-JAM: What is your view regarding Intelligence Service? With the disbanding of the Iranian Organization of Intelligence Service in Iran during the revolution, what plans did you have for the creation of another intelligence service?

Bakhtiar: Don't think I was so inexperienced in political and social affairs not to understand the importance of an intelligence service for the country. The Intelligence Service we had at that time, except for a short period when it was run by Major General Pakravan, was terrible, corrupt, and inefficient that interfered in every aspect of the country. Some people believe that if the Intelligence Service were not disbanded, Iran would not have suffered like this. After 24 hours from disbanding the Iranian Intelligence Service, I set a procedure on how to run the Service by 40 days, and until that time it would continue its duties. According to my evaluation, during the final 3-4 weeks, the Iranian Intelligence Service did not perform its duties in the same way as in the past.

As I mentioned before, the duty of the Intelligence Service is to collect information inside and outside of the country, to analyze it, and put it at the disposal of the central government. In this case I agree that no country in the world can do without it, but if the Intelligence Service would interfere in the affairs of families, or seize someone's property, would remove someone's nails, or torture, I can not allow it.

All eastern and western countries have Intelligence Services and they torture some people. It is not a good reason that we accept that. I believe if someone has ideas different from mine, he should not be tortured. If in Iran someone says that he prefers a republic, tell him that: "according to the Constitution, the government is a constitutional monarchy". It states that if he were in the majority, a republic would be established, of course not Islamic-democratic one, and not other nonsense like that. Well, such a person ought not be tortured or imprisoned, but if he made grenades, and wanted to explode armaments or arranged armed riots, he should be taken to court. In this case, the administration of justice should do its job, try him, send him to prison, years and years, and if necessary the death sentence be issued. This respect for the law and the spirit of the law is my principle of freedom of thought.

I can not agree that an organization which has been founded for intelligence and security of the country gives wrong information and endangers its own security. I suggested that it be disbanded. I think all the Iranian people know that even the officials of Shah's regime did not disagree; whereas when I suggested to the late His Majesty, that it be disbanded within the framework of the government program, he replied that there was no problem. He replied positively, but he asked what could substitute for that. I explained the same explanation as I am explaining here, extensively, and he said: "but there was no torture recently".

I said: "Maybe there wasn't, maybe they didn't use torture at the time of Pakravan, but how about Nassiri"[10]?

No! I could not tolerate such a regime. Even now I believe that disbanding the former Intelligence Service was the right thing to do, but no government can continue its ordinary political activities without an intelligence service.

JAAM-E-JAM: As the last question, may I ask you to express your views about the Iran-Iraq war, its consequences, and how it will end?

Bakhtiar: I have discussed this question not only in books, conferences etc., but in three announcements which were translated into English and French. We did not have any conflict with Iraq before the arrival of Khomeini. I should say that there have been differences and disputes, even fights, but then an agreement was reached in Algeria between the

---

[10] Pakravan and Nassiri were heads of SAVAK, the State Organization for Intelligence during the Shah's regime.

late Shah and the current Ba'ath regime of Iraq, which I have always said that I respect.

This is the way a normal, mentally balanced person thinks. But while Khomeini was against the Shah on the one hand, because he was deported from Iraq, he cancelled the treaty when he arrived [in Iran]. Why? What was wrong with the treaty and for what reason should it be cancelled? It was foolish to cancel it because it was signed by the Shah and Saddam Hussein. I can say that since the beginning, Khomeini started to send funds, people and other means for igniting the fire of war between Shiites and Sunnites, and "Real Islam", "Semi Real Islam" and "Unreal Islam".

No government is able to allow its neighbor to resort to causing such instability after conclusion of a peace treaty and resume these activities. Thus it can be said that Khomeini initiated the war.

But, Iraq made a great mistake in thinking that Khomeini and the nation of Iran were united and the same. Iraq wanted to attack Khomeini, and set the nation of Iran against itself. It is a historical and psychological mistake to imagine that the nation of Iran does not have nationalistic emotions; it does have very much. As the consequence of that, you saw the results.

By the way, during this period, some Muslim groups and groups from non-allied countries, neutral countries, Dr. Kurt Waldheim, the former Secretary General of the United Nations, visited Iran in order to help achieve a cease fire. They asked Khomeini to stop the bloodshed in which hundreds of thousands of people were killed, tens of billions of dollars in financial cost, refineries, railways and other assets were damaged, but he did not agree with them. The reason for that was explained by him about ten days ago. Khomeini said: "As long as I live, the war between Iran and Iraq will continue because my life and the survival of the regime of the Islamic Republic is dependent on this war". In fact, he himself says: "I have caused the war. I have caused the death of Iranians. I have caused the death of Iraqis".

I know that they are also human beings with emotions towards their wives, children, friends, relatives and compatriots. Instead of helping with the reconstruction of the country, of what was necessary to be reconstructed, his actions were killing, destroying and ruining the country. Foreign countries found it to be satisfactory. Israel is not on good terms with Iraq; its administrations often sell weapons to Khomeini, and they say he sells oil at low prices, purchases arms from us, and attacks Iraq. A few countries which have high technology believed that after the two countries would be ruined, they would ask their help for reconstruction of their countries and would have to sell them oil at a low price. Thus they ruined the resources of the country because they committed a foolish deed.

If I were asked who was responsible for this war, I would say: first Khomeini, second Khomeini, and third Khomeini.

I repeat again that the Iraqis made a mistake by thinking that because a part of the army was destroyed, humiliated, or killed by Khomeini; it can not stand against the Iraqis. We saw that for the reason I mentioned, the Iraqis made wrong evaluations.

JAAM-E-JAM: Thank you Dr. Bakhtiar. Wishing you victory in liberating Iran, I thank you again on behalf of JAAM-E-JAM.

Bakhtiar: Thank you very much. I wish success for everybody.

Shapour Bakhtiar

June 1983

JAAM-E-JAM: Dear viewers, beginning this week, we will broadcast Dr. Shapour Bakhtiar's speech which he delivered on his visit to Los Angeles and a question-and-answer session from the audience comprised of Iranians residing in California. This program has been exclusively produced by the mobile crew of JAAM-E-JAM Television.

Professor Abbas Amiri: With the permission of Dr. Bakhtiar, I am stating that our session is formal. This program begins at 4:30 and will end at 5:45. After the speech of Dr. Bakhtiar, if you have any questions, please raise your hand, they will bring you paper, and write your questions. I will submit the questions to Dr. Bakhtiar and he will answer your questions.

Shapour Bakhtiar: Ladies and Gentlemen, twenty-two years ago, at the Jalalieh Square, I was one of the speakers, and I began my statement with this poem from Hafez[11] and I continue to believe in the philosophy and the path that this valuable poet particularly in this segment of the poem which he wrote, and that poem is the one that after twenty-two years—despite all the turmoil in which our country has experienced unfortunately due to the causes which you know has been in the turmoil caused by the conspiracy of some unpatriotic mullahs—I still believe that we ought to continue the principle and the philosophy outlined in this poem.

---

[11]   The Persian poet of the 14th Century.

[Shapour Bakhtiar recited the poem from Hafez]

I hereby send my regards to all of friends and acquaintances living far away from the homeland, and my warm regards to all Iranians who despite bearing all hardships did not surrender to and will never surrender to the cruelty imposed by the government of Mullahs, and try to remain Iranian forever along with their children.

I do not think that any Iranian, any nationalist Iranian, would be my enemy, but I repeat forever that differences of opinion or even ideology should not turn us, Iranians, against one another.

Since I was young, my policy has been based on two principles:

First: Liberty, that means to wish freedom for all and not just for one's self. Second: Nationalism, which means every Iranian nationalist, regardless of opinion which may differ from others, is our brother and deserves respect. In my old age, I am standing here with pride, and all of you know that all my life my deeds have been the same with what I have written and what I have said. I have fought Hitler, some of the Mullahs, and I have and will continue to struggle against any other regime which stands against freedom and humanity. What is going on in Iran is a plot planned by some Mullahs to destroy the characteristics of us Iranians and annihilate an ancient nation. How did this conspiracy and disaster happen? How did a very ancient country with a rich cultural background and so well-organized—although it had its shortcomings, but those shortcomings are defendable in today's world—in a short time we faced this situation where you the Iranian people are wandering around this city while other Iranians are wandering near the border of Turkey-Iran, some Iranian people are wandering around in Pakistan, Germany, France and England?

These events took place so unexpectedly and almost suddenly, that for people like us who are fighting; it does not permit us to understand what had caused them.

It is your duty, the young people who are the future researchers and writers of history to investigate how a nation that did not go through foreign invasion, without external bombardment and military attack, did not have any economic problem regarding natural and economical resources, fell into such a destiny. I know that there are many reasons that are more or less clear to all of us, but scientific research ought to be conducted by the younger generation so that the nation of Iran, the future generations learn not to surrender to the forces whom they do not know and have not tested them, that do not believe in patriotism, liberalism and love for Iran.

So, it is the duty of every Iranian to fight, resist, and also strive for the preservation of the culture and existence of Iran. The existence of Iran is possible only if the enemies of Iran in any form are put aside. I know each one of you has many questions on your mind, and I will try to answer them considering the brief time that we have. I am sure that one of the subjects we'll talk about is what Europeans would call "Opposition", which in fact means those who are against the current cruel and oppressing regime of the Islamic Republic in Iran.

The opposition issue, i.e. the opposition to the Islamic Republic, should in fact be considered from two points of view: First—the agony, torture, helplessness and disaster of the Iranian people who live without any law, the result of which is that 36 million Iranian people are in mourning and are wandering around in the cities and are suffering due to a foolish war imposed on Iran. The people in Iran are in such situation that to be fair, the real opposition against the Islamic Republic exists in Iran and not here.

Regarding the Iranian opposition to the Islamic Republic that has been created by some Iranian people living overseas, they did not accept these conditions and this regime, i.e. the Islamic Republic, and announced that they will not surrender. They emphasized that they are human beings first and only then Iranians and only then Muslims. This was my motto, which I followed and will continue to follow forever, being one of your humblest compatriots.

The issue which is under discussion now, the question I occasionally hear is why the members of the Iranian opposition to the Islamic Republic who are outside the country do not unite?

The meaning of opposition ought to be recognized and be clear. How can a noble and nationalist Iranian person sit at the table and talk about unity with murderers in the Islamic Republic who have been the architects of this regime, i.e. the Islamic Republic? The latter, either could not continue to stay there any longer or had to leave since the regime of the Islamic Republic turned against them. These people have started to call for freedom and nationalism!

Is it possible to negotiate about the future of the people of Iran with members holding the highest positions at the Republic of Khomeini and sitting on the Revolutionary Committee of the Islamic Republic, gave the orders to execute the officers of the Imperial Iranian military? These people are now saying: "The army is with us!"

Is it possible to negotiate with those who gave the orders to the Revolutionary Committees to set fire, to ruin Iran, disregarding the fact that a million or two of Iranians would die because of what they called their "superior idealism"?

There are people who gave orders and collaborated with the executioners, most of whom were not Iranians and together with the very leaders [of the Islamic Republic] had collaborated in terrorism there—who gave the orders to kill without trial.

These people are talking today—in the streets of Washington or London or Paris—about peoples' government, freedom, and national sovereignty.

If you want to get help from these people, whose number is not few—I did not mention their names, but they are guilty on different levels—for saving Iran, you are trying in vain; in fact you will be helping Khomeini.

Is it possible for one who believes in nationalism and patriotism to convince such a people [former Khomeini's elements] that an officer, a clerk, or a businessman is innocent, or if he has committed a crime, he should have been punished according to the severity of his deeds? What was important to them was just bloodshed for threatening, frightening and terror in order to prevent people to breath.

Iran wanted and needed serious reforms. It is impossible to continue without them in Iran in the future—considering the population of Iran. Considering the young people under 20, who make up 55 percent of the Iranian population, it will be impossible to go back to the former situation. We tried to implement social and economic reforms and what was needed to initiate progress in Iran.

We tried to carry out all the reforms. We placed the result of 25 years of our campaigns at their disposal. We said to them that those were the reforms you wanted and we did carry out most of these reforms in the minimum amount of time, but they did not want these reforms. They wanted the country to be delivered to illiterate people, some of them studied in "Feiziyeh",[12] and schools of that kind, and whatever they wished did happen. Of course, the foreign countries helped them [these people] in the final stages.

Thus if the unification of opposition to the Islamic Republic means coordination among Iranian nationalist forces and Iran lovers, I have always been ready and I am ready for that, although there may be some differences of opinions and ideas, which is to be expected. I am always ready to repeat what I have said or written for my people.

I am responsible for what I have said, written, or put forward in other means myself, and what I have said in my speeches, because the National Resistance Movement of Iran, it is not a political party and I am not the leader of any political party. I believe that the National Resistance Movement of Iran forms a broad spectrum—If you put these two spectrums aside, on one side of which there are those hired by foreigners, while on the other side, there are the superficial Mullahs—what is left are Iranians who are capable of cooperating although there may be some differences regarding some principles I have mentioned earlier.

When Iran is liberated and there is rule of law, you will be able to form any political party, group, or organization that suits your thoughts and ideas. In this kind of government, no discrimination should exist.

---

[12] Islamic seminary in the city of Qom in Iran.

On the days of that winter in Iran, I sent messages to those calling for measures to be taken, like freedom of the press, release of political prisoners and transfer of the Pahlavi Funds to the government, etc. All of that was accomplished, but when Mr. Khomeini started to express contempt, I answered him that up to now many innocent people have been killed—there may have been some guilty people among them—but from now on that freedom would be given to people, you would be responsible for any possible future bloodshed.

I emphasize that I am resolute in the opinion that, up until now, that I am standing before you, those who led Iran to this situation are responsible for any Iranian people who were killed.

Therefore, do not ask me to talk as a political party leader who is an individual. I have always tried to convene most Iranians who have similar opinions; I mean those who, like me, do not change their ideas from one day to another. You have rarely heard that I have changed my ideas. I will always follow the Constitutional Law. But I will say briefly, since there may be some points that are unclear, that when I was in my hiding place on 7 Farvardin 1358 [March 27, 1979], they were preparing for the referendum [in Iran]. From my hiding place, with all the difficult situation that existed at that time, I had sent a message to Mr. Khomeini—recorded on a cassette which also reached abroad—that I will never vote for Islamic Republic and will never recognize it either. I added that in my opinion this republic is a dark parenthesis in the history of Iran and that this parenthesis ought to be closed as soon as possible.

This was my assessment and you know that there were some people who not only voted for Islamic Republic, but were also among the founders and architects of this system and did everything to help establish the regime of the Islamic Republic. After their leaders fired them, or may be they were not able to cope with him [Khomeini], they chose to fight for freedom of Iran! Such people, eager to reach high positions had turned to him, without knowing what the Islamic republic is about.

The future of Iran, therefore, depends on the Constitution [of 1906]. I would like to emphasize that we have had the Constitution for 77 years, but it has not been enforced for even 7 years. If it had been enforced, there would not have been any place for illiterate Mullahs.

We could have respected the law and believed in the right of freedom for all. We could have observed the Constitutional Law despite its deficiencies. Thus we could have enjoyed its advantages. We could have amended the Law in the case of ambiguity or if there are points that are unacceptable. Although the Law was approved 77 years ago, it does not mean that it should be discarded. Amendment of the Constitution took place even in America, France, and Germany. In America, since the era of Jefferson, you can see that Amendments to the Constitution have been made; also in France, in Germany, and all other countries.

In the future Iran should be governed first by a provisional government based on the Constitution [of 1906]. In this situation, the leader of the government should not follow the path of dictatorship. He should consult with the people of all levels of Iranian society. I believe that what ruined Iran was the lack of people's control over their fate. In the past, we Iranians did not have the right to participate in social or political affairs, and if we did, it had been according to a formula that was different from freedom and liberty. If we are supposed to go from a dictatorship to a different type of dictatorship, this is something I cannot accept, and if you are ready to put up with another dictatorship, you should separate my struggle from yourselves.

I am sure that I will not be alone in the struggle for liberty; I am sure the people of Iran do not think the same as they did four years ago.

Unfortunately some intellectuals and intelligent people were deceived, and you know what some leaders did in spite of their long records. I repeat, the future of Iran should be based on the principles of nationalism, a government based on nationalism, and national sovereignty. I accept the Constitutional Law and Constitutional Monarchy. National sovereignty is included in the Constitution [of 1906]. All types of power are mentioned in the Law and are derived from the Iranian people. In this way, sovereignty is national sovereignty. The important question in this subject is whether the nation should be able to have an influence upon its destiny, or whether others would determine the way it should be?

When you are able to let the nation participate in their affairs, even though you will not immediately be as advanced as Switzerland or Sweden, but you have to take the steps, and you will be able to say to the villagers in Iran that they are able to choose the head of their village; and that this affair is not relevant to Tehran. This day will be the beginning of democracy in Iran. In this case we should respect the law and if someone doesn't respect the law, it would cause the country of Iran to be ruined as it has been. However, this respect for the Law must exist in a regime in which the people participate and the majority of the people determine their destiny. Rather than a regime in which a few people, mostly corrupt ones, would possess all the authority, and the nation of Iran itself would have no power to make any decisions.

I assume that that you may have some questions regarding my visit to America. In all my life, I had never come to America, and truly I have come in order that I would perhaps be helpful in solving the problem of Iran. I went to England once. I have lived in France. And, in my opinion, England, France, and America are all equal to us and are foreigners. It is our interest that ought to be [inaudible] if our destiny is in our own hands we should share this destiny with others with all sincerity. Don't fear accusations. This is not important. We will live long enough for people to understand who was who and in what stages who had courage, and others how they were under the influence of others.

About my visit to America, I should mention that I visit this country following the recommendation of some of my friends—American and Iranian—to speak about Iran in one or two universities and in American circles. Therefore, I made speeches in some cities including New York, Washington and Chicago, the text of which will be at your disposal.

It is very important to me that people in the West know who we are and what we want. The issue of Khomeini is still not clear to most of Americans and Europeans. It was necessary that a group of people, who know about this issue, address the issue. I addressed the issues the best I could considering my background and experience.

I told them that: "whether you like it or not, Iran and the Iranians have the right to fight for their freedom and independence; therefore, if you are opposed to it, you are opposed to the will of the nation of Iran. If you help Khomeini, due to your own interests whether or not you are aware of your real interests, it is not relevant to us. We will not let the nation of Iran get used to this kind of regime, i.e. the Islamic Republic."

This was briefly the kind of negotiations I had with American leaders and with different people in the academic and various circles. I can say that the consequences and the results of the trip were much better than what I had thought. I repeat that for the sake of freedom of Iran, I am ready to go to any part of the world and talk and negotiate with any political regime and any person in order to save our country from its current situation, emphasizing that the people living inside Iran are the prisoners and not us. We are wanderers but not prisoners.

Another subject you may like to know about is how Khomeini should be overthrown. The only thing which is definitely meaningless is to organize an army and hire some men and invade from a corner of Iran while the others try to do the same from another corner in order to overthrow the regime of the Islamic Republic.

Khomeini's regime should be overthrown from the inside, i.e. through having connections with the army, tribes, intellectuals and all those who mistakenly regarded him as a savior.

I am informed about what is going on in Iran day by day and know which forces inside Iran are established, and which individuals have roots in Iran and who does not. I know what kind of persons do not have a good record or reputation in Iran. Exaggerating abroad—especially if instructed by foreigners—is very easy. The day we started our campaign, nobody had told us to wait, or whether there is green or red light. No matter what is going to happen in the future, this campaign will continue. Surely, no noble forces of struggle have ever failed and have always led to victory.

Iran of tomorrow, considering what I have mentioned, will be much different from what it had been in the past few years because tens of thousands—even hundreds of thousands of people, because there are no accurate figures—were killed, families were ruined and cities were destroyed. This reminds me about the role of the Iranian military. You are so young, but I remember since I was a young child when the establishment of the modern Iranian military occurred in Iran. This is the first time in history that the Iranian military has defended against the aggressors and proved to be Iranian. It fought not for Khomeini, but for Iran.

Those who think Khomeini is the symbol of Iran are wrong. Don't assume that the Russians fighting in Stalingrad fought for Stalin's sake. But it would not be fair to compare Stalin to Khomeini. At least he had a doctrine, a program, or something to say whether acceptable by us or not. But in their case, in order for Khomeini to be calm and be busy, he resorts to war, bloodshed, and riots, receiving inspiration with such changes on a daily basis; one day democracy, one day Divine Order, and another day Imam's Fatva [decree]. All these cause the people in Iran to be confused. This Iranian army is not what it used to be before. This Iranian military is not the Mullah's Military. The Mullahs are trying to destroy this Iranian military. The Mullahs are trying to establish an Islamic nation military. We should try to make our army a nationalistic and an Iranian one.

I would like to use this opportunity to announce my willingness to cooperate without any pre-conditions with Iranian officers, especially with the young ones, regardless of what their political ideas may be. Iran is above everything and I will always love those who love Iran. It was a long introduction and we do not have much time.

Questions from the Audience:

Read and Answered by Shapour Bakhtiar

Bakhtiar: I just received a note with a question from "Mr. Moradi": He writes as follows:

> "Mr. Bakhtiar, the Shah delivered Iran to you", and after showing some affection he continues in a commanding tone:

> "Why did you deliver it to a . . . man like Khomeini?"

> —Signed: "Moradi".

Bakhtiar: Secrets were not supposed to be disclosed. I should have been called to run the country, instead of people like Hoveida and Sharif-Emami and others. While the cancer of Khomeini was spreading to all the body organs of Iran, I had two options: either I would have taken a stance that was popular at the time and would not have interfered, or I would have shouted in support of the establishment of Islamic Republic as did others. I chose to accept the order of the Shah and I tried my best.

*Another gentleman has kindly written:

"Mr. Bakhtiar. We have heard your ideas about the future, but what is the opinion of Council of National Resistance of Iran about this matter?"

Bakhtiar: I guess by Council of National Resistance of Iran he means the organization of Mr. Rajavi and Bani Sadr. In this case you ought to ask them and not me.

Theirs is the idea of Pol Pot. Their views change according to a given situation; [on their flags], one day there are verses of the Koran along with sickle and hammer, one day Kalashnikov with other things, but I have always had one flag, and it is this one [pointing to the flag of Iran with the lion and sun].

*Mr. Davood Amir Ghasemi aka Mr. Hadi Nazer wrote: "Mr. Bakhtiar, the legal Prime Minister of the Royal Government of Iran: Respectfully, the supporters of Royal Regime of Iran . . . ."

Bakhtair: I once wrote something like this in my book, but [generally] I do not sign this way. I once wrote that during the past four years, and I am explaining it to you who most likely are a monarchist. I infer it from your words.

I once wrote: "Prime Minister Shapour Bakhtiar" on flowers I sent to Cairo when His Majesty passed away. I wrote that to show that, contrary to the ambassadors and ministers who accumulated wealth through the Shah's regime and then turned their backs, I was not [not audible]. I thank you for the title you gave me. I am grateful to [not audible] and I think that all my life I have been a follower of the Constitution [of 1906].

I would like to say something to you that I am sure is surprising for you:

About two or three years ago, I was talking to the Queen and the Crown Prince of Iran in Cairo. Among the issues discussed was the issue of the system of government, a republic in Iran, and I told them that a Republic is not in itself a [not audible], but from the geopolitical point of view, situation and traditions of Iran, constitutional monarchy is more useful. I told this without intending to be flattering. I said that because I believe this is the right way, otherwise I would say the opposite.

*Mr. Safyari has written [to me] as follows:

"Mr. Robert Dreyfuss has written in his book, entitled "Hostage to Khomeini", that the revolution in Iran was brought about by the British, do you agree with his opinion?"

Bakhtair: As I have said before, certainly, especially the propaganda of the British caused us damage as much as they could, especially during the last stages of the regime of the Shah prior to Khomeini. They intrigued against us as much as they could. I would like to recommend another book I have written in French [entitled Ma Fidalite] which was translated by one of my friends into Persian [entitled Yek Rangi]. In this book, I have mentioned that the harm caused by the B.B.C of London to the government of Iran in the Shah's regime, or in the rise of Khomeini's government to power is clear and I provided evidence there of what happened at that time. Now regarding the issue that the English had a role in this matter.

I know Mr. Robert Dreyfuss. He and an American man called Mr. LaRouche—whom I think is his representative and he was a candidate in the presidential elections—came to my house two or three times for talks. He believes, and I have mentioned it in my book, that Khomeini and, in general, the Mullahs have always been agents and elements of the British who have always been in the hands of the British who the British utilized time and time to harm the nation of Iran. I agree with this belief in principle. But because we saw Seyyed Abolghassem Kashi and Behbehani and him and these [elements], I essentially agree with this thought. But there is something worse than that: since the reign of the Sassanid sultans up until now, every misery and failure taking place in Iran had been caused by the interfering of Mullahs of that time or this time.

*Mr. Shahab Ghods has asked a question.

Bakhtair: Yes, as I have written in my book, I said something to the late Sadat whom I highly respected. I might have written about this. I told him that Iranians are either monarchist or republicans, although there are differences between these two ideas, but both groups highly respect you and know you as a great man. Those who are monarchists are grateful to you for the way you treated the Shah. People who are not monarchists and belong to other groups—even though they may have different opinions—still respect you because you were the only one who had the courage to give the Shah temporary shelter at a [critical] time.

In one of the sessions, the Late Sadat—whom I highly respected—as he used to speak in his own way and like most of the presidents and kings of Arab states addressing people by their first name, said to me: "Shabour—this was the way he pronounced my name because [in Arabic] the letter "P" does not exist. Sadat said: "I told Mohammad, my brother" at first I didn't know that he meant Mohammad Reza Shah, "that he could order the Air Force to land here in our airports, anywhere in Egypt, our full establishment, in case we may launch a move together with your air force which is the greatest and almost as strong as Israel's. The Shah did not respond. The next day, when I presented the issue, he said with sadness: 'Do you think the Iranian Army and the Air Force are under my command?'" Then Sadat said nothing and I didn't ask any questions. Because the disaster that occurred to me with regard to Fardust and Gharabaghi was indicative of that.

Bakhtiar: Youssef Zadeh has asked a question.

We fully observe democracy. Even if you ask [me] with [tendency towards] opposition or agreement, I will reply honestly.

He asks: "Did the Shah of Iran have to leave? Was it not possible for him to stay and manage the affairs [of the country so that it would not be disrupted]?"

Bakhtiar: If it had occurred to His Majesty to stop giving power to incompetent people, and had he changed the situation two months before, the people would have contempt for the Prime Minister and other people, then we did not have to face such a problem.

If we [not audible] hold an investigation among the resolutions issued by the Mullahs and The Tudeh [the Communists Party of Iran] until the time of Sharif-Emami and the latest stages [of the Shah's regime], we will find out that the issue was not that the Shah should leave; the issues were free elections, free press, and similar issues—with which I, you, and most of the gentlemen agree with. Nobody said the Shah should leave. The situation, [however], had changed. Little by little the Iranian people started to talk about it, and Knomeini as usual kept emphasizing and requesting the Shah's departure. Thus, unfortunately, little by little, people turned to be more aggressive. That's why I say that if His Majesty had made genuine changes—not reassigning the former political figures—the issue would not have arisen and neither America nor England or Soviet Union would have had the courage to raise the issue.

Here is another question:

"At the beginning of your tenure as a Prime Minister, had you been informed that the members of the National Front of Iran were supporters of Khomeini?"

Bakhtiar: Yes, despite that I accepted this position. One should be proud of it.

"Did they help you to hide and help you leave Iran?

Bakhtiar: I tell you, neither any of the National Front of Iran members neither Bazargan nor others knew where I was in Iran. I left Iran six months later with the help of my friends who were not members of the National Front of Iran.

"If the answers to my first two questions are positive, why did you leave the country and deliver it to others?"

Bakhtiar: My dear brother. I had been in my hiding place and I wanted to come here so that you, at least, would [hear] me inside and outside of Iran. You should say this to Mr. Rajavi who is 35, and can fight at the border of Iraq. I stopped fighting when I was 35.

Mr. Razm Ara asks:

"Regarding the future government you [plan] for Iran what people and officials will take part? Why haven't you introduced them to the people?"

Bakhtiar: In response to your question, I will just give an example. When General De Gaulle was in England, do you think that even if he had determined his cabinet he would have announced that on Television or radio? For people who live in Iran it is very dangerous to be publicly known as [future cabinet] ministers. Surely they wouldn't like it.

I should remark that we have just five minutes left to answer the questions, and then they will ask us to leave here [the Ambassador Hotel].

A compatriot asks:

"You have mentioned in your book "Yekrangi", that one of Dr. Mossadegh's mistakes was that he did not have any specific political party to support him at the time he needed it."

Bakhtiar: That's true. Dr. Mossadegh had the same feelings as the Iranian people, but he neither wanted nor agreed with the establishment of a political party. Therefore this was one of the factors that contributed to his fall. There were other reasons. Just like me, who has been a member of the "Iran Party" for the past 30 years, and do not intend to establish a new political party. I have reached the age and stage in my life to bring together different people and political parties. Mossadegh did not like to establish a political party and as a result separate people from one another. As I told you, the National Resistance Movement of Iran is not a political party. It has the characteristics of an organization which wants to bring together various individuals regarding general issues and the overthrow of the Islamic Republic.

Once freedom is achieved, anybody could establish a political party and everything will start all over again.

Next question:

"For what purpose did you allow Khomeini to enter Iran?"

Bakhtair: There are two reasons for this issue. Either you accept respect for Law, or not. Two issues forced me to accept that Khomeini enter Iran. One was that there was no other option. There was only one way which was to order General Rabiee to shoot down his airplane when flying towards the Iranian border. There was no other option. There was only one way, and I had assessed everything. When I wanted to go to Paris, of course it was not intended for seeing his . . . face but to bring him to the negotiating table, and therefore to make him descend from the highly holy position which he had made for himself, and negotiate with him as two Iranians—obviously, if he could be considered an Iranian.

Now, why didn't I do that? Considering humanity, human rights, I am not the type of person who would have done that. But, another reason, more important than the rest, was that 72 Arabs who had differences of opinion in a desert in Karbala were killed. Even after 1,400 years, we still beat our chests and mourn. If I had done that, you would have seen that they would have said that the Mahdi whom they were waiting for was coming and that the son of Shemr (me!) attacked him and forced him to leave!

The audience: Viva Bakhtiar.

Amir Taheri

Journalist and Scholar; Author of several books on the Middle East, Contributor to many newspapers and magazines, Editor-In-Chief, Kayhan International prior to the Iranian Revolution.

The Assassination of Shapour Bakhtiar

Manouchehr Bibiyan's Interview with Amir Taheri

August 11, 1991

JAAM-E-JAM: In this part of our program, we are going to broadcast the discussion of Mr. Manouchehr Bibiyan with Mr. Amir Taheri, the International political commentator and journalist based in Paris.

Manouchehr Bibiyan: Mr. Taheri, how do you assess the request of the Islamic Republic's Foreign Minister from the Government of France to prevent the activities of Iranian opposition against the Islamic Republic in Paris, and how do you interpret the assassination of Dr. Shahpour Bakhtiar?

Amir Taheri: As you know, Paris has always been the center of activities of the Iranian opposition to the Islamic Regime in Iran. Since 12 years ago, the Islamic Government in Iran has tried to convince the different French cabinets to prevent the activities of the Iranian opposition against the Islamic Republic in Paris. France is a democratic country which is ruled by law, and I do not think that the Islamic Republic will be successful regarding this matter.

Regarding the assassination of Dr. Bakhtiar, there are different views and hypotheses but it can be said that the assassination was directly or indirectly the result of the violence existing in the political life of Iran since the beginning of the Islamic Revolution. It is not important who is personally and directly responsible for the assassination. What is important is that unfortunately the politics of Iran, the political life of Iran is still continuing its violence and terror, [inaudible].

The assassination of Dr. Bakhtiar will not put an end to the activities of the Iranian opposition abroad against the Islamic Republic. The National Resistance Movement of Iran whose founder and leader was Dr. Bakhtiar had recently chosen a new leader. The new leader intended to act independently of Dr. Bakhtiar because the late Dr. Bakhtiar intended to minimize his activities due to his old age, and act as the founding father of the movement.

The activities of this movement are going to continue, and I think that other Iranian opposition groups against the Islamic Republic will become stronger following the assassination, and expand their activities contrary to the expectations of the Islamic Republic.

Currently, many political activities in Paris and in other cities in France and Europe are being conducted in common in honor of Dr.

Bakhtiar, the late Prime Minister of Iran. The negotiations which have previously started will expand. The telephone contacts with the leaders of the opponents of the Islamic Regime inside and outside of Iran have proven to be a counter reaction rather than a submissive attitude. The assassination of Bakhtiar is an indication of the weakness of the regime of the Islamic Republic rather than its strength. No doubt those who were afraid of a retired politician—who was going to stay away from the day to day arena of political activities—are weak people.

The situation of the Islamic Republic is chaotic and ruined, and there are so many conflicts among themselves. These terrorist activities cannot solve their problems.

from left:
Manouchehr Bibiyan, Ali Amini
1989 At Amini's Residence

from left: Shapour Bakhtiar; Dr. Lailee Bakhtiar (it was with her help that JAAM-E-JAM's contact with a television station was established to broadcast JAAM-E-JAM programs); Manouchehr Bibiyan

from left:
sitting: Ali Amini
standing: Manouchehr Bibiyan; Dokhi
At JAAM-E-JAM Studio 1984

Shapour Bakhtiar

from left: Reza Pahlavi; Manouchehr Bibiyan

from left: Manouchehr Bibiyan; Reza Pahlavi; and
JAAM-E-JAM Colleagues Goli Yahyavi and Sattar Deldar

from left: Manouchehr Bibiyan, Ardeshir Zahedi
1994

from left: Manouchehr Bibiyan, Ardeshir Zahedi
2004

from left: Manouchehr Bibiyan, Daryoush Homayoun

Abdolazim Valian

from left: Benjamin Netanyahu; Manouchehr Bibiyan

from left: Manouchehr Bibiyan, Moshe Katsav

from left: Sir Anthony Parsons; Manouchehr Bibiyan

from left: Manouk Khodabakhshian; Farhang Farahi; Ahmad
Madani; Manouchehr Bibiyan; Manouchehr Omidvar
The Interview of Some of JAAM-E-JAM Colleagues
during the past 30 years with Ahmad Madani
At JAAM-E-JAM Studio

Shahin Fatemi

from left: Manouchehr Bibiyan; Amir Taheri

from left: Manouchehr Bibiyan; Marvin Zonis

from left:
Standing: Kourosh Bibiyan, Lili Ahmadi, Parviz Sayad,
Sitting: Manouchehr Bibiyan, Shohreh Aghdashlu
Some of JAAM-E-JAM Colleagues during the past 30 years

from left, Shohreh Aghdashlu, Homa Sarshar,
Manouchehr Bibiyan, Parviz Sayad, Parviz Kardan
Some of JAAM-E-JAM Colleagues during the past 30 years

from left: Goli Yahyavi; Manouchehr Bibiyan; Hoda
Some of JAAM-E-JAM Colleagues during the past 30
years
The first years of JAAM-E-JAM Television

from left: standing: Lili Ahmadi; Mansour Sepehrband;
Farhang Farahi, Anahita Khalatbari, Kioumars
Bouzarjoumehri; Sattar Deldar
Sitting: Manouchehr Bibiyan
Some of JAAM-E-JAM Colleagues during the past 30
years

Reza Pahlavi

Heir to the Iranian Throne

Reza Pahlavi

Broadcast: June 15, June 22, & June 29, 1986

Reza Pahlavi: Well, gentlemen, I see you work hard. I would like to thank you for your efforts in producing these programs. It is important to maintain high morale. I see that you work hard despite the problems and difficulties you encounter. As an Iranian, I would like to encourage you and say that what you are doing is very effective. And, may be you should be more selective regarding your viewers because your viewers do not have the same opinions. It is the policy of your program to appeal to which type of viewers with which perspective.

You are obviously producing programs mostly for people with a specific way of thinking who understand to some extent better than others or expect to view these programs. But, there is a certain class of people who are used to watching TV on Sundays as a hobby. These people's attention should be drawn as well. I am very glad to see that your programs are well prepared and well established. Being a perfectionist, I would like to see even more. I hope that you continue your activities that you have had with continued success.

JAAM-E-JAM: On behalf of Jaam-E-Jam TV and its viewers who are mostly self—exiled Iranians, please accept my congratulations to you on your marriage to your dear wife; we wish success to both of you.

Reza Pahlavi: Thank you very much.

JAAM-E-JAM: As you know, JAAM-E-JAM Television network has been engaged in a serious struggle solely for the freedom and liberation of Iran for over 5 years, and has not given up its professional honor and patriotism in exchange for anything either moral or material, and therefore JAAM-E-JAM Television is not indebted to anyone. The president and executive-producer of JAAM-E-JAM Television Network, Mr. Manouchehr Bibiyan, and his colleagues are proud to work hard in exile for the creation of an Iranian media in exile that is reliable and honorable despite limited possibilities.

Manouchehr Bibiyan: I, Manouchehr Bibiyan, the president and executive producer of JAAM-E-JAM Television Network, before having my colleagues ask questions that have been prepared at JAAM-E-JAM about current issues, would like to ask my first question about your marriage. Usually, marriage is a turning point in the life of any young couple, and the beginning of a new stage. What does this beginning mean to you while living far away from the homeland? And, does it make you more resolute and steadfast in the political struggle, or would it be resultant that you would prefer a calm and worriless family life to fighting an uneven and difficult war?

Reza Pahlavi: What I can tell you and perhaps it is more a question is that can it be claimed that the decision-making power of a single man be more than a married man? I think that regarding I and many other individuals, a stability in life would be found more. It is this way for me and I have in any case many times referred to the point that my personal life will not intervene in my political life, and in this issue, a new situation would be created for me. Until now, I knew myself as the child of Iran, one day perhaps when I myself become a father, I would know the pain and responsibilities of fathers and families. Today, I can see from the perspective about these issues much more as a man who has a family, rather than personally as a single man. And, this might be very important that in a leader usually when he has a family he feels a degree of more responsibility. I think that this must be a good sign and my compatriots to know that this not only does have an opposite effect on me, no exactly the opposite, it will be very positive also, and certainly it will have a positive effect on my decision-making.

JAAM-E-JAM: Now that we are talking about your marriage, many people are very interested to know how you met Ms. Yasmin.

Reza Pahlavi: Well, in three days, it will be our first anniversary. We met each other very accidentally. After completing her studies, she arrived at Washington to visit a family member. I had also gone to Washington when we met at the airport. This was the beginning of our acquaintance. Later, we knew each other which led to love and marriage.

JAAM-E-JAM: Is she in politics?

Reza Pahlavi: Well, You should ask her about it.

Manouchehr Bibiyan: In the Constitution of 1906 there are Articles implemented from 1906 to the revolution in 1979 that have not protected the rights of religious minorities in Iran. For example, participating in elections, candidacy for Majlis [parliament]—[they could solely elect one representative from their respective religion], holding government or military positions, etc. If you become king, will these religious discriminations remain or will they change?

Reza Pahlavi: This is a very interesting question. In our Constitution, it is exactly written that the King of Iran is the promoter of Shi'a Asna Ashari [Twelver Shi'ism]. In any case, this exists in that Law. I have not written that Law. There had been a Majlise Moassessan [Constitutional Assembly] and in this way the Law has been written.

If you want my personal opinion which is separate from the legal duty that I have to that Law, essentially, that if the discussion is regarding religion, religion is an issue that is relevant to a person and the relationship of that person with his/her God. Whether the religion of Islam, Christianity, Judaism, etc. Meanwhile, I believe that religion ought not to become a form of government or intervene in politics. It is possible that it has impact. In any case we are a Muslim country and in majority. Well, the way of thinking and outlook on issues is certainly under influence.

But essentially if we want to mix religion with government, it is neither to the advantage of religion nor to the advantage of government. At least it can be seen in today's progressive countries in the world, democratic countries. But, instead of raising the issue of what issues possibly might exist now which there exist different thoughts about it, I want to express the issue this way that according to that Law if it will be necessary that issues that exist in the Constitution change, there is a formula for this.

The Majlis [Parliament] establishes a Majlise Moassessan [Constitutional Assembly] with a specific goal that what part of a Law or a reform or amendment or in any case all of the law or the way it has been predicted, they convene and change those articles in the Constitution. And, in any case to the extent that I understand the Law it seems that this possibility exists in that Law. Whatever it is, I believe that we are entering the 21st century and there are many issues that should be—considering the progress of time and change in people's thoughts—changed and there be a flexibility and changes be made in the Constitution [of 1906].

In any case, as time progresses there ought to be review regarding some issues. I can give a simple example. The Constitution says that the King is the commander of ground forces and navy. Well, there was not an Iranian Air Force at that time. Now, if you ask me that whether I am the commander of the Iranian Air Force or not, well according to the Law—because it is not stated—perhaps I am not. But, well, Air Force is part of the Armed Forces. In any case, I believe that this possibility exists regarding the Law, as I have understood the Law up until now.

JAAM-E-JAM: In the interviews we had with Dr. Ali Amini, a suggestion was made saying that the Shah of Iran would land in Iran and settle in a province near the border in order to lead the Iran Liberation Staff. Do you have any comment regarding this matter? Do you think this plan is enforceable?

Reza Pahlavi: Different scenarios will be noticeable and relevant only when they fit the situation that goes with it. I do not have any extant plans regarding this issue. In such cases, everything would depend on the situation of the country.

However, I do not reject this idea. It might be necessary for me to land inside the country with a group of people. I do not reject it, but everything depends on the situation at hand. You mentioned the Commanding Staff. It was discussed in general, but it is a new issue for me and if necessary, I will talk to the gentlemen in Paris immediately, or any suggestions that have been made by others. At present, I neither reject nor confirm any possibilities.

JAAM-E-JAM: In your last interview, you mentioned that the demonstration of thousands of Iranian people—in one voice—in Washington D.C. opened a new window of hope for you. In this regard, what has been the reaction of the politicians with influence in the region's politics?

Reza Pahlavi: What you have mentioned not only me, but many of our fellow compatriots, well, they would be happy and hopeful. I believe it certainly had a great impact on foreign policies of states. When they hear our people in loud voice and always talking about our country, and revealing the situation inside Iran, it makes them pay attention to this issue, especially the people living in this country as you do—surely know how much impact public opinion has on politicians in this country, more than in any other country. Thus, the more they witness these demonstrations, the easier it make our task, especially for me because there is no need to speak of it, because I have seen it and witnessed it. The cooperation among my fellow compatriots multiplies our strength. The potential strength existing among we Iranians would help us no longer feel that we have a piece of homeland that can be divided but rather that we are a living nation belonging to that land, aware, and vocal.

If we are indifferent or do not express ourselves, how can we expect politicians from other countries to pay any attention to us? The louder our voice is, the more can we help our country.

JAAM-E-JAM: JAAM-E-JAM is making arrangements to have an interview with Queen Shahbanu Farah in order to inform people about the last days of the late Shah's life. In the book entitled "Answer to History", which has been published in other languages, we see that the texts are incompatible, and even its translations into Persian are different. Is it not the best answer for the Iranian people that the Queen, Shahbanou Farah, participate in a dialogue in which she would speak with an Iranian media, for example, JAAM-E-JAM, for the first time?

Reza Pahlavi: Well, this is a question you should ask her. Surely, the hardships we experienced during that period may include interesting points for our fellow compatriots as well. Some of them have even witnessed the events that had taken place while my father was alive. Anyway, these events were all part of the attempt to force the Shah out of the country. Maybe she [Queen Farah] will have the opportunity to talk to our people in the future about what we have gone through and what happened to our family according to our point of view.

JAAM-E-JAM: May I ask what your wishes are?

Reza Pahlavi: Yes. I wish to have children. I would like them to grow up in an atmosphere like that of Tehran rather than Washington. You see here that although parents send their children to Persian classes, read books and so on, it does not replace Iran. They may speak Persian, but alas with American accent; there is a limit to everything. I wish I could go back to my country and start life there, to live the kind of life that will help me to contribute to my nation in every aspect.

There is no difference between others and me. I also wish to raise children who will serve the country in the future. I would rather have my children raised with the view of Damavand Mountain, see the view of Shemiran and, well, the south Tehranis not be upset, the south of Tehran too.

JAAM-E-JAM: Have you ever thought on utilizing talents?

Reza Pahlavi: I believe that an intelligent person should be able to reach any position one likes, regardless of one's family background, position, religion, or education. I really think that it is not necessary to have education or political experience in order to be a leader or lead people. One may be illiterate, but be people believe in him. In fact, our national capital is not the dollars that are earned by selling oil, but the talents of the people of that country.

Manouchehr Bibiyan's Interview with Reza Pahlavi

Date of Broadcast: February 12, 1989

Farhang Farrahi, JAAM-E-JAM: This week was significant. It was a week in which Crown Prince Reza Pahlavi talked to the media, met representatives of Iranian youth, women, artists and Iranian officers, and in all these meetings, during a 90 minute private meeting, the Crown Prince emphasized two major points: First, independence and national sovereignty for Iran as a goal, and then, uniting all nationalist forces as a means for achieving that goal.

Mr. Manouk Khodabakhshian, considering the fact that Crown Prince Reza Pahlavi would not interfere with the executive affairs, and leave the task of organizing to others, what is the best way of creating cooperation, or call on the opposition against the Islamic Republic to cooperate?

Manouk Khodabakhshian, JAAM-E-JAM: Mr. Farrahi, the goal is clear and the means to achieve it is clear too, the only issue left is strategy. The problem of entering Iran, as he has said many times, is not the same as the arrival of Benazir Bhutto. Bhutto entered like Khomeini did. The point is that when Khomeini was in Paris, all groups formed a coalition and a platform for him to take action. In those days, there were organizations like the Iranian Students Confederation, National Front of Iran, Iranian Mujahedin-i-Khalgh, Iranian Fadaiyan-i-Khalgh who, together with millions of Iranian people allowed Khomeni to enter Iran very easily and settle there. Today our goal is clear, on what basis can we form a coalition? Benazir Bhutto was supported by the Peoples Party, Rajiv Gandhi was supported by the League Elements, but what about us? What do we have? The problem is that we have many powerful political personalities, but because they do not act together, they do not possess any strategic value; they should converge, and form a winning card. I mean those who believe in national sovereignty, have nothing to add to it. He also speaks about national sovereignty. The goal of Reza Pahlavi's supporters is to overthrow the Khomeini regime, so their goal is clear. A national coalition should be formed inside the country to make it easier to settle there.

Farrahi, JAAM-E-JAM: The dreadful regime in Iran, i.e. the Islamic Republic celebrated the tenth anniversary of the Iranian revolution by showing admiration and honoring the Iranian revolutionary forces killed in the past 10 years, whereas on its 10th anniversary, many of the best children of Iran who fought for the freedom of their country are imprisoned or executed in Iran. Through the memory of those who fought for freedom, an intellectual revolution among Iranians is being based outside of the country. This great intellectual revolution begins with what is developing, i.e. national unity. And it will lead towards achieving national unity. Considering the responses of Crown Prince Reza Pahlavi to Mr. Manouchehr Bibiyan, we see that the greatest obstacle to the unity of our nationalist forces is behind us.

Until now, there was a great obstacle in the way of unification of political forces, and it was that: 1) Reza Pahlavi is interfering in executive affairs, and therefore, he should not, as a king assume the role of coordinator. 2) he had not made clear his role vis-à-vis the nationalist forces.

The answers that Crown Prince Reza Pahlavi gave to the important questions asked by Mr. Manouchehr Bibiyan, President and Executive Producer of JAAM-E-JAM, determine the fate and removes the biggest obstacle to uniting the nationalist forces.

Manouchehr Bibiyan: In discussing nationalism and national sovereignty, Dr. Mossadegh, for nationalizing the Iranian oil industry and his emphasis on the principle that the Shah must reign, not rule, has left his mark on Iran's history in the last fifty years, more than any other individual. What is your opinion regarding this issue?

Reza Pahlavi: I think Dr. Mossadegh has been one of the most prominent nationalist figures in Iranian history, and he should be considered a very important individual in our history. What he said was very true. In order to clarify misunderstandings, I should say that the faithful followers of Dr. Mossadegh have always told me that he was a real monarchist and believed in this system. He knew that there were major differences between a king, who is a symbol of the state and a leader or a prime minister of the state or a leader of a party. I would like to say now that allegations made against Mossadegh are unfounded. I believe that Dr. Mossadegh has been and will be considered one of the greatest men in the history of Iran.

I will always have great respect for him for his historic activities of patriotism and nationalism. I think that people who do not appreciate him, are unfortunately unable to firmly believe in the nationalism of Iran.

Ardeshir Zahedi

Iran's Last Ambassador to the United States; son-in-law and Adviser to Mohammad Reza Shah Pahlavi; Foreign Minister; Ambassador to England; Deputy Director of the Point Four Program in Iran prior to the Iranian Revolution.

Manouchehr Bibiyan's interview with Ardeshir Zahedi

May 8, 1994

Location of the Interview: Los Angeles

Manouchehr Bibiyan: Mr. Zahedi, the book which has been published under the Shah's name, entitled *Answer to History*, you know, the French version of this book differs from its English version. The Persian version of this book differs from its French and English versions. Do you think that this book, entitled *Answer to History*, was really written by the Shah?

Ardeshir Zahedi: I was against it. His Majesty, in the last months, was infinitely ill. Unfortunately, the Queen Shahbanou and others interfered in the written text. And, this man could not even talk about his daily life. Unfortunately, this is a book for a man who reigned for 37 years, and he struggled in order to maintain the situation, Azerbaijan, the land reform and distribution of lands, and other contributions. A few—four people—have written these under his name. It is truly unfortunate.

Manouchehr Bibiyan: One of the reasons that I respect President Nixon is that when the Shah was displaced and ill, he visited the Shah.

Ardeshir Zahedi: I took him there. I went because he was sick. I rearranged the visit that had been previously delayed. He [Nixon] came to [Cuernavaca] and met with His Majesty. I would like to mention that he was the one who came to the funeral. All the other Heads of State and others kept their distance from him, but he came like a brave gentleman.

Once, [President Nixon] wanted to come to Iran. During that time of unfortunate events and problems, unfortunately they misled His Majesty and he ordered: "No, he ought not come." I told him not to come. After that, he had interviews, and then he wrote something, he wrote an article in which he said that this is a dark page in the history of America.

Manouchehr Bibiyan: Don't you think that had Watergate not occurred, had Nixon remained in power, the U.S.-Iran relations perhaps might have been better, and the Shah could have had stronger support from the United States?

Ardeshir Zahedi: Well, this comes back to the other event. Certainly, if Nixon had remained in power the political situation in the world would not have changed the way it has, because he was a powerful man and it might have been possible that our circumstances would have changed. But, it could have been one of the reasons, yes, and other reasons. Unfortunately, we come back to ourselves because when Pinochet came to power, Pinochet is still in power, and he has brought democracy to his country. They did not hang anybody and have not destroyed anyone. The economic condition of his country is one of the best in the world. Therefore, one, the blame is with the leadership and also, to some extent, with the groups or the Administrations—whatever they could be called. We maintained this Administration for thirteen years. What results did we obtain? We caused the people to be dissatisfied. We changed the place of Ministers, and in the end, when we needed them, they all packed their luggage and ran away earlier than anyone. One said that he had pain in his waist; the other said he had pain in his neck! They said to me that I was wrong to go there! Well, this is a point of view, unfortunately everything altogether.

Manouchehr Bibiyan: Mr. Zahedi, to the extent that I have information, I don't know whether this information is accurate or not, you were one of the individuals who were opposed to the departure of the Shah from Iran.

Ardeshir Zahedi: That was my opinion and it still is. I believe that if His Majesty had not left Iran, Khomeini would not have dared to enter Iran. Furthermore, the army would surely not have been destroyed, because the army knew His Majesty as God's shadow. In this way, the army would always have been under the control of their commander. After the Shah left Iran, the armed forces felt they had lost their father. They felt they had lost their leader. Khomeini had said several times that he would not enter Iran before the Shah left. That was because he did not dare to come. It did not occur to him to enter Iran, and when he did, he could not believe that he had managed to capture the country so easily. Unfortunately, it happened anyway. I still believe that the Shah should not have left the country. I commented on this in his presence many times and explained my reasons, but I was just one person and the others said other things. I do not want to say that I was a man of insight, because everyone [inaudible]; I had a duty to perform. I told him the truth as I viewed it—with conscience and honor. I don't mean to say that what I said was correct or not. It is not I who render a judgment; history and others would judge. There were other people around [him] who were advisers, who were older and more knowledgeable and experienced than I, God knows.

Manouchehr Bibiyan: Mr. Zahedi, you are the only person who knew what was occurring behind the scenes—meaning, at least in the United States. Twelve years ago, when we talked, I believe you said that there was a division, here, in the United States regarding the Shah's leaving or remaining, and you went to Iran to prevent the Shah from leaving Iran. And, I don't know whether they had told you to do so, or you yourself went there to prevent this. Why didn't you succeed?

Ardeshir Zahedi: The historical aspect is that for a long time I told His Majesty that as I hear the situation in Iran is not good. His Majesty was almost my boss, my commander. He was dear to me, and I always wanted to tell him the truth.

I am going to tell you where and when that Gentleman Agreement started. It was on a summer day in Saad Abad Palace. At that time my father was alive. I always reported to him the truth, facts, and sometimes he accepted my remarks and other times he thought I was exaggerating or was not right.

The day before my meeting with Carter, I was having dinner with the former Vice President, Mr. Rockefeller, in New York, when Zbignew Brzezinski called and said that President Carter would like to meet me. The meeting lasted from 10:00 A.M. to 1:30 P.M.

In this meeting, the President told me: "I have heard that you are going to be either Prime Minister or Court Minister, either of which may be helpful!"

I told him: "I am a candidate neither for Prime Minister nor for Court Minister. I love my country and am interested in the Shah, thus whatever I am able to do, I'll do, and I do everything according to my conscience."

In the meeting, Mr. Zbignew Brzezinski and two other people were present. They asked me: "So what are you doing here? Go to Iran." I replied: "I am the Ambassador of His Majesty, the Shah." At that point he said, with good intentions, that he might be able to manage our embassy—I think Brzezinski has written about this in his book. "I will perform the task for you", he said.

During this period I went to Iran twice. The first time was in the summer when I took the Crown Prince to San Francisco to help familiarize him with the situation in America. At that time he was studying in the Air Force here. One night I talked to His Majesty and felt that he was upset. He stated that I go to Iran. Right away I placed the Crown Prince under the protection of Dr. Kazemian and flew to Washington in a small army plane and a few hours later I was on my way to Iran. I stayed there for two weeks and at that time, the Prime Minister of China, and a high ranking Japanese authority were visiting Iran.

The second occasion was at the end of summer, and I was here. It was a few days before his departure, and His Majesty insisted that I return to Iran. In fact, I did not want to leave Iran. This is another story of which I will tell you later. Any way, I went.

At that time, I felt that there were two groups within the American Administration: the first group believed that the Shah should leave Iran for a short time, and the other group did not insist on this, but did not express their opinion explicitly. As a result, I could not have a definite evaluation of the situation. That was why I said to His Majesty—and I also said it to him one night in the presence of the Queen Shahbanou—that if he left Iran the events of 28 of Mordad [1953] would not be repeated. I believed so, and said so at that time.

Later on, after dinner, one of my American friends who was with me said something and from what he said I felt that they would prefer His Majesty to leave Iran and then abdicate. For this reason I insisted that the Shah ought not to leave, and in Iran I also tried to state to him, but I was not quite sure and did not want to say anything. I did not have any proof to show that something specific would happen. I did not have any document in my hand; it was just my feeling, right or wrong.

Manouchehr Bibiyan: Mr. Zahedi, don't you think that in the last months of the Shah's regime, the change of three prime ministers rapidly—and the prime ministers who came to power none of them had the courage and policy of this position, these prime ministers that came to power towards the end. I am not speaking of Bakhtiar, rather Mr. Emami came, General Azhari came. Don't you think that one of the reasons for the defeat of the Shah's regime in Iran was the coming to power of a few prime ministers in a short period of time?

Ardeshir Zahedi: I do not remember if I mentioned this in our discussions, which was in any case my opinion, and many times I told His Majesty, that Administrations should not serve for a long time—especially in a Monarchy. This is because when people are unsatisfied with the administration, and they feel that the Shah supports that Administration, indirectly they turn against the Shah himself. Administrations are responsible; they must come and go. If they work well, they must get credit, and if they work badly, they must be warned. This is my opinion, when I resigned and His Majesty insisted that I stay, I told him that one of the reasons that I leave is that at least those people who are on bad terms with me would be on good terms with His Majesty and that Administrations should not be in charge for a long time. Therefore, two defects: Administrations empowered for too short a time or too long a time, in my view are bad for a country.

In an Administration that stays for too long, the cabinet ministers because they work so increasingly, etc., they loose contact with people, and consequently, they will act like horses wearing blinkers. And, also, the cabinet ministers, little by little, become interested in their positions, which leads to corruption and they will do anything to keep their positions. In a country like ours, where the Administration is responsible to the King and tries not to do anything against his will, this gradually leads to flattery and lying, and slowly, the groups unite with each other to maintain their positions.

That is why I think Administrations anywhere ought not remain too long. Maybe I am mistaken, but I state my opinion to you. Over a short time, Administrations do not have time to accomplish tasks. In one of my interviews with the BBC—I think it was for a program on their English Service when I was asked—I said that were you to change Prime

Minister 3-4 times during one and half years, two years, your situation would be unstable.

Once, when I went to Iran and at that time we were searching to choose a Court Minister for His Majesty. I talked to different people and ultimately to the late Dr. Ardalan who was at the Mayo Clinic. I talked to him. I telephoned His Majesty and it was arranged that he be assigned as Court Minister. However, prior to this issue when he was in Iran, two to three weeks before, I had talked to the late Entezam, Abdollah Entezam, Nasrollah Entezam, and Dr. Siassi.

One day the late Dr. Amini had come to see me. We were in Hessarak. He used to come to visit me a few times a week. I arranged that on my first trip that I would go to [Iran], the late Amini and Entezam could have the honor of being in the presence of His Majesty to express their views and opinions.

I said to him—at that time he was against the Administration of Sharif-Emami—I told him that the issue is not one of agreement or disagreement. This Administration has only been in power for ten days and changing the Administration will weaken the Shah's regime; today what we should do is to support the administration—whoever serves in that administration—in order to enable it to work. Rightly or wrongly. What I meant was that the Administrations should not be changed too frequently. This would have a negative psychological impact on people and on those who work for the government—whether they are military personnel or civilians. Well, it might have been one of the causes or as is said one of the pillars that we destroyed.

In this respect, I think I have the same view as you regarding changing Administrations repeatedly within a short time. First, in my view the last time I said to His Majesty to permit to meet

Congresspersons, most of whom had come to see me, even some of the Congresswomen. My answer to them was "why do you ask me? Have you not taken an oath of loyalty to His Majesty and to your country? This time, go and [express] what you believe [to him]—they meant the late Bakhtiar. Later on, one or two of these gentlemen who were close to Bakhtiar told him. Bakhtiar had either called His Majesty or had gone to see him.

His Majesty called me and said "What do these people say?"

I answered, "Who am I, His Majesty? I am your Ambassador in Washington. I have come here to, does not anyone have the right to ask me a question or listen?" And, I told them: "go yourselves." We had arranged a gathering of some of the heads of the country and had prepared a gathering for them—afternoon tea, dinner, etc. They would come to be in the presence of His Majesty. And, His Majesty would tell them—including the leaders of both Majlises [the National Assembly, and the Senate] about the country's situation. His Majesty could tell them about the situation of the country, perhaps saying: "I am tired, choose three persons from among yourselves, and out of the three, I will choose one."

My reason for suggesting this was the experience of my father who described that in the past—at election time, we stated that unsuitable candidates ought to be disallowed and the rest should be chosen according to the vote of people.

This would result in, especially in Iran where everyone has a close relationship with each other—we went to the same school, or played soccer together, or share a family relationship. Our country has a tribal tradition. It is a country in which in every part of the country, our tradition emphasizes respect for parents and teachers. Therefore, in this way, when the people of Khorassan, Hamadan, Shiraz, and Isfahan choose someone from among themselves, because they are then themselves engaged, and the [election] is not semi-official anymore, they try to help the person whom they have elected. Today, to an extent, we see this situation in Japan. Undoubtedly, mistakes have been made, and, little by little, they compounded and the result was the situation that occurred, which despite should not have had these results.

This is what I believe, but sometimes it is too late. A year prior, we began to weaken the country. With maintaining an Administration—maintaining it for thirteen years was another [policy] that weakened the country. Well, we began to wither, and well, other issues, regarding your question, the illness of His Majesty, was very significant. The few people—five people, or perhaps four people—knew that His Majesty was ill; these people instead of suggesting to His Majesty that the people should know—and I believe that had they told the people, and I stated to him, the people would have cried for him—this is another issue, the interference of officials. You have forgotten that a number of people who had become millionaires from the Shah's regime and the country of Iran, and they had the best life, it was heard that some of them helped 200-250 million Touman of that time to Khomeini, in the last days they thought that they could obtain positions. Well, you saw that they themselves drowned.

Manouchehr Bibiyan: There are a few issues that I will discuss in the coming weeks when I'll visit you in Geneva.

Ardeshir Zahedi: My pleasure.

Manouchehr Bibiyan: But I can not refrain from stating two issues. The first issue is that everything that was implemented in Iran—whether right or wrong—was said that "it has received royal

approval" and they recorded these issues in his name. The second factor that contributed to the revolution was the nondisclosure of the tapes that reached Iran from outside the country, especially the speeches of Ayatollah Khomeini. Had the Shah's regime given the people the freedom of choice so that the people would know that Khomeini who was coming to Iran, what does he essentially say, would our intellectuals have also followed these issues? Also, was it a right measure that the Shah took when he said to the people—I don't know who wrote the text of the speech that the Shah gave, because it has been refuted; some say it was written by Shojaedin Shafa, others say by another individual—when the Shah said regarding the revolution: "I heard the message of your revolution." These are among the issues and questions that we will discuss in the coming weeks.

Ardeshir Zahedi: With great interest.

Manouchehr Bibiyan: But, the principal question that I want to ask you is that you have come to the United States to participate in the funeral of Richard Nixon. In your opinion, what are the contributions of Nixon, as a historical figure, to world peace and to the strengthening of Iran-United States relations? I don't want to say that you are the only individual, but you are the best individual to answer this question because Nixon was a friend of yours, and I also know of his friendship with the royal family of Iran.

Ardeshir Zahedi: The establishment and strengthening of Iran-U.S. relations, of course, began a short time prior to WWII. But, it was principally after World War II and at the time of Truman when Truman rendered his greatest help to Iran—it was regarding the issue of Azarbaijan, which God willing because the issue is the late Nixon—we will talk about these issues.

Nixon traveled to Iran in 1953 as the Vice President of the United States. It is very interesting that, prior to his visit to Iran, Henderson, the American Ambassador, called me and asked me to convey to the Prime Minister and also to His Majesty, that if he would come and during their meetings with Nixon, if they hear anything from him that we did not like, they should know it is because there was insufficient time to brief him. Of course, we heard later that they had tried to brief [him] for hours. He listened for a certain amount of time, but later they had thought that he was not listening. Thus, they said that now and then Nixon would make mistakes. When Nixon came to Iran—I had the honor of being present during both his meetings with the Prime Minister and His Majesty—everybody was surprised, and I became more and more worried that statements that they [the government] might think that I had stated at my own initiative, and that they [the government] might think that there had not been a message. This is an example showing that Nixon was intelligent and an example of his interest, and an example of his knowledge of geopolitics.

At that point, I saw that he was [knowledgeable] regarding Iran. You should consider that Iran [at that time was in the era of] post war, after the time of Mossadegh, which [at that time] the situation of the misery and economics and everything was at the worst level. From the north, the Soviet Union of those days at the time, Stalin with that power and with that situation, [and the extent of his activities] against our country and the Tudeh Party [the Communist Party of Iran] which was [engaged] in such activities

In our surroundings whether in the East, Pakistan, which had newly gained independence in 1956, or Afghanistan which had its own situation of chaos, or in the Persian Gulf which most of our neighbors on that side did not have independence at all, these never existed, and

Iraq, which after some developments, the Baghdad Pact and CENTO. We saw the revolution also [which occurred in Iraq], a situation like this that we faced, and this man saw all of these.

I was relatively young, but I truly formed an opinion about Nixon. In the short time after 1959, it was the first time that I came to Washington as the Ambassador, and I was there until 1962. The president was Eisenhower, whom I respected very much. Well, for this reason, I truly tried to have closer relations with the Vice President for the relations of the two countries. From here when I left, I became the Ambassador to England. I kept my communication with Nixon, until the time I became Foreign Minister, and when I became the Foreign Minister, he was no longer Vice President; he had been defeated in California, he had been defeated in Chicago by 130,000 votes (which was said that there were issues unstated about it), but for this man there was upheaval in his life, for this reason I respect him). He was always interested in Iran and I was a witness. When he wanted to come, I sent him a message that whenever you want to come, come as my guest.

He came to Iran, at my residence in Hesarak, we talked until 4:30 in the morning. I took him to His Majesty; he had an audience [with the Shah]. They had arranged a half-hour agenda for him, [but] the meeting lasted two hours. At that time he was neither a presidential candidate nor anyone thought that he would have this chance. At that time, he had come from Vietnam, and I saw how interested he was in world peace, and how much effort he had, and in those days he believed that they ought to withdraw their forces from Vietnam as soon as possible.

People might have regarded all this as a joke. Is it possible, 50,000 forces? With all these issues considered, when Nixon became president, he accomplished this task. I had come to see the then president, President Johnson, and Dean Rusk, the Secretary of State, regarding the issue of Bahrain [which was] approaching and regarding the issue of oil. It was regarding the Persian Gulf, and other issues. When I went to New York, the Arab-Israeli war had [occurred], I had dinner with Nixon and another person who was there, William Rogers the Secretary of State, after that dinner, I felt that the discussions were [indicative] that Nixon would be a presidential candidate, from the Republican Party—would he win or not? I was not certain. I stated to His Majesty via telephone; His Majesty was surprised, and he was justified, not many months after this issue, Nixon became a presidential candidate from the Republican Party. Fortunately, later the elections occurred and we saw that he won.

What I saw in Nixon, one day I had an audience with His Majesty, and he was complaining. I was again coming to the United States regarding the same issue of Bahrain. When we went to the Oval Office, Nixon told me:

"As long as you spend this oil revenue for the welfare of your country and the progress of your country, complain to me, fight me, and I would agree also. Go and continue your work." He was interested in Iran, His Majesty, and peace.

Nixon knew what the danger of Communism was. For this reason, we see that this man accomplished tasks that seemed impossible. It was the [opening of diplomatic] relations with China in 1969. I accompanied His Majesty here, he [Nixon] had recently become president. After the ceremonies ended, William Rogers, the Secretary of State, while we were walking on the lawn of the White House—I have the photograph of that time—he talked to me about establishing closer relations with China. I did not believe it. I told him: "Well, inform His Majesty." I went to His Majesty and told His Majesty, and His Majesty was surprised. They had problems at that time, regarding Poland. We arranged, and Iran was very effective here [U.S.-China relations], which achieved the entry of Pakistan, and later Henry Kissinger came, and later Henry Kissinger went to China. The rest is all the events that you know, but these segments had remained untold. This was another example of the interest of Nixon in peace. He wanted to play [that game] with China, and also with the Soviet Union, both of which were Communist [states], to render these two as rivals, and ultimately achieve what we see : one of them [inaudible] and the other is incomplete.

This was a man who came that day, regarding Détente he was ready to go to Helsinki. He went there and spoke there. He was a man who was [interested] in conciliation [the negotiations regarding Strategic Arms Limitation negotiations], he went there, and we saw the results. Regarding the Middle East war, in the Arab-Israeli war, he said that the United States ought to be evenhanded, like a father who guides both, so that they would arrive at peace.

Well, the Watergate issue caused him much damage, but in my opinion this was also regarding the interest that he had in his colleagues, because Nixon was in my opinion a very good father; Nixon was a very good husband, Nixon loved his country infinitely. The only thing that disturbed him—we saw the issue of Khrushchev and Nixon in Moscow—was something that would cause his country harm, or insult. It was the same with his colleagues—at the same time he had influence, and was a political figure, he was respected also. I believe that one day it will be proven to the world what he did—was due to his kindness to his colleagues. He wanted to defend them, and he ruined himself. In my opinion, in these few days, there has been much tribute to Nixon, everyone is paying attention to what political and international figure he had been, but I believe that perhaps five years, ten years, fifteen years in the future, history, and perhaps in the next twenty years, render more judgment regarding this late [political figure], and this courageous man, that what international figure he had been. Of course, opinions are different, you asked my opinion, and I stated my opinion to you, and another was that he was Luti, he was a friend to his friends. When His Majesty died, he came [to Cairo].

Manouchehr Bibiyan: I think that one of the causes of the occurrence of Watergate was the illness that Nixon had. You know, he had paranoia.

Ardeshir Zahedi: Of course. I myself went to visit him. I was the only one. He has written in his book also. Another characteristic that Nixon had which I respect was that this man was a friend of his friends, as we say ourselves he was Luti, a friend of his friends and enemy of his enemies.

Manouchehr Bibiyan: As you are famous for having this characteristic.

Ardeshir Zahedi: Thank you, this person was grateful. He tried to defend whoever accomplished a good deed for him, to keep him. For this reason, due to his Lutiness deeds, perhaps for this reason, due to the same gratefulness he caused jealousy toward himself, both enemy and also those individuals who perhaps he had been grateful toward them, and he was kind to them, [but] they did not deserve it. Therefore, to some extent it is also the fault of those individuals, perhaps. We see this in every country. We see this regarding the issues in our country also.

We have seen it in our history many times. Regarding England, at that time I was the Ambassador, the issue of Parifimo or Mr. MacMillan, I saw this issue, I saw this issue in De Gaulle's surroundings. Well, there are some such individuals, this man was a person who despite all the bitterness that he had faced he became ill here and he was almost dying [but] he did not give up, he fought.

I was close to him. I knew that Nixon did not want to resign. Nixon wanted to pursue the issue to the last level. Some time ago I was talking to one or two American friends, some of them also arrived at this conclusion, at this opinion, but now whether true or not, but in any case I knew. Nixon even wanted to proceed to impeachment vote, I reported to His Majesty.

I told His Majesty again, that now he wants to resign. That day when I called [the Shah] he did not believe it. Because he thought, why [between] the two reports that I had relayed, during this time, the situation had changed? The reason that I think that [Nixon] did not follow this [process], one of the [reasons], was that he was interested in his country; he thought that by going to Congress and defending himself, he would become a lame duck president and he could not do anything. The situation in the world in those days was something [particular], the superpowers, the Soviet Union considering the possession of its nuclear weapons, from the other side, China, England, France, therefore he might have caused damage to not only himself but to the United States, also to world peace. A small mistake could have sparked a crisis. But the economic [situation] in the world was not good [either], this issue could have caused damage [to the economy]. Thus, perhaps, in the last moments, he had concluded that "well, I will sacrifice myself, but prevent the [occurrence] of danger", and in my opinion, perhaps again this might have been a wise thought. [But I believe] that this man, not only the tribute that you see today, he did not want his body to be taken to the United States' Congress. He wanted a very simple [funeral] such as the funeral of his wife.

Last year I came here to his wife's funeral. She was a model wife and Nixon was in love with his wife, and this family was close and loved each other.

Manouchehr Bibiyan: Nixon's weeping was indicative.

Ardeshir Zahedi: He wept so much there where I was, when I came, I told those who accompanied me: "I am afraid that he would be ruined."

The paper that I had received from him exactly three weeks prior—before I went to the Greece Conference—a three page letter which he had written in his own handwriting because this man was such a Luti, when people were afraid to say hello to me in the streets—in the beginning when the situation had changed—but he came to Switzerland—with his wife who was a true Lady. She was paralyzed on one side of her body and had suffered a stroke—they went to the Montreux Palace and they came to Montreux to visit my mother and I. My mother had cancer, at that time we had lost everything, thus it was not just because a personality is king.

[Nixon] was a friend to his friends. Through all the upheavals. And, to the last moments he tried to help them. Whoever approached Nixon, he [accomplished] whatever he could for them. I was witness to an issue where an Iranian youth, she was visiting abroad, he wrote a two page letter to their Ambassador, Vernon Walters at the United Nations "see what you can do for this individual." [Nixon] had characteristics and Luttiness that unfortunately, today we see less. Now, "Lutti" might not be a good word, but I call him "Lutti" because as we say ourselves, we say:

> "This person is a Lutti! Meaning that he is a person who wants to help everyone, or perhaps I [inaudible].

Manouchehr Bibiyan: This is part of our culture; Luttiness is popular for the Iranian people, because Lutiness has many meanings. In any case, I know that you are visiting America for a short time, I will visit you in Switzerland and we will talk extensively. You are a very effective individual in enlightening the history of Iran, and I hope that you will help that we shed light on some of the chapters of the history of Iran.

Ardeshir Zahedi: With pleasure. Thank you very much.

Manouchehr Bibiyan's Interview with Ardeshir Zahedi

Broadcast Date: May 15-June 5, 1994
Location of the Interview: Switzerland

Manouchehr Bibiyan: Recently, you went to America to participate in the funeral of Richard Nixon. In your opinion, what are the contributions of Nixon, as a historical figure, to world peace, and also to the strengthening of Iran-United States relations?

Ardeshir Zahedi: During the times of Truman, Eisenhower and then during the Nixon Administration, the United States and Iran developed closer relations. One factor was the National Independent Policy we followed during the reign of His Majesty. At that time, Iran was willing to have closer relations with the neighboring states as well as with the free world. At that stage, Nixon first traveled to Iran as Vice President, then he came to Iran as a private citizen and had the honor of having an audience with His Majesty, and finally [again] when he was President. During the Arab-Israeli war, Iran tried to play a greater role. Then, if you remember, Iran tried to find a solution for peace. We were very active in the approval of United Nations Resolution 242. At that time the problem of a fire incident at the Aqsa Mosque occurred which [not audible] of principle of Iranian policy. We were instrumental in ensuring that the first Islamic Conference was held in Rabat.

With respect to that policy principle, after the October War in 1967—if I am not mistaken—Nixon became the President, and Governor Stetson, who was running [not audible] for the presidency, came to Iran as the president's special representative. Later, Elliot Richardson, who later became the Secretary of Defense, visited, and then the Attorney General came. Those people came, and also

William Rogers, who at that time was Secretary of State. William Rogers used to say that they wanted to play a neutral role—as they say, "have an even-handed policy." We were very active in this matter to make our Arab brothers feel that it was the best chance to create the pre-conditions for peace. Based on this policy, when Nixon was elected President of the United States, and His Majesty traveled to the United States—I think it was in 1973—in accordance with a previously designed policy, it was decided that Iran would play a greater role in the Middle East Peace Process. At that time, we had friendly relations with Egypt, which terminated when Nasser came to power. The political relation was later renewed due to the efforts of the [Egyptian] Foreign Minister, with whom we had close relations, and also after negotiations between His Majesty and [President] Sadat, who in my opinion is one of the greatest men in history.

Now that we are discussing the past, it would be good to talk about Sadat. As an Iranian citizen, I appreciate him for helping our country and us. The hospitality the Egyptian President and his people showed us led to bilateral relations and meetings. There were negotiations before the October War (1973) and it was agreed that President Sadat would send a representative. The negotiations started here, in the house in which you are present. Mr. Ashraf Arbal proposed a principle that, had all [parties] agreed to it, could have prevented the October War, but at that time the Egyptians insisted that His Majesty confirm and guarantee the treaty. The Americans were [also] not prepared [to accept the principle] at that time because they had to [first] talk to Israel to know its opinion. This took place when Nixon was in Sacramento, California. We had telephone contact with the President and Kissinger, the Chairman of the National Security Council, who later was appointed Secretary of State. The endeavors did not produce a good result and finally the war began. Then also,

Iran and [especially] His Majesty and, I can say, Nixon, played a great role. I believe that if the Watergate affair had not occurred, the peace that we now see progressing would have been so much closer and the situation might have been much better.

Of course, this is my opinion [not audible]—there were other factors besides political relations, because Iran was of great geopolitical importance to the United States and the free world. Iran had friendly relations with its neighbors at that time and, with respect to leadership, Iran [not audible] in the south, [in] the Persian Gulf, in the north we had a problem with the Communists, and also with Afghanistan, Pakistan, Lebanon and Iraq, the last of which did not dare act against us. These factors caused conditions in Iran to [not audible], even though—as you remember—there was a time when the economic situation in Iran was so bad and Truman's Point Four helped this country. Aid started from $500,000 and reached $3,000,000.

At that time, Iran could help other countries, including the African states, and Iran could help [not audible] European countries as well. I can say that President Nixon played a great role in the bilateral relations between Iran and the United States.

Manouchehr Bibiyan: You answered a few questions that I had written, but a few points remain unclear here. One is that don't you think that this war, the 1973 war, the Six Day War, which you talked about, caused an increase in the revenues of Iran and the many fold increase in the price of Iran's petroleum.

Ardeshir Zahedi: No. I believe not. Iranian oil didn't go up because of the war. As you know, oil is a product whose price depends on supply and demand. The world needed oil and they obtained it from Iran or other countries at a low price—a little over a dollar. If you remember, His Majesty was the person to initiate oil price increases, and these were probably instrumental in his [inaudible], because he created many enemies for himself, but, as a patriot, he played a great role and caused the price of oil to increase to $23. It must not be forgotten that the modern world, with a population of 5 billion, needs energy and cannot rely solely on oil. Some specialists believed and still believe that if the world tries to substitute other energy sources, such as nuclear power, shells, stones, or alcohol, for oil, it will cost $30 to $40 for the countries who want to prepare it. You may remember that [the price] was $18 to $20. The assistance Iran provided the free world constituted refraining from cooperating with the Arab countries that had decided not to export oil. The decision was made after Nixon called His Majesty at 2:00 a.m. and requested it of him. At that time, the American Diego Garcia Base—all over Asia and Southern Asia—needed oil and energy. Iran agreed to place oil generously at their disposal. At that time, Iran was [inaudible] and [not audible] ensured we provide oil to them. This action brought appreciation from the West, especially from the United States.

Manouchehr Bibiyan: Mr. Zahedi, during the past fifteen years, you have mostly kept silent regarding the events of Iran. Yet, now I am in your house and I see your sincere friendship and relations with tens of presidents and the most influential personalities in the world, both past leaders and present. You know thousands of memorable events and thousands of events that have occurred in the world. Why have you chosen silence in these fifteen, sixteen years, and have not expressed any opinion?

Ardeshir Zahedi: Well, to tell the truth, I believe the less said the better. Talking too much causes problems. Today, if I want to speak according to my conscience about some issues, it may cause trouble for some people who are living in that non-democratic country—whose relatives have sincerely helped the country. Yet, if I don't mention their names, it would be unjust. That was one of the reasons. On the other hand, if we want today's youth, or those who will be born tomorrow, to run the country well, we should judge history objectively. In the present situation, you will agree that it may be hard to judge objectively, thus in the future I will try to let people know about facts and figures and readers decide who was right and who was wrong. In the book, I have published my reports to His Majesty and his responses, and also my own points of view, otherwise it is easy to claim "I warned the Shah." [Whereas] they did not have the right or the courage even to shake hands with His Majesty. Nowadays they consider themselves like the "Conqueror of Stalingrad" [not audible].

Manouchehr Bibiyan: When the Iran Desk was established in the State Department during the Carter Administration, did Americans give you, the Iranian Ambassador, any information regarding the change in their policy regarding the Shah's regime?

Ardeshir Zahedi: First, I state to you that this Iran Desk was not established at that time. In every Foreign Ministry, there is a section regarding a country or a region. And, their duty is that they obtain and gather these. About the Iran Desk that you mentioned, I should say that its duty is to gather intelligence: Iran also ran a section, known as the Fourth Office, to collect intelligence relevant to our relationships with the United States and Canada, and there was another section monitoring the affairs of Persian Gulf and Arab countries. But at that time, there was a kind of excessive activity and movement at the Iran Desk. Of course, the State Department and the Secretary of State, and in another section, at the White House the National Security Council convenes, and tries to coordinate with the Department of State, and there are sections of the Department of Defense, sections of the CIA, and they all try to coordinate with each other and submit a report to the president or to their own bosses. But, regarding my own opinion, at first I believed that [not audible] Carter should travel to Iran. At that time, I insisted that Carter should first visit Iran, but His Majesty [not audible] accepted that [inaudible]. The details of the matter will one day be revealed. Carter constantly assured me—during our several-hour meeting at the White House—to tell His Majesty that "we are one hundred percent interested", but they followed an inconsistent policy. Today they would say one thing and tomorrow another. The Secretary of State stated one thing, the president said another and their ambassador in Iran said something else again. His Majesty has referred to this issue, thus perhaps, it was a little confusing, but basically, I apologize for saying this, we should not have placed so much emphasis on foreign policy. I mean, we followed the National Independent Policy [according to] which we should have implemented policies for the benefit of our country, no matter whether they were acceptable to foreigners or not. We ought to try to act logically and to do so according to principles. Foreign policy is important, but it cannot dictate to us. I believe foreign policy is only one of the pillars for running the country.

Manouchehr Bibiyan: If you were the Shah of Iran, would you have left the country in this situation?

Ardeshir Zahedi: Of course, I have never been and will never be the Shah of Iran. I have been in the service of the Shah of Iran and have served my king and country. I had told His Majesty many times that he should not leave the country. I did not agree that he should leave Iran and told him that if he left the country, his return would be impossible. In a meeting in the presence of Her Majesty and a few people, I even tried to upset him in order that my words would influence him; I said to him that if he would leave, he would never come back. I even mentioned the event of the 28 of Mordad [1953]. Right or wrong, I believed that His Majesty should not leave the country. If His Majesty had not left the country, the Imperial Iranian military's situation would have been quite different and it would not have been destroyed. I believe that Khomeini would not have dared to enter Iran and also Iraq would not have dared to attack Iran. I have always thought this way—is it correct or not? God knows. I don't know.

Manouchehr Bibiyan: Please tell us where you were on the 22 of Bahman, the day of the revolution and how did you feel when the revolution occurred in Iran?

Ardeshir Zahedi: I was in Morocco in the service of His Majesty when I heard the news. I must say that it was the worst and saddest moment of my life. Besides, I witnessed how His Majesty was feeling sad and despairing. Incidentally, it occurs to me that I always disagreed with His Majesty leaving; when he was in the hospital in New York, on the same day that he had had an operation on his shoulder, and there were still tubes in place, unfortunately Mujahedin-i-Khalgh [People's Mojahedin] and others demonstrated outside. His Majesty was very sad. On that day, he said to me: "I wish I had listened to you and had not left." I said: "It is too late now." Thus, I think His Majesty himself realized that he should not have left.

Manouchehr Bibiyan: Mr. Zahedi, at the time of the occurrence of the revolution, Iran's Embassy in Washington was akin to a depository of documents and information regarding Iran-United States relations. Did you transfer these documents to another

location before you left the embassy? Or did the succeeding regime, i.e. the Islamic Republic acquire them?

Ardeshir Zahedi: I will not answer this question now. Maybe I will do so in the future or maybe in my book, because one should not gladden his enemies, so now I will only say, No comment. I will answer this question later.

Manouchehr Bibiyan: Did you meet the Shah when he was outside of Iran? And, if you met him, please tell us a memory about him that people should know.

Ardeshir Zahedi: Once His Majesty had left the country, first I accompanied the Crown Prince to Morocco. In these travels I used to come and go whether to Morocco, Egypt and Mexico, and I arranged His Majesty's going to Mexico and to Panama and also his return to Egypt and his telephone discussions with the Egyptian President and also with Ashraf Gharbal, the Ambassador of Egypt. Therefore, I was at his service most of the time, from morning until night. There are many memories about which you will read or I will talk about later.

Manouchehr Bibiyan: You, as a statesman who has much information regarding the contemporary history of Iran, do you intend to publish your memoirs? You mentioned that you would publish your book, but you mention if . . .

Ardeshir Zahedi: As I mentioned, I hesitate to do so for the sake of the families who helped their country, and Iran is indebted to them. I have to consider this fact—to do otherwise would be unconscionable. Nonetheless, I hope it will be published in one or two years in a volume or two.

Manouchehr Bibiyan: We have heard that a book is being written about the life of Brigadier General Zahedi. What can you explain about this issue?

Ardeshir Zahedi: Incidentally, it may have been one of the reasons for my hesitation. I hesitate that what I say about my father may be interpreted as my own personal admiration of him. I loved this man. We were [like] brothers, friends, and co-warriors, besides being a father and son. I have heard that there are one or two books, be they good or not—and that I may want to confirm or rebut statements made in these books, but the best policy is to wait until my book is published. A few people called me to get information for their books. It was helpful for them and for me too. I have heard one of the books will be published soon and I will be happy to read it.

Manouchehr Bibiyan: Mr. Zahedi, considering that in addition to having the position of Foreign Minister, you were the Ambassador of the Shah's regime in the United States during the most critical period. Can you tell us what happened on the 22 of Bahman; was it a revolution or mostly an international conspiracy?

Ardeshir Zahedi: Well, the answer is very long and it is not possible to state it easily. A revolution? First, I have never accepted this revolution. And, then we must see how it reached this situation. If what I said before and the reasons I mentioned before, if those would have occurred perhaps this revolution would not have occurred. And the foreigners are not in love with us, they want their own interests. Therefore, when they see—I also said this to His Majesty once, when he was on his way abroad. I particularly told him that if you leave—it was during a summer when I was in Iran for a few months. I told him that usually, when they see the leadership, that leadership does not have that much power, they implement their policy from another direction. I believe that, in the beginning, the foreigners because they needed Iran, an independent Iran playing a leadership role in the region. As I said to His Majesty that night—Sadat also called that night from Camp David—they might have decided to punch His Majesty and wanted to make His Majesty upset. His Majesty often used to attack the English and Americans and they wanted to retaliate for that, as in boxing. But, without any doubt this was not what they wanted. But, at that time there was no leadership in the United States, at that time the Western countries were not close and harmonious with each other. Therefore, yes, perhaps one of the factors, it is possible. But, I hope that I will be able to answer it with documents at the right time.

Manouchehr Bibiyan's interview with Ardeshir Zahedi

Date of the Interview: July 22, 2004
Interview conducted at Ardeshir Zahedi's residence in Montreux, Switzerland

JAAM-E-JAM: Ardeshir Zahedi is a descendant of two families that have shaped the history of Modern Iran. In the last two decades of the Pahlavi Dynasty, Ardeshir Zahedi served as Ambassador to the United States, to the Court of Saint James and five years as Foreign Minister of Iran. He married the Shah's first born "Princess Shahnaz". He separated from her 8 years later. Ardeshir Zahedi remained a close confidant and friend of the Shah until the Monarch's death in 1980.

Today, Ardeshir Zahedi lives on the side of a lake in the city of Montreux in Switzerland in his father's former residence, among more than 150 pieces of photographs some of which you witnessed.

And, now, together we will watch the historic interview that Mr. Manouchehr Bibiyan, executive producer and president of JAAM-E-JAM Television, had with Mr. Zahedi, and we understand the secrets of the Iranian Revolution and the contemporary history of Iran. This interview was conducted on July 22, 2004, this year, at the residence of Mr. Ardeshir Zahedi.

In this interview, he revealed many untold stories of inside the Shah's royal court and Iran's relation with the western world.

The first two questions that Mr. Manouchehr Bibiyan asked Mr. Ardeshir Zahedi were the following:

1. **Regarding the illness of Mohammad Reza Shah Pahlavi and**

2. **Who encouraged Mohammad Reza Shah Pahlavi in Iran to leave the country during the revolution?**

And Mr. Ardeshir Zahedi answered:

Ardeshir Zahedi: The question that you ask—the illness of the Shah. He might not have been well. Because I asked him. But because no more than five persons were informed of the issue. As he, himself stated.

Regarding the illness of His Majesty. Regarding this part, one of the criticisms that I stated to His Majesty after we left Iran was that: "Why didn't you tell me?"

He replied: "If I had told you, you would have said it."

Actually, my point is regarding the very same issue, because a king ought not to hide his illness from his nation. At that time, there was a rumor that His Majesty was ill. I told him in person several times. I also asked him in telephone conversation. He replied: "No, it's nothing".

And once he stated he had gout, and I jokingly said that it is said: "those who had gout, have long lives, it is not important."

For this reason because there was another rumor that there had been an assassination attempt against His Majesty, and this is why he went to the north because it was said that he had not been seen in public. When this occurred, I arranged that Barbara Walters went to Iran, to the Caspian Sea, and when Their Majesties were water-skiing their pictures be taken so that the rumors would no longer . . .

And, regarding the departure of His Majesty from Iran: I was against it, I still have the same opinion: His Majesty ought not have left Iran, because had His Majesty remained in Iran, Khomeini would not have dared to come. Had Khomeini not come to Iran, the situation of the Imperial Iranian military would not have resulted in this manner, and ultimately His Majesty was the father of the Imperial Iranian military and Commander-in-Chief of the Imperial Iranian armed forces. Therefore, this was my opinion and still is and will always be my opinion.

There is a possibility that it is right or wrong considering all the evil that these Mullahs have done in Iran, I can now say that in this regard, I might have been wrong and that the Shah was right. Because they severely shed blood and killed these persons.

The first time I felt that His Majesty was ill was when—Usually when the Crown Prince was studying in the United States, I took him to see various places in America so that he would become familiar with that country. At the same time, it was for him a flight exercise. At that time, he had come to that part of the air force. When we were in San Francisco at the invitation of Shirley Temple and General Haig, when we went there, I received a message that His Majesty had called, and I immediately came to the hotel and called him. I felt that His Majesty was ill. Her Majesty Shahbanou the Queen also talked on the phone. At that point it was decided that I go to Iran. I placed the Crown Prince under the guidance of Dr. Kazemian who had a position at the Embassy and conducted our cultural affairs and helped the students in their issues. And, also General Oveissi, one of our closest individuals to take care of the Crown Prince.

I came to Washington. I thought that prior to going to Iran, it perhaps would be good to conduct a few meetings. In this way, I had a meeting with Zbigniew Brzezinski; I had a meeting with Mr. Turner; I had a meeting with Mr. Mondale, and also I had a meeting with President Carter which lasted for four hours. They have themselves written about it in their books. And, in order to know what they were thinking, these were the meetings.

When I went to Iran and arrived in Iran because it was night time when I arrived in Iran—it was 11:30, 12:00 at night when I entered the airport, and I saw that a few of the leaders of the Imperial Iranian military were there—my friends—it was questionable for me. The Iranian Foreign Minister Mr. Amir Khosrow Afshar was there. And, it is questionable why, despite the fact that I had come confidentially, why has this occurred? It was later that I knew that all of them were concerned, because Amir Khosrow Afshar also when I was in Washington told me on the telephone twice that: "If you don't come, the Twenty-Third would be repeated". I didn't know what he meant by the Twenty-Third. Ultimately, he sent a letter via a trusted person.

And, I went there, and when I wanted to go to the Sa'ad Abad Palace from the airport, at that time Amir Khosrow Afshar said that if it is possible I want to come with you. He came with me as I drove my automobile to go to Sa'ad Abaad, because His Majesty was waiting. On our way, Amir Khosrow Afshar briefed me of what was occurring—and I was wondering that at that time when the president of China had come to Iran—or the Prime Minister for a visit in the Administration of Sharif-Emami, why their attention was more focused on my arrival.

When we entered the Palace they told me that: "Her Majesty the Queen is waiting for you". When I entered, Her Majesty told me that: "His Majesty is not feeling well and is ill don't say anything that he would become upset". Of course, because I was in a hurry, I didn't answer her, and I was going to proceed—and she said that "if he becomes upset it is possible that he would commit suicide". For this reason, when I had the audience I told His Majesty: "Sir, His Majesty is tired and also I have come directly from the United States—and from San Francisco I had been in airplane. Permit me to present to you my reports in the morning." He stated: "No. Come sit here." He ordered the servants to bring tea and when they brought tea, His Majesty wanted to take a pill. I panicked very much. I thought that God-forbid. Next, in summary, I reported regarding the negotiations.

Since that time, I had the opinion that first His Majesty ought to take a strong stance. But at the same time make the decision that small issues be conducted by the state. In order that it would not be resultant that it would be carried out under the name of His Majesty. Even regarding the issue of martial law, we had a long discussion. And this was regarding the first stage of the summer.

The second time that I returned to Iran, there was a meeting there. First, we had dinner with His Majesty and Her Majesty came, and from there we went to the Library room, which is in front of the room for family cinema room. There I stated to His Majesty: "if you leave [the country] neither this woman," who I meant Her Majesty the Queen, "nor your son," whom I meant the Crown Prince, "would be able to run the country." Such that the servant who brought tea, because he was there since the time of Reza Shah—I believe his name was Akbar Khan—placed the tea down and hug and kissed me, which caused me much discomfort.

And, I was persistent that first, that His Majesty continue his official visits and not cancel them—in order that it would not be interpreted as weakness. We spoke regarding Huyser, and I several times requested that they "permit me that I order to arrest Huyser." He stated: "you want to start a war?" I stated that: "very well, then we state that the Iranian military police there direct him to airplane and return him. With whose permission has he come here? You are the Chief of State and you were not informed." He stated: "tell the American Ambassador".

The response to your question: Yes, I was opposed to His Majesty leaving Iran and to come abroad. I believed that if he came abroad, his return would be difficult. For this reason, I was persistent, and when I saw that he is determined to come outside and [there were] several days of discussion regarding his tiredness and other issues.

I was opposed to His Majesty going to the United States. Because a close friend of mine, an honorable person, told me confidentially that: "we, here, are interested that if the Shah comes, there have been negotiations that he abdicate". On this basis I contacted a president whom I respected. The name of this president is Anwar Sadat. I had arranged the establishment of relations between Iran and Egypt. I met him during his tenure as the Deputy in the Islamic Conference. At that time, I wanted to forge closer relations between Iran and Egypt. I contacted him. And, I talked on the phone with him and His Majesty King Hassan, the King of Morocco. Also, I sent a message to His Majesty King Hussein. Later, King Hussein told me that I received your message late. But, President Sadat invited His Majesty [to Egypt]. Also, His Majesty Hassan. His Majesty Hassan and President Sadat wanted to talk to His Majesty and invite him. His Majesty didn't want to talk [to them]. On this basis, I told His Majesty: "Sir, I won't leave until you express your decision and answer them". It was during the Bakhtiar Administration then. His Majesty promised to answer their telephone calls.

At first, His Majesty thought that I had planned with them so that they convince His Majesty not to leave Iran. The exact opposite: they wanted to invite him. I have heard that Lady Jahan Sadat also had tried to talk to Her Majesty the Queen.

Therefore, yes, I was opposed that the Shah leave Iran. I still have the same opinion. A few years ago, also, the BBC had a half hour program entitled "As I Recall", which exactly a week prior to my interview the Prime Minister of Egypt participated, also the Prime Minister of Israel. It was a program in which there were regular interviews with various figures, in any case, they interviewed me for thirty minutes, and it was broadcast worldwide. This was my opinion. And this is what occurred.

Manouchehr Bibiyan: Prior to the revolution, it is possible that everyone considered whether the Shah was ill or not; whether it was a rumor or it was not. However, after the revolution, everyone knew that the Shah had really been ill. I want to know who was effective in the Shah's decision-making to leave Iran?

Ardeshir Zahedi: There is no doubt that unfortunately one of the mistakes that the Shah made—one day I stated to him. Her Majesty was there, and his family, the children, were there. It was in Mexico. I stated to him: "Sir, five persons betrayed the country: one of them is yourself because you didn't tell the people. The second, it is said, is Her Majesty. The third was your Prime Minister. The fourth was your Court Minister who knew and had encouraged you. Regarding the fifth person, I changed my mind. His Majesty looked continuously. We were having lunch in Cuernavaca . I stated that: "the fifth person, I wanted to say the Doctor, but I acquit him because a doctor has no right to reveal the secrets of the life of individuals. Therefore, this doctor had his duty as physician, not political." Unfortunately, the people didn't know.

What you stated, regarding the rumors, since years before whether the Communists, etc., due to enmity, they always tried to spread these rumors, and the first time that I also—at first I was shocked—was when I had arranged that Her Majesty come to the United States and give a speech in Aspen, Colorado. When we were in Aspen, Colorado, a call was received that His Majesty wanted to speak. Here, His Majesty became very depressed because from one side Dr. Ala'a in Tehran was listening to the conversation on the phone, from another side Her Majesty was on the phone. On another side, via the Embassy we had equipment at that time that few Embassies or perhaps countries had and we could conduct conference calls. Now, it is available everywhere. And, I made that conference call—I arranged it from the other side so that from one side was Dr. Gul in New York, the Director of cancer center at the New York Hospital. The other was Dr. Haul who was once Eisenhower and his wife's doctor, and I arranged that they go to Iran. But at that time, it was not for the Shah. At that time, it was for the Queen Mother Pahlavi, the mother of His Majesty. When Dr. Gul was having dinner with me he told me; "I have really an extraordinary respect for your Shah. Because I had heard how he is very knowledgeable whether on economic issues and whether on military issues, etc. But when I talked to His Majesty, the questions which he asked were like a doctor speaking to me—his questions and answers". Of course, this issue was regarding the Queen Mother because when the Queen Mother Pahlavi was in Iran, no one knew that the Queen Mother had cancer or they concealed it from her. Perhaps the only one who knew was Dr. Ala'a. Here, the questions that His Majesty asked were regarding his mother. For this reason, I went to New York Hospital because there was a detailed report regarding cancer and how they can prevent the young people and others, and children from getting cancer, and how a father had come to donate his own bone marrow, how all of the marrow was—I sent complete reports and His Majesty became very depressed and for this reason he helped one million to the cancer center there in the name of the Queen Mother Pahlavi.

Manouchehr Bibiyan: The absence of the Shah before the revolution—the Shah was absent for a few months and people did not see him anywhere and there was no news about him. And, in the streets there were many rumors—including one that the son of Ashraf had stabbed him, and many other rumors.

Ardeshir Zahedi: No, they said that the son of Ashraf—one of these things—a person. Perhaps. I was in any case in Washington.

Manouchehr Bibiyan: This was one of the rumors.

Ardeshir Zahedi: That is right, and for this reason, they said that His Majesty was shot in the foot.

Manouchehr Bibiyan: Now, do you know what was the reason for this absence?

Ardeshir Zahedi: First, we had an agreement with each other since the day I had the honor to be the Shah's confidant. It began when in 1948 when His Majesty was in Arizona—that picture which you see with President Harris—all through my life, the 28th of Mordad, etc. We promised each other not to ever lie to each other. For this reason, even if the relations of my personal life also, while at that time I had a wife and my wife was the daughter of the king.

If God forbid something would occur the first person who ought to have known was the Shah himself. Therefore, I had the expectation to be informed. Her Majesty the Queen talked to me regarding His Majesty's illness several times, but the only thing that I couldn't understand was this. For this reason, I arranged that Dr. Pirnia would come and examine His Majesty. I arranged that he come confidentially to the Palace and he examined the Shah with two-three of his specialists. He told me that His Majesty's heart and lungs are entirely well.

In the meeting with President Carter—the picture is there—President Carter, Mr. Zbigniew Berzezinski, Mr. Mondel, and later Vance, in the meeting that the five of us had at the White House, a discussion occurred—now, I again return to the days of His Majesty's illness. They told me that based on the report of the CIA which Turner and they had studied, His Majesty was healthy, only that he seemed tired. There, I said that usually when His Majesty cannot sleep at night he takes one or two 5 mg of Valium. There, I don't know whether it was the president or one of the people there who said to me; "ask His Majesty that please take less valium".

My way was that regarding very confidential issues, I first wrote a brief telegram—regarding the negotiations between Iran and the United States. There, in the brief telegram that I sent to His Majesty, I again referred to this issue. Also, I briefly stated to him via telephone. Usually, it was customary that I wrote the reports extensively from A to Z, solely in my own handwriting, and I would place it in a box which His Majesty had one of the keys and I one. I used to send it via a special messenger. It would arrive in Iran within 15-20 hours, and he answered it. Therefore, these rumors existed.

Manouchehr Bibiyan: Considering that for years Alam was one of the Shah's confidants and Minister of Court, the closeness of the Shah and Alam is not unknown to anyone. Would you express your opinion regarding Alam's book?

Ardeshir Zahedi: I unfortunately have not read Alam's book either. I have only read parts of Alam's book, and a few British friends such as Lord Shawcross had commented regarding this. It is a book that has first been written in English in one volume, later I heard it is in three-four volumes. I read parts of this whether in Rahe Zendegi, or in Kayhan, or in Nimrouz, piece by piece. First, from what I know about Alam—he was my friend, I called him Amir—he was not close to such a degree that some think. I doubt it. The confidential issues of the Shah and I will be gone with me. Regarding whether all this—what the persons have talked to me—in some of these sections, especially in the English part which I have read, he contradicts himself. Now, for example, because I read about myself, for example, in one place in his book he says that Minister Abba Eban[13] is coming to Iran and the Foreign Minister does not know. In the next few pages or another place, he says that he had lunch with Zahedi. First, I had known Abba Eban. Second, since especially the first time I knew him, of course—now I know that the person who looked after my father was at the time a British Major, I read in books that he was Abba Eban. Because at that time my father wanted to give me power of attorney when I was a child, but that also is part of history.

I met him in London when I was Ambassador there. Because I often had close relations with those Embassies—it is the duty of every Ambassador—it was at that time also despite the fact that we had no

---

[13]   Abba Eban, the then Foreign Minister of Israel.

diplomatic relations with Israel. Later, I became close with Abba Eban when he was Foreign Minister, and we saw each other in New York, and we had often messages. Also, often the Ambassador in Tehran, Mr., I think, Ezri, no?

Manouchehr Bibiyan: For a period, Ezri was also.

Ardeshir Zahedi: Was there at the meeting. He invited that they come. Also, you know Abba Eban spoke Persian very well.

Manouchehr Bibiyan: Yes.

Ardeshir Zahedi: And the last time I saw him it was the fiftieth anniversary of the death of the late Truman—the picture of it is there, and I had respect for him very much. And, for this reason we talked to each other very openly. In the morning, he came to Hesarak [in Iran] until noon. I told him, even in that meeting, that this war—and this was my opinion, it is, and it will be. "That until the day that you would not end the Arab-Israeli war, this conflict of terror, and insecurity would exist in the Middle East." I believed in this, and I have always insisted. Therefore, I told him: "Dear friend, why you as the Foreign Minister have to come to a corner of the airport at 4:00 in the morning. I hope that one day these conflicts would be resolved so that when you come you would be greeted with red carpet like other foreign ministers".

Now, regarding Abba Eban—but Alam has contradicted himself.

I had friendship with both Alam and his wife. I brought my daughter to visit him at New York Hospital. When he used to come here, we would go either to the South. But, because he had cancer, Mr. Alam had cancer, and I knew that he was on certain medications which was for chemotherapy which caused him severe body pain. I remember that I was playing backgammon with him in the South of France and the doctor brought these medications in ice box—they brought the medications from Paris or Belgium. It caused him severe leg pain. I mean when a person takes this medication in this manner, I am not sure that the memoirs that he wrote in those days—what issues he has written about.

Manouchehr Bibiyan: It has been years and years that Iranians consider the British government responsible for the removal of the Shah's government from power and the victory of the Mullahs in Iran; of course, many people believe that these statements are Uncle Napoleon like—I don't know whether you have seen the film of Uncle Napoleon or whether you have not seen it.

Ardeshir Zahedi: I have read the book.

Manouchehr Bibiyan: Some think this way.

Ardeshir Zahedi: He is an interesting person and he has written well.

Manouchehr Bibiyan: Yes, but we cannot disregard the role of the BBC in the Iranian Revolution of 1979 either—now if possible express your opinion.

Ardeshir Zahedi: The role of any establishment—whether it is television or radio—is important, and especially today, it has been proven in the world that these good propaganda or bad and uninformed propaganda how it could have an impact. For this reason also you who live in the United States now, and in England, or anywhere else, when elections occur they spend millions so that anyone could leave an impact with his/her words. Even a few days ago, I went to see a film regarding 9/11. See how that could impact you. And, whether England or the United States, to state my opinion, at that time we used to see very much that even Mr. Sharif-Emami the then Prime Minister, and Amir Khosrow whether at the time that he was Ambassador and whether at the time that he was Foreign Minister, and also His Majesty, we respected foreigners too much. This goes back to that poem: "It is our mistake, what has occurred to us." If we knew what to do that would be popular, BBC and others could not have had impact. When we placed our attention to a very much extent, first, this increases the image of the BBC. Moreover, if BBC states something wrong, one could have informed the people. If we had good radio and television in Iran, if we had good propaganda, no one would have listened to the BBC. Therefore, that from the perspective of psychology it is possible that it would have impact. But I don't believe it. I don't consider foreigners that important to come and so easily bring a government to power and to overthrow that government. And, they ought not to have the right to do this. But, some have these beliefs. I even heard that at a time it was fashionable that was said that if someone had twins they said that this is the work of the British. Unfortunately, one time I had a discussion regarding intelligence, and one-two individuals who were close to the Shah's regime in Iran and with foreigners. And, they said that, for example, in Iran we don't have enough persons who could go and research. Therefore this was a lesson that they gave to the Savak officials—the Americans and the British—that we have to act somehow as though, that they would be afraid and imagine that in every meeting that occurs, one of them, one is spying for them. These from the perspective of psychology some had this belief. But I don't know whether this belief could be accurate today or not. Especially today that we are talking with each other we see that a superpower such as the

United states and other states such as England, also the CIA, also its State Department, and also its White House, with wrong information they started a war. Now, they say that they made a mistake. Therefore, I don't know to what extent it could have impact. But, I believe that if one accomplished something that benefited the people, and that you would not cause the dissatisfaction of the people without reason, these propaganda could not have the impact that it was designed to have.

Manouchehr Bibiyan: I had an interview with Parsons in England several years ago and I asked him the same question. He stated that before 50 years ago your statement was accurate, and that we had power in Iran and in the book if you read it

Ardeshir Zahedi: Yes, I have read his book.

Manouchehr Bibiyan: Yes, he accepted that "yes, we had influence in Iran, and we had much influence". Of course, I remember.

Ardeshir Zahedi: When a foreign minister of a country privately speaks with the Ambassador of another country and says bad things about the Shah's regime in which he himself is a part of, solely that he keep his position for an additional four days, their influence is people like Alam—I don't want to name names because they are all dead. It was these people. People don't have any fault here. To have spies is one thing, and certainly at that time as you state—first, the person such as Mr. Parsons, I don't remember to have ever seen him, but later, in the book that Zandfar in his book I see here that he was there. All that time, he bowed to and praised His Majesty. He lied to him. Then, Mrs. Thatcher sent him to the United States when the Shah was in the hospital, the person who spoke against the Shah was Mr. Parsons. Of course, I don't have any criticism regarding them, because every person has the responsibility of his/her country. My criticism is regarding these people who sold themselves. This is true today also. Now, we have lost a country. That one constantly says the United States ought to provide money. That one to come to our country. I am against these statements. My statement is perhaps wrong. But, basically if their statements are true, they don't need foreigners. The need to collaborate—Azerbaijan was saved by many things, but here one of the factors that was very important and helped us, how the United States, it did not bring troops and forces. The United States came to the United Nations and supported our thesis. Their message was the message of Truman. At that time, Truman sent a message to Stalin either "you are getting out, otherwise we get in".

Manouchehr Bibiyan: Yes.

Ardeshir Zahedi: Considering these issues, in my view, it is necessary that the foreign policy of a country be very good and in friendship. But certainly any one would like to have influence. When His Majesty came to the United States and I had an interview—the only person who wrote this was Mr. Amirani in the Khandaniha. They censored it and did not permit it to be published, and one of these people is now in the United States. And he sent me a tape—his interview with me at the arrival of His Majesty.

When we have an important country such as Iran, it certainly has international significance. Certainly governments need Iran. Iran is in Asia and Europe. Iran has existed since ancient times until today.

Manouchehr Bibiyan: Well, but we have to accept that the people of Iran did not have political information, and the Shah's regime did

not try so that the people would have more information regarding the country's political affairs.

Ardeshir Zahedi: When you state the Shah's regime, in any regime there is good and bad—in any family there is good and bad. Here, you cannot hold the Shah responsible. You have to consider the Administration's responsible.

Manouchehr Bibiyan: We are talking about the regime.

Ardeshir Zahedi: Yes, I want to know, did the Administrations perform their work well? The mistake was that we kept a prime minister for thirteen years and a half. We had cabinet ministers who were in the cabinet for seventeen-eighteen years. Therefore, because I wrote about this to His Majesty—it is said that the Akhunds have the papers; I have the original. Regarding the issue of political parties, I wrote to His Majesty. I also talked to him about it via telephone call. Especially when Mr. Alam had quoted me as saying that I have become a member.

All of my colleagues are now in the United States with you. I wrote to His Majesty: "Sir, first to have a single political party is wrong. Second, the persons that you want to remove, to bring him/her here, is wrong. Third, we need renewal"—to initiate a new program. Therefore, when we brought these people, there was no difference. Also my colleagues—there was a letter from the Ministry of Foreign Affairs that whoever wants to become a member, I stated that: I would not become a member. I also wrote a letter to His Majesty—the letter exists that because when these letters arrived, they were written in the handwriting of His Majesty. I told my colleagues that: "I would not sign it. You are free to become member if you believe in it. Otherwise, as Ambassador and representative—and implementation—I don't recommend it to you. This is a letter that has come from the Ministry of Foreign Affairs in Iran." Essentially, I did not believe that the Ministry of Foreign Affairs or the Imperial Iranian Military should become a member of a political party or an establishment.

Manouchehr Bibiyan: Several years prior to the revolution—perhaps fifteen years prior to the revolution, works of arts were placed under the approval of the Ministry of Information and Intelligence. Such as Savak, which the criticism that they had was not right, and they created dissatisfaction of some groups. For example, a lyric which we had given to—

Ardeshir Zahedi: Those who were in an establishment, if they believed to do this and have placed themselves under Savak—are at fault. If they didn't believe in it, they are again at fault. Why didn't they resign? It has become fashionable today that everyone says that we went and told the Shah. What did they [inaudible] the Shah? I witnessed some people—the very same Alam, I have written in my writings—when there was a shooting against His Majesty, I became angry, and what I said.

Manouchehr Bibiyan: I was saying that see to what extent this had reached that a lyric entitled:

Ardeshir Zahedi: And when we were having dinner last night, also

Manouchehr Bibiyan: the lyric was entitled "the story of frozen lips" This lyric was rejected by the Ministry of Information and Intelligence. The radio rejected it. When we objected, they said that in Iran no person's lips are frozen.

And that lyric had to be created anew, and its music had to be created anew that when a lyric is ruined all the expenses that have been spent are ruined. Any lyric that contained "chain", "knife", "red flower", and many others they prevented. And the very same without the poet knowing what the issue is caused that that poet who wrote the poem in Lalehzar and contained "red flower", and this lyric was 50 Toumans, when this lyric was banned, the poems of this poet would become 1,000 Toumans, 500 Toumans.

Ardeshir Zahedi, You have an example of this in the film 9/11. The United States wanted to prevent its release. That man went to South of France and received an Oscar for it also. Now, it has been released worldwide, and now everyone stands in line to see it also. Not regarding this, but because you stated the Shah's regime—the Shah, I can honorably state to you that it has occurred many times, I, because I would be saying and I don't want to say I, I, and I all the time—even those people who had committed terrible deeds against the Shah, and that the Shah considered this unimportant, anytime I had a problem or statement, I would state it to His Majesty. His Majesty ordered. Because had I not stated it, I would have hidden it from him. Therefore a group had promised each other not to [reveal] to His Majesty at all the issue as to say not to upset him. The example was regarding the Queen, which I said. There are other issues—I will tell all of it. But when all this existed, unfortunately, what can a person do? The criticism is not directed at the Shah. The criticism is directed at those individuals who had sworn to their country and their king to be righteous. And it was their duty also but they did not, I consider them at fault.

Manouchehr Bibiyan: Well, we did not have any means to communicate with him. Once, we were able to, in one of the newspapers, our complaint what had occurred to the artists,

they had been under pressure, this was written in one of the newspapers. The next morning the Shah himself intervened and it was resolved.

Ardeshir Zahedi: My office, a person in Iran—what I say is my opinion, not that it is right or wrong, the judgment is yours, and those listening, or reading. See, in the Court, one of the most significant issues that I am proud of, there was an establishment entitled Special Office, whether during the time of Reza Shah that I hear, whether during the time of Mohammad Reza Shah. First, you had someone such as [inaudible] and also a person such as

Manouchehr Bibiyan: Moeinian.

Ardeshir Zahedi: Moeinian. I consider both of these persons, to

Manouchehr Bibiyan: They had good names.

Ardeshir Zahedi: Righteous. That the details, if there was complaints, something, they would give it to the Shah to read it. However, if that establishment did not follow the issue, then the Shah no longer has faults here. I went to see His Majesty. It was regarding the celebration of the 2,500 year Anniversary.

Manouchehr Bibiyan: One of the questions that I wanted to ask you was the same issue.

Ardeshir Zahedi: I went to His Majesty and stated that: "Sir"—now the reason why it occurred, and that this was not the duty of Foreign Minister. Two-three servants that grew up in our house since the time of my father. Their behavior towards me was a behavior like I was their brother or son. They were nannies. When I was a child, if I wanted to go to school late, either they would place me on their shoulders, I would struggle and say that I made a mistake so that my reputation would be saved in front of school and Mash Akbar.

One day I was having breakfast with my daughter, they came and said "Dear Sir, they are arresting some people including my child and his child." I said: "what is the issue? He said: "The issue is regarding bus line." Very well, then we said that the issue be pursued. I went there—actually here, I must say that Her Majesty helped here. At that time she was expecting and was in Iran. The late Ms. Farideh was also at Darband. I talked to the prime minister. I said that "at this moment get"—the late Nikpay and Javad also came to the prime minister's office. I sated it to him. Mr. Prime Minister at that time was recording these. And, I criticized him: "Mr. why do you record these talks?" His Majesty stated that we organize a meeting. This meeting was organized. There were people from Savak there, all of the cabinet ministers were there. I told General Nassiri, and General Moghadam, the head of Savak, that this is my view. At that meting they became convinced that they had arrested these people unjustly. I myself went to the university at night time. There the meeting of Thursday night lasted for many hours. His Majesty was at St. Moritz, there the issue was reported to him, and the gentlemen were all at the table. Of course, an issue occurred that made me feel hurt and I wanted to resign. Because His Majesty stated that "you—the fourteen-fifteen individuals—were not able to manage one individual". Later, I realized that His Majesty said: "I said this to encourage you." At that night it was agreed to release all the students. General Mobaser came and told me that: "We will arrest them. They have ordered us. The order has come from the Ministry of Foreign Affairs". The issue was a bus line company that the government considered at fault and corrupt.

They had also arrested the director of the bus line company and imprisoned him.

This issue was resultant that people's bloodshed be prevented. At that time, I had never known Mr. Daryoush Homayoun. They said that there is a newspaper that is published in the morning by the name of Ayandegan, we stated: "immediately publish this"—and the university academics read it—and the radio that night because it was Thursday night—and we said: "distribute this".

I told Moghadam that they have to be to a great extent [inaudible], he said that time was required. I said whatever it is, they have to be released tomorrow morning—whether time is required or not. He accepted. The late Nassiri, all of them did this. When His Majesty came, I presented my resignation. The details have been written.

Manouchehr Bibiyan: The Shah in his last interviews believed that oil companies were responsible for the riots in Iran and the fall of his regime. Considering that the Consortium Agreement was to end in 1979, and the Shah did not extend the previous agreement, in your view, to what extent the oil companies had impact on the Iranian Revolution? In your view, did other factors in the years of the revolution resulted in the fall of monarchy in Iran?

Ardeshir Zahedi: At that time, once-twice I stated to him that: "Sir, in this part, perhaps you are exaggerating." Once he answered me, and once he laughed at me. Now, after thirty some years, I have to say that I realized that here His Majesty was right. There is no doubt that the oil companies exert their power for their interests. And, today we see that even a superpower such as the United States because it only has 25% of its own energy and needs energy from the outside, for years tried to deal with Saudi Arabia and strengthen them. Also, the war that occurred in Iraq. Therefore, and in the conferences—during the past years I have been participating in conferences. At that time, I had a conflict regarding Iran. I believe that both the BBC and the Voice of America broadcasted it. And, it was regarding whether Iran's oil, the oil of Iran's neighbors would be brought to the outside world via Iran, or—when it was during those difficult conflict and the Taliban, now we see that they themselves, some of these American gentlemen, had relations with the Taliban. At that time, pipeline it via Afghanistan in order to give something to the then president of Pakistan. Or, by several times that expense pipeline it via Turkey and to Ceyhan. Therefore, in this part, I believe that His Majesty was right. But, I can say it this way, in my opinion this is one of the reasons of the problem and the fall of Iran. No doubt, there have been other things; they have all combined . . .

Manouchehr Bibiyan: I asked this question because if we remember, if I say it accurately, some time prior to the occurrence of these riots, the representatives of oil companies came to Iran and they talked with the Shah regarding extending the contract. At that time the Shah believed—we heard—that the Shah had stated that: "I want the destiny of oil to be absolutely Iran's decision from now on".

Ardeshir Zahedi: He was right.

Manouchehr Bibiyan: And he stated that because in the future the Crown Prince would succeed him, he wanted him to be comfortable, and for this reason he did not accept. Of course, in the last years also to some extent the Shah, it was said, had become too proud to an unlimited extent including what he used to say such as

blue-eyed people and other talks he had regarding the Europeans or Americans. And suddenly the riots that occurred in Tabriz, that even Savak denied and didn't know about these riots

Ardeshir Zahedi: I believe it was in 1979 or 1978

Manouchehr Bibiyan: Yes, approximately around that time

Ardeshir Zahedi: If I am not mistaken, at the time His Majesty was in Egypt and they wanted him to return soon. Was it not the Amouzegar Administration?

Manouchehr Bibiyan: That's right.

Ardeshir Zahedi: Next, problems, the first riots if I am not mistaken.

Manouchehr Bibiyan: Yes, it was in Tabriz itself.

Ardeshir Zahedi: Well, my judgment here is very limited because at that time I was the Ambassador in the United States, and I was not in Iran. Following this, I went to Iran and remained there, and Mr. Carter also asked me to come. It was therefore that His Majesty wanted to have a country that—His Majesty was a patriotic person. His Majesty loved his country, and he wanted . . . He liked himself also. Because of his interest in himself, and as you stated to that son—there you see that picture

Manouchehr Bibiyan: Yes.

Ardeshir Zahedi: There is a story about it, what my enemies against me did. There I had taken the Crown Prince to acquaint him with Carter.

My enemies had said to His Majesty that I was planning to dethrone him; to replace the Shah with the son. I was very

Yes, His Majesty loved his country. He was interested in the future of his son. To make everything comfortable for him. Therefore, there is no doubt that foreigners were hurt from this perspective. The mistake perhaps, we could refer to the past. A few prime ministers, the personality such as Qavam, and also I as a cabinet minister always stated to him that: "Sir, whenever they have an issue permit us to resolve it." Once he told me: "they'll kill you." I said: "What would occur if they killed. One person would be killed. If God forbid something would happen to you, then what would occur?" Therefore, at the beginning when they went to him, His Majesty often accepted these terms. The day came when he could no longer accept these terms. He had become more open-minded. Also, our country had become stronger. And also, our economy. Therefore, when he said no to them, they certainly began their opposition to the Shah's regime.

Now, some people say that he was arrogant. These are personal issues—and I many times stated to him. But, no, we return to the very statement that you made regarding oil: this was one of the columns that has contributed to our problem and in the loss of our country. There is no doubt. I mean, this is what I think. But, for history, I have an advice—because I don't know to what extent a teacher knows and could talk about it. But today, the issues are open. I have most of them. I have sent people, and obtained them and studied them. Today, even, I have the documents of Russia and France also, one after another. The best place is there where the best libraries are near you, or the State Department, or here the documents of England—when you go there, the documents are open and released after thirty-forty years, you can derive from it, and then your judgment would be better than mine, because I don't know whether I know the extent that is here because I was not an expert on oil.

Manouchehr Bibiyan: I have assistance. My daughter has a doctorate in history and political science, and she even teaches at universities in America.

Therefore, regarding this book, or other issues, she assists me. She goes on the internet, and she prepares anything that I want.

Ardeshir Zahedi: Congratulations. Because to write an essential book. Our biggest mistake was that we never liked to have a team. The only thing that in my opinion brings success—I had a team in the Ministry of Foreign Affairs. When I used to see that they accomplished good work, I used to include that work—now we see that a book has come from Iran, by Zandfar, who has written about the issue of Bahrain. I congratulate you that you have such assistance, and the issues of today are different from the issues of yesterday.

Manouchehr Bibiyan: Now you see another person who is recording this interview today, and provides other help also, she is a doctor.

Ardeshir Zahedi: Congratulations. You have people who are interested in you. Not every daughter or son can because she has the capability. Congratulations.

Manouchehr Bibiyan: Thank you.

Ardeshir Zahedi: She has the means to go to England, Russia, these documents are accessible at many places.

Manouchehr Bibiyan: In Alam's Diary, it has been written that

Ardeshir Zahedi: I have not read Alam's Diary yet.

Manouchehr Bibiyan: that the Palestinians received much assistance.

Ardeshir Zahedi: I'll tell you now

Manouchehr Bibiyan: that after the development of the Palestinians' closer ties with Iraq, the Shah ceased this assistance. And, during the revolution, and after the revolution, Iran provided much assistance to Yasser Arafat. With the outbreak of the Iran-Iraq War, Yasser Arafat immediately turned against Iran, and provided his fighters to the advantage of Iraq and against Iran. How, despite the fact that the Palestinians several times turned against Iran, still these assistance—whether in the form of cash or arms, or political—continues?

Ardeshir Zahedi: First, it is said that once it was said to a so-called important figure of Iran—it is similar to the old Iranian saying: one day a person knocks on the door and asks "is the Khan here?" The other person says no. After that he says "he is not that important, so what if he is not here."

You state Yasser Arafat, who was he? What power did he have so that he would support Iraq, what was even Iraq itself compared to us.

And, regarding assistance. I have not read this book. Mostly, the information that he states is based on what I have heard. At that time, I was the Foreign Minister. This information is regarding that era. They were interested that we have closer ties with the Palestinians, and not to, because they considered us pro-Israel. The Arabs considered us such.

Manouchehr Bibiyan: Yes.

Ardeshir Zahedi: It was His Majesty King Hassan. It was the Egyptian president Sadat. In this regard—I am 90% sure that it is in Rahavard Journal. It is regarding the fire at the Al Aqsa Mosque and how I made the Shah aware of this issue and how I requested to see the Ambassadors, etc. I will not go into details so not to waste our time. There, after . . . it was decided that we found a meeting, it was named the Islamic Conference. And, at that time, we did not want to take sides, we did not have diplomatic relations with Egypt. At that time I had a good friend named Ihsan Sabri . . . who even became the president of Turkey. He was the head of the senate; he was cabinet minister for many years. And we wanted to have an independent policy—not to develop closer ties with any country—and Ihsan Sabri used to say: "cast any vote that you want, it is also my vote". He couldn't come to the opening of the Islamic Conference.

There when the leaders came there were two problems. One was the Palestinian problem. And the other problem was India—which was not an Islamic country. In order to embark on a middle ground, I reached the conclusion with the foreign ministers at the Conference that because we wanted to reach a successful policy, that it would be better if the Palestinians conduct their own policy and not enter [the Conference]. Until ultimately His Majesty King Hassan stated that: "they come, they are in my country, and be observers." And that at the same time assistance be provided. If I am not mistaken, after 40 years I still remember it 99% that there was a check approximately $750,000 which I gave to Ahmad Alikhan Bahrami who was our Ambassador there to provide him with.

And later, a representative of . . . one of the heads of . . . came to Iran when the late Zelli was the Political Deputy of the Ministry of Foreign Affairs. We brought him to a house that belonged to General Bakhtiar. Later, the government took possession of it, and later Mr. Hoveida went there and made it his home stating that he has no place. At that time, sometimes when during these visits when we didn't have a place and didn't want to place any of them in a hotel, and this person went there. And also Yasser Arafat had written a program for His Majesty and I gave that program to His Majesty. This is the issue that I am informed of. And the rest, I left the Ministry of Foreign Affairs. If Alam had information that I have not read, I don't know. And after that I don't believe—

Manouchehr Bibiyan: After that is regarding after the revolution.

Ardeshir Zahedi: At the time of the problems—in the few months before the revolution—there were two groups. Again, we come to the issue that you raised regarding propaganda. One group wanted to attack the Shah and they used to say that the Israelis have brought forces to Iran in order to fight for the Shah. The other group used to say that no, the Palestinians have brought people for Khomeini and the Mullahs, for them, and against the government. These were parts of rumors. I don't know whether either is true or false.

Manouchehr Bibiyan: Well, a few years ago, one of the leaders of the same Palestinians accepted that they helped the Iranian Revolution, and they themselves accepted.

Ardeshir Zahedi: Well, there is no doubt in this regard, because they also named the street after him. That street belongs to my father. The street was also named in the name of my father. Hesarak which the Akhunds took over. That man, Khomeini, went there. And they placed that man's name there. This exists. Yes.

From the perspective of principle, a person had turned against us. A principle—that as long as the problem of the Arab-Israeli War and Conflict is not resolved, these problems will continue.

Manouchehr Bibiyan: Do you think that the West wants that this issue

Ardeshir Zahedi: The West wants it. The United States doesn't. The United States did not keep its word. And to some extent I consider the termination of the Nixon Administration to be the cause. This even handed policy—the person whose picture you see there—William Rogers. He came to Iran and he was my guest. The person who with a message from the president of the United States . . . who himself was a presidential candidate . . . the United States never implemented this even handed policy. It was always pro-Israel. Therefore, now, in the newspaper it has been written that Israel has stated that: the West—meaning all European countries—are no longer neutral because they have voted at the United Nations—the 150 votes which have been cast against the . . . Wall. I was against it also.

Regarding Czechoslovakia, I told Gromyko about the issue of territorial issues—taking what is one's own territory and also what is others' territory. The Shah also became very upset because he was afraid that our relations would deteriorate. And, later when we wanted to go there I told the Soviet Union that I would come on the pre-condition that the relations between the two countries would only be bilateral. But, well, today I have to tell the West about these—and I stated this in a conference 14-15 months ago. And, this is what I told them.

Manouchehr Bibiyan: Well, of course, I don't think that the Israeli-Palestinian issue would be resolved so easily.

Ardeshir Zahedi: Unfortunately.

Manouchehr Bibiyan: Because the issue is not nationalism. The issue is religious fanaticism—from both sides. And, as long as religious fundamentalism exists—

Ardeshir Zahedi: Yes, I very much respect your opinion. And, what you state is true. Until the day that we learn—by we I am not referring to the Arabs and the Israelis, rather human beings. Last night when we were having dinner we also talked about ourselves and our country and how the people can live together. Khrushchev pioneered the issue of peaceful coexistence. But as long as human beings cannot accept and have forgiveness and this requires education to not to infringe on other people's rights so that that person's own rights would not be infringed. But this interaction. Well, it was said some time ago that we should not have had diplomatic relations with Egypt. They consider me responsible. Still some groups. I have the honor to have opened diplomatic relations with Egypt and Anwar Sadat to the degree that at least a place were found to burry my king and respectfully such that the Ambassador of Israel participated in the funeral. I have the picture also.

Manouchehr Bibiyan: Sadat is a person whose good name will remain in the world.

Ardeshir Zahedi: Certainly. He was a patriotic man. What he did was to devote himself to his country. Unfortunately we ourselves—yes, by we I mean the public—still haven't learned this that we have to decide whether we want Iran for our own sake or whether we want to devote ourselves for Iran. This often, unfortunately—

Manouchehr Bibiyan: Now, I have to ask you a question that I asked Bani Sadr and received the response, regarding the oil in the North Sea. That when he became president what decision did he take regarding the oil of the North Sea. Because Iran had a share in the oil of the North Sea—that of course he stated some issues which will be published in the book. And, he knew about this and he had also talked to Khomeini regarding this issue, and a conclusion had not been reached—this is as he stated it, and that they did not follow-up on it.

Ardeshir Zahedi: Yes.

Manouchehr Bibiyan: What ultimately occurred in Iran's share in the petroleum of the North Sea?

Ardeshir Zahedi: You mean the North meaning here (Europe). Certainly, we wanted to have shares. Yes, Iran was interested to be share holder here and to have discussed. Northern oil, you mean, British oil, and Norwegian oil.

Manouchehr Bibiyan: A few European countries.

Ardeshir Zahedi: Yes, as far as I am informed, we were interested to be share holders, and I believe that we also became share holders. All of these documents exist. Because these are not confidential issues. Ask with one telephone call to the BP, etc. I would guess.

Manouchehr Bibiyan: Thank you very much.

Ardeshir Zahedi: I accept that, yes.

Manouchehr Bibiyan: Because energy is one of the important necessities of the world.

Ardeshir Zahedi: But what Khomeini did, and what these Akhunds did—essentially I believe that no one would consider them important to discuss with them [regarding this issue].

Manouchehr Bibiyan: Queen Farah has written in her most recent book that the she wrote the text of the will of Mohammad Reza Shah Pahlavi a day after his death. Does this will have historical significance? Also the book, *Answer to History*, which has been published in several languages including Persian, English, and French—and they are all contradictory. Considering the knowledge that you have regarding the character of Mohammad Reza Shah, has this book been written by him?

Ardeshir Zahedi: After the death of His Majesty and there was a meeting. In that meeting there were persons such as, whom I believe was the president of a university in Azerbaijan named Montasari—if I am not mistaken—there was another person, General Moeinian, General—

Manouchehr Bibiyan: Moeinzadeh.

Ardeshir Zahedi: Moeinzadeh who I believe once was in Savak in London. And, Ghotbi. A few individuals who were close to the Royal Court or the Queen. There, there was a discussion regarding the writing of a will for His Majesty. I was against this issue. Because I believed that this is betrayal to history, and especially since a person who was the king of this country for thirty-seven, thirty-eight years. Therefore, I warned that if this would occur, unfortunately, I would be forced to announce it.

And you know after His Majesty died, the late Sadat with all honor and arranged such ceremony—and later after the funeral he organized an interview in the room—Sadat, I, and the Crown Prince participated for worldwide broadcast.

After these issues, they were convinced not to declare it the will [of the Shah]. This is the first time that I am now hearing this when you stated it. Therefore, they said that they would declare it—if I am not mistaken—as an announcement—that what they would declare would be their inspiration from his statements. And, therefore to the extent that I know—and I am almost certain—His Majesty did not have a will regarding the country. In fact, he was not in a situation to issue it, because he was very ill—and the operations that he had.

Regarding the book, some people came and offered their suggestions. I was personally against this. To write this book—after two surgeries, and the travels, etc., His Majesty was not in a situation to write the book or read it.

Of course, the beginning of this was in Mexico. I believe—if I am not mistaken—it was Mr. Shojaedin Shafa who came with a few French individuals to conduct an interview with His Majesty. One or two afternoons they came for about one to two hours, had audience with His Majesty, and asked some questions and he answered them. After that Her Majesty and her entourage completed the book. His Majesty was very ill when correcting it. Therefore, I don't know to what extent he had said what is there, and to what extent other persons have interfered in the writing.

Manouchehr Bibiyan: Thank you very much.

Ardeshir Zahedi: Did I answer your question?

Manouchehr Bibiyan: You tried.

We know that for more than half a century the ethnic and religious conflicts in the Middle East have been in the day's headlines. What was the Shah's role, and your role, who were the Foreign Minister and Ambassador of Iran to the United States, regarding this issue?

Ardeshir Zahedi: The general policy of Iran, foreign policy, which His Majesty named National Independent Policy, was based on conduct that we identified as our national interests. And, not to take sides, this task continued until the day we lost our country. There were two groups. One, in the beginning—when I was young and I was the deputy of His Majesty—was the Baghdad Pact, which later became CENTO, which was a defense pact. And, many times we talked with Khrushchev also—His Majesty's opinion was different there. The other was RCD—and this pact consisted of three countries: Pakistan, Iran, and Turkey. This was an economic pact. And, the Baghdad pact . . . with Iran, Pakistan, Turkey and England. At first the Americans supported this, after that they became similar to observers. Then that man, the invader, came and it was ruined.

However, regarding the foreign policy of Iran. Since the day His Majesty gave me this honor—in the talks that we conducted whether in Hungary, Paris, or London and when he asked me to come—and at that time I did not want to come because of certain reasons (my life, etc)—it was agreed that when we would come we have to try that first to, the countries which we live with to bring this up at the level of Foreign Ministry. Meaning that they—whether it was Pakistan, or the Soviet Union, or Iraq, or Afghanistan—they had vital importance to us. And, also the South. All of these sheikdoms of Kuwait in the south of the Persian Gulf.

And, from the perspective of politics, we implemented our national interests. For this reason, when none of the Arabs dared to speak a word—we proceeded to an extremely strong approach in the Czechoslovakia issue. And even in the negotiations that I had with Gromyko, I told him—when he wanted to prove to me that the Czechs themselves wanted—I told him: "you want to tell me that the territory that belongs to you is yours, and the territory that belongs to others is either yours or up for negotiations and deals." I also told him at the United Nations. At that time because the poor Arabs were pawns of the Soviet Union, they were forced not to say anything about the Soviet Union. However, because we considered ourselves independent, and we were independent, we always expressed our will. The same is true regarding our independent policy.

And, regarding our policy in the Persian Gulf. Regarding this part, I recommend Fereydoun Zandfar's book. He has worked hard in writing it, and it was published in Iran—I was surprised how this book was published there. Because you know when I came there, I established an establishment responsible only for the south Persian Gulf countries. Therefore, this was our policy.

Manouchehr Bibiyan: But, the issue of Bahrain. Don't you think that Iran lost Bahrain very easily, and the three islands

Ardeshir Zahedi: You may think so. The issue of Bahrain. First, because once I did not know the issue, I was severely against it. Actually I see that Mr. Fereydoun Zandfar also has referred to here in his book. I even took my colleagues from the Foreign Ministry to have an audience with His Majesty. Because what we thought [about the issue], we told him. But today—also if I did not believe in this issue then, I would have resigned. Therefore, I accept this responsibility. No one gave me an order. My speech exists, regarding Congress. However, what were we doing? Mr. Mesbahzadeh is living

Manouchehr Bibiyan: Yes.

Ardeshir Zahedi: Ask him. Mr. Masoudi was there. University academics were there. I first organized a meeting. The gentlemen from the Imperial Iranian Military, General Arteshbod Jam came. Oveissi was there. Aryana was there. At that time General Jam was the successor at the [Iranian] embassy [in the U.S.]. I first told them because at that time . . . and once regarding the issue of Shatt-al-Arab and we exerted diplomatic pressure with the conclusion that the very president of Iraq came and signed the Shatt-al-Arab agreement. Because these were our two problems.

Regarding Bahrain, I asked the Imperial Iranian Military: "You tell me, if we want to take Bahrain, what would happen?" They became very happy. They went and later brought a program. Then later we said: "What you have brought, tell us how much armament we need? How many people might be killed?" The result was that we would have reached a dead-end. That similar to 150 years prior to that, that we would have faced superpower states. And the result, today you see whether in the Falkland Island or whether the issue of Cyprus which is still one of—we wanted to have good neighborly relations with the neighboring states so that the problems would have been resolved. At that time we told England. It was stated at the United Nations also. The negotiations began in this very house at the time I was cabinet minister. Mr. Amir Khosrow and a group of others were here; the reports exist in the British documents. His Majesty the Shah, I, and the cabinet ministers, and the people who worked for the government also, any person if they believed that it was a wrong decision, they should have resigned.

We reach this conclusion that it would have been in the interests of Iran to have good relations with these neighbors. Especially when at that time it was stated that the oil of Bahrain would not last for a long period. And, it is true, and as you know Bahrain does not have much pearl either. And from the perspective of geopolitics, entirely, it is located in the south of the Persian Gulf. And, I told a few people in the organization that we had a small problem and now face a larger problem. At the time the British suggested to Iran that "we'll help you so that we will take Bahrain from the Portuguese for you and we'll give you Bahrain." This is the essence of the story of Bahrain. After . . . it was not under Portuguese rule, but it became under British rule. For years under their rule. And every time the Iranian government—even prior to the Pahlavi's reign—wanted to go there, they said: "until, you don't have troops, I'll bring it for you." If you want the details, I again recommend Fereydoun Zandfar's book—because he is in Iran and you don't have access to him. Another person is Dr. Tadjbakhsh who has written his dissertation on this issue. He is in the United States. Before he has reached a more advanced age, meet him. It is possible that it will be against my statements and opinions, but for you who have written history it is important.

Therefore, yes. We stated that we neither accept that it become part of Saudi Arabia. Nor do we accept that the British government gives Bahrain as a present to anyone. And, nor do we agree that Bahrain become a British protectorate. Therefore, after long negotiations and extended negotiations occurred, we said that whatever the people of Bahrain want, we would accept. However, we have preconditions. One, that the Islands belong to us. Another, that there ought to be a referendum conducted. Referendum occurred. The people voted. We asked the United Nations to send a representative. Bahrain was gone. Now, a group believes they have a right they—are severely patriotic and nationalist—they state that we ought not to have had there. I accept this responsibility which occurred during my time. And, had I not been convinced in this issue, I would not have proceeded this way. If I were opposed, I would have resigned.

Manouchehr Bibiyan: Regarding the three Islands, the Tombs and Abu Musa, the British who evacuated the three Islands, was it them who agreed that Iran capture the Islands?

Ardeshir Zahedi: Everyone ought to have agreed. At the time when, as they say, because they thought that when England left, they wanted to break their promise. There, they saw that Iran captured. Iran had the right. It belonged to, it belongs to and it will belong to Iran.

Regarding this issue whether with Mr. George Brown, and other cabinet ministers, Prime Minister, Foreign Minister, and the first Secretariat who was the Foreign Minister of Italy. With these figures. All of these countries. To all of these countries, we stated Iran's right, and they all endorsed Iran's right. Therefore, no one could . . . essentially, because this is historic, it will be in my forthcoming book also. However, it is possible that I would die and not be here until that time.

Therefore, what occurred to him, what intrigues existed, what occurred that here His Majesty called me. Why did they request to see me, how my airplane had technical problems, how did we enter, how His Majesty's tears were in his eyes. Later I went and I myself read the views for him. Later Sardar Fakher, Friday Imam, Ala'a. At that time these two were not on good terms with me. Both Ala'a and Eghbal.

We organized that meting with Abdullah Khan Hedayat. We went and visited the commander of war. Because there the issue was only this. And, he recorded my statements. It is available in its entirety, and you have access to it. Because for my own book also, I want to obtain it.

Manouchehr Bibiyan: Okay.

Ardeshir Zahedi: You see. But, ask your question—whatever you want.

Manouchehr Bibiyan: No. My question is that

Ardeshir Zahedi: This is historic.

Manouchehr Bibiyan: Yes.

Ardeshir Zahedi: When will your book be published?

Manouchehr Bibiyan: This book, I think approximately, in six to seven months.

Ardeshir Zahedi: Well, your book will be published before my book. If my book is not published until then, then again, you accomplished better than me. With all honor. Because it is historic.

Manouchehr Bibiyan: Exactly ten years ago, in 1994, I visited you at your residence here.

Ardeshir Zahedi: I remember very well.

Manouchehr Bibiyan: And, we had an interview

Ardeshir Zahedi: It was here.

Manouchehr Bibiyan: At that time, I asked you regarding an interview with Queen Soraya which was not conducted because she was not here in Switzerland at that time.

Ardeshir Zahedi: I remember, that firstly here.

Manouchehr Bibiyan: You know that the Shah was in love with Soraya.

Ardeshir Zahedi: Yes.

Manouchehr Bibiyan: And, now, for the reasons that we all know, the Shah divorced her. But, for years and years, he protected her. And, it is important for me to know that at the time she was the Queen of Iran, how was she treated at the Royal Court.

Ardeshir Zahedi: In its entirety. My acquaintance with Queen Soraya was established when my father was the Commander of Forces in Isfahan and she was one of the daughters of the Khans who had family relations with our family. Soraya and my sister went to the same school. And, I went to a school named Adab near there. Later, in 1949 the first time that I saw her was in Zurich. Later, it was her marriage, and later the Royal Court, and in the end what occurred, which persons had views regarding these issues. How His Majesty wanted to decide. And at that time I was here because I wanted to seek my father's advice. They asked me to go to Tehran. Later they came and I answered them again. And how it was arranged that Queen Soraya came to St. Moritz. She was here. After that she went to Germany, to be with her parents. What delegation was arranged to visit her in Germany and state this statements to her so that she would be given the title of Her Royal Highness. And, in that period also there was no longer direct line of contact for a long time because I was close to His Majesty, and her relations to me as my Queen and at the same time I loved her like a sister. There was confidential relations between, there was no relations, there were questions and messages which were said until the day that His Majesty became ill and it had been arranged that he would have surgery. Despite the fact that she did not like to fly by airplane, she came here and visited me. Because a few hours prior to my going there I told His Majesty regarding this. It was agreed that I arrange that they see each other. But, unfortunately because at that time His Majesty was ill I did not want His Majesty, or that she would not see His Majesty in that situation.

Yes, His Majesty loved his wife. To the extent that I have witnessed, His Majesty at that time was very much under the influence of Queen Soraya. There were family problems. And, in the end, certainly, this friendly relations and respect between this husband and wife, was divorce. And I have respect for both of them that they never mixed personal issues with political issues.

Manouchehr Bibiyan: Thank you. Another question. The last question that I want to ask you is regarding your article in one of the reliable economic newspapers of the United states in which you have mentioned that three decades ago meaning in the era of Mohammad Reza Pahlavi, Iran was among the first signers of the Nuclear Nonproliferation Treaty (NPT). And you as the Foreign Minister signed this treaty. Of course, the then Foreign Minister.

Ardeshir Zahedi: Certainly.

Manouchehr Bibiyan: This year, the United States and European Countries have exerted diplomatic pressure vis-à-vis the Islamic Republic to not conceal its nuclear activities. During your era, did Iran act transparently regarding this treaty? Would you provide more information regarding this issue?

Ardeshir Zahedi: Iran every time, in every diverse issue, I can promise that it was both transparent and honorable during the era that I was witness to. Iran was not afraid of anybody. I knew that it is not good to tell lies. And, I personally hate lies. Because the person who lies, the liar, ruins his/her own reputation. Yes, I wrote a letter regarding this to the Wall Street Journal. It exists; I'll provide it to you. It was published worldwide. Not only in the Wall Street Journal in the United States, but it was also published in Europe. With four days difference. I had an interview with Radio Farda. I provided a complete version of the issue because in that newspaper it was not placed there. I stated my own views regarding Iran. I believe because both not to waste your time and also I don't remember the details. It is better that I provide you with both. You can utilize anything from it.

Manouchehr Bibiyan: I said the last question. Do you have a statement that I have not asked you but it is necessary that you refer to it?

Ardeshir Zahedi: First, excellent, you always ask everything in your interview and get the answer. Your questions are all excellent. And, you also get the answers in every case. The issues might be many. But right now because I was prepared to answer your questions, I am thinking. And, you saw that I did not have notes. It is possible. I hope that I would be fortunate that if I would come there, and God willing I feel better I want to certainly come and to meet each other in Los Angeles. And, of course I would be happier if you would come to Switzerland again with your daughter to meet each other here. Regarding these issues what comes to my mind, in this period also if there are questions, because I am writing my memoirs, I'll tell you via telephone.

Daryoush Homayoun

Journalist; Minister of Information (1977-1978) during the Iranian Revolution; Deputy Secretary-General, the Rastakhiz Party (in the Shah's regime); Editor-in-Chief, Ayandegaan (in the Shah's regime)

Daryoush Homayoun

Broadcast Date: September 4, 1983-October 23, 1983
Location of the Interview: JAAM-E-JAM Studios

This interview with Daryoush Homayoun has been translated by Daryoush Homayoun

JAAM-E-JAM: Dear viewers, in today's Open Forum program, we have conducted an interview with Mr. Daryoush Homayoun—one of the political figures of our country. Mr. Homayoun held the position of Minister of Information in Dr. Jamshid Amouzegar's Administration—a critical position in the cabinet.

JAAM-E-JAM: The era of the premiership of Dr. Jamshid Amouzegar and his administration and the cabinet, is considered one of the most critical eras of the history of Iran and a turning

point in the political history of Iran and the destiny of our country. The first sparks of the riots and the revolutionary situation emerging in this period. Many people still believe that the political policies and the political behavior of the Amouzegar administration caused the beginning of this riot and the Islamic Revolution—the publication of a letter against Ayatollah Khomeini in the press of Iran; the cessation of the Akhound's endowments by the government; Wagfs; and many other issues had motivated the people to launch this riot and the revolution.

Mr. Homayoun, who is a gifted writer and for many years was the president and editor-in-chief of the Ayandegan newspaper, is a key statesman who can shed light on many of these events.

During the premiership of Mr. Amouzegar and his administration the people's first stage of demonstrations and riots began. The demonstrations and the people's involvement with the government forces resulted in the fall of the Amouzegar cabinet. In that era which was a time of much riots, Mr. Homayoun was a Cabinet Minister in the Amouzegar cabinet and he witnessed many of the events of that period.

At the beginning of our interview, we ask Mr. Daryoush Homayoun to provide a summary of his life in the past as well as his political activities—especially during the time when Dr. Mossadegh was in power—when he was an extremist member of the nationalist groups.

Daryoush Homayoun: I don't think my life is interesting in itself, but as I have lived during an important period of the Iranian history, I think talking about some periods of my political life would help the coming generations.

I was born during Reza Shah's reign. The Russo-British Invasion of Iran (1941) sparked the first signs of political consciousness in me and my peers. We were the Reza Shah generation, born in a period of exceptional national pride. The generation that followed us could not feel the same exalted sense of being Iranian. It was only because of the extraordinary changes Reza Shah brought to Iran and the deep impression it made on our young minds. The sudden collapse of that idealized world was a tremendous shock to us. However, it did not lead us to despair, and awakened a spirit of struggle and resistance in many of us, even though we were mere teenagers. I was among those who started a life of political activism right from then. My journalism also started well before my 20th birthday. The first journal I published was a political-artistic magazine, incidentally called "Jaam-e-Jam". During Dr. Mossadegh's term and the campaign for the nationalization of oil industry, I was related to the extremist rightist-nationalist organizations, among which was a secret group which targeted the communist "Toudeh Party" and another group known as the English party. Almost all of those groups supported the campaign for the nationalization of the oil industry. We were part of the popular uprising of 1952 to re-install Dr. Mossadegh to premiership. Many of us joined the demonstrations against Mossadegh on 28th of Mordad (19th of August 1953) to bring back the Shah from exile. The reason being that during 1952-53 many things had changed in Iran and our national struggle had deviated from its path. We thought that Iran without the King would be in danger, and not Dr. Mossadegh but the Toudeh Party would emerge victor from the struggle for power. Dr. Mossadegh was playing the same role as Krensky during the Russian Revolution. I remember that I had written an article mentioning this similarity. I wrote in a newspaper published by our organization that Mossadegh might be the Krensky of Iran and that our country may fall into the hands of Communists.

This is the story of my activism during that time. Later on, in 1954, I ended my membership in the right extremist organizations and chose a moderate stance. I adopted a more centrist and liberal worldview as I grew older and better educated, a process still continuing. This worldview contains the elements of nationalism, liberal democracy, progressivism, and social justice in various degrees. Later on, I decided to work in the publishing field. I established the Organization of Pocket Books in Iran. It was the first publishing house of pocket books in Iran and it continued to publish for several years. We published many fine books. Finally I realized that the media at that time was not suitable to make my ideas publicly known, so I decided to establish the 'Ayandegan' daily, which is a long story.

JAAM-E-JAM: Mr. Homayoun, you mentioned that in the years after, you turned into a moderate person, and of course some groups, that as far as I know, became a monarchist. Did this change occur solely due to your advancing age as well as the advancement in your education that you decided to turn from a nationalist into a moderate person and supporting the Monarchy?

Homayoun: Even at the time I was a member of the extremist nationalist organizations, I was a supporter of Monarchy and as I mentioned, I took part in August 1953 demonstrations. I should emphasize that there is a difference between one who believes in monarchy as a form of government and a "royalist" who puts the Shah and kingship at the center of political universe. The person of a Shah cannot serve as a symbol to the entire monarchy. For almost 3,000 years of the history of Iran, we have had numerous kings, the majority of them were not people we could love. There were also great and respectable men among those kings. I, therefore, differentiate between them as personalities and the institution of monarchy in the course of Iranian history. My political views at the early stages of my life emanated from my reaction to the traumatic events of that period and the blow to our national pride leading many of us to the extremes.

JAAM-E-JAM: We will ask you some short questions to let you give longer explanations. Let us talk about the Ayandegan Newspaper. How did it start and what happened to it at the end?

Homayoun: I started "Ayandegan" in 1967 as a company owned by share holders with the cooperation of some of my friends and colleagues. It was an interesting enterprise, and as we had expected, it had great impact on the Iranian press and served as an example for them. Ayandegan caused an uproar, especially among the morning dailies which were many but small and devoid of professionalism. Some of those papers started a campaign of smear against me whose impact lasted for years. We started the newspaper with a small capital and had big problems. I think we were the first or the only newspaper who used to pay salaries to the staff by promissory notes! This situation continued until the economic boom of the 1970s. The newspaper never grew as much as my colleagues and I expected, but it was very influential and had disproportionate intellectual and political impact. In 1977, 10 years after the establishment of the paper, I joined the government and passed on the newspaper to some of my senior colleagues with the agreement that all the staff would gradually become shareholders. With the resignation of Amouzegar's cabinet, I returned to the newspaper to solve some problems but left in a few days and no more did I interfere with the affairs of the newspaper. In the early months of the Revolution (February 1979) Ayandegan was the only newspaper that started a major campaign against Khomeini and the Islamic regime in Iran to the point that Khomeini unprecedentedly announced: "I do not read Ayandegan." I remember that when I was living in hiding underground, it was written on the walls: "I do not read Ayandegan because I am illiterate. Signed: Imam Khomeini"! The newspaper continued its struggle until August 1979 when "Pasdaran" raided the premises, confiscated everything and arrested 11 staff members. The newspaper was closed down and another newspaper replaced it.

JAAM-E-JAM: Mr. Homayoun, there was a newspaper article saying that the machines of the Ayandegan's printing press were given to you as a gift by Israel. Is it true? If so, what was the relationship between you and the State of Israel? Why did the Israeli government give you the machinery?

Homayoun: That was exactly the pretext the agents of the Islamic regime in Iran used to confiscate the newspaper. They claimed that Israel had helped Ayandegan with its printing press. The truth is that in 1970, some three years into Ayandegan, I realized that it was impossible to continue printing the paper in two printing shops and binding it in another establishment. I talked to Dr. Mesbahzadeh, the publisher of Kayhan Newspapers. Kahyan had a second hand rotary machine too small for their use but more than enough for our operation. The machine was mortgaged by the Omarn Bank as a guaranty for Kayhan's loan for it. Both the machine and the loan were transferred to Ayandegan. But Omran Bank demanded more guaranty from us. Here my colleagues, Dr. Cyrous Amouzegar, mortgaged his house and I secured the loan from Omran Bank. My connection to Israel was to the extent that I was once invited by the State of Israel to visit that country. I was not the only one who was

SECRETS OF THE IRANIAN REVOLUTION

invited. Hundreds maybe thousands including government authorities, businessmen, journalists, university staff and students visited Israel during those years. No, these are just accusations now used by the Islamic Republic.

JAAM-E-JAM: Mr. Homayoun, as it was mentioned at the beginning of the interview, some events took place at the time of Jamshid Amouzegar that could have been prevented. As a cabinet member, why did you neglect the solution of these problems? How do you explain what had happened in the past?

It is too easy to give simple explanations for complex phenomena. Human mind usually tends to do that since it is very difficult to investigate the real reasons. In my opinion, it would be incorrect to state that Dr. Amouzegar's cabinet caused the revolution to break out. The start of the Islamic Revolution goes back to the time of Islam. By Islamization of Iranian society it became a political force in Iran. Thus, part of the explanation goes to the Islamic nature of our society and the relationship between religion and politics. Besides, one of the causes for the Islamic Revolution was that oil prices quadrupled, as a result of which the country suffered grave disruption in every aspect of national life.

Three years prior to the revolution our country experienced extraordinary changes which could be named disorganization at all levels. The oil income was too high for the country to absorb. And it was spent by bad planning.

When we came to power in the summer of 1977 inflation was rampant and electricity in Tehran and other cities was cut off several hours a day. People were resentful. One of the steps taken by our cabinet was to reduce inflation and remove shortages. The roots of the revolution go much deeper. I would like to talk about it not for the purpose of exonerating ourselves. There is no need for that. Anybody who made a mistake or committed any sin in this revolution, has been duly punished. The reason I am giving an explanation is that people should not consider the events or their mistakes in such a trivial way, so that the same experiences would not be repeated. In order to prevent this, and in order not to live as we did in the past, we should know our past well and acknowledge our mistakes in order not to repeat them. I told you about the role of the religion. The religious opposition, i.e. the Islamic opposition was all the time active right under the reign of government of Iran in the Shah's regime and used the state institutions against it. Then there was the broad coalescing of Marxist and leftist forces with this religious opposition, i.e. with the Islamic opposition, the so called red and black coalition or "Islamic Marxists". It was ridiculed at the time, but later proved to be the case. Those were active elements in the revolution, but passive elements were even more numerous.

Iranian society during 1960s and 1970s had experienced transformations that were beyond its capacity. Not that the changes were too fast, but because they were too inadequate. We pursued a way of development that proved unable to meet the needs of society and made social problems worse.

At the beginning of the 1960s, half of the population of Tehran did not live in slums. They lived in their own villages where they had a life they were used to. As a result of our policies the population of Tehran at the end of the 1970s had reached 4.5 millions and most of this population lived in despicable conditions and with heightened expectations. These were the people who filled the streets in their multitude and brought this group to power. They had no water, no electricity, and had to put up with the terrible traffic jams, heat and air pollution of Tehran which is no better than that of Los Angles! And then the inflation, the shortages, the hardening of imported cements in Bandar Abbas customs area, the rusting of 2000 heavy trucks imported and left under the sun and rain . . . . I myself saw a terrible scene of these trucks scattered in the desert. There were eventually some plans to use their chassis for storage! We, at the ministry were going to use them as roadside tea houses. To drive those trucks valued at millions of Dollars, south Korean drivers were to be hired while thousands of Iranians were unemployed. There were many such examples. We failed in educating our people as well. We could not educate the manpower necessary for our industry and services while every year, tens of thousands of students graduated without proper qualification. All these factors created dissatisfaction leading to revolution. In principle revolutions take place when two conditions are present. The first when the system fails. The second when the leadership loses the will to defend itself. In Iran the leadership did not posses that will and readily surrendered. These were the factors which caused the revolution in Iran. Obviously, during Amouzegar's cabinet, some events took place, and you are right to point them out and I shall explain them.

JAAM-E-JAM: Mr. Homayoun, as it was mentioned at the second part of the interview, and of course, you provided an answer. Regarding what some believe that the Amouzegar cabinet caused the dissatisfaction of the people and at that time, of course you were one of the cabinet ministers and had shared responsibility with other cabinet ministers. How and why did you neglect the prevention of the occurrence of these events and the solution of these problem? Who do you consider at fault regarding these factors?

Homayoun: As I mentioned last week, when Amouzegar was appointed, the dissatisfaction among people was at its peak. Frequent electricity blackouts was the most visible of government's failure. House prices and rents were too high. Inflation was rampant, there were shortages everywhere. The ports could not handle the ever increasing imports. Interestingly enough with the Amouzegar's cabinet, there was a sigh of relief among people. They hoped that the situation would improve. The new cabinet definitely did not come to cause a revolution and give the country to Khomeini. It is against all logic. Amouzegar's cabinet started its work with the intention of solving the country's problems, and passing it on to a successor in a better shape. It is natural that one who accepts a responsibility wishes to do his best. It is unimaginable to think that 20-30 people, with years of political and social activity and good records in administration came to power with the intention of ruining the Shah's regime. This is meaningless. We thought that, basically, the problems of Iran were inflation, agriculture, education and housing. We tried to solve these problems. We also tried to improve the administrative machinery in lethargy after 13 years under the same prime minister. We undertook our responsibilities with such aspirations, but soon were confronted with a threatening situation. Hardly into our second month in office the universities opened after the summer recess, and universities were revolutionary centers not only at that year of 1977 but long before. The strange occurrence of that year was that university unrest rapidly took an Islamic turn. The Minister of Education reported that female students had occupied the first rows of the classrooms in Islamic attire. It was shocking. I remember that during one cabinet session, I warned about the rapid growth in building mosques in the cities. Something was happening in society, which we had not been aware of. We were trying to improve the administrative aspects of the government, bringing inflation down and reconnect electricity, but the problem is that when you bring inflation down, unemployment goes up. Many construction workers had rushed to Tehran from villages and other cities due to high wages there. With the slowdown in those sectors some became unemployed.

Budget cuts lead to a degree of recession and the slowdown of economy. This is true here in the country in which we living. Since 1980 until now, you can see the kind of recession they have been facing as a result of taming inflation. There was going to be a double-digit inflation rate. Currently, the inflation rate is lower than 4%, but 11.5 million people are unemployed. These are the problems that are unavoidable. You have to either put up with unemployment or with inflation. Of course, if we were aware of the consequences of unemployment, we would not do this. I am telling you, it didn't occur to any member of the cabinet that we would be heading toward a revolutionary path by bringing inflation down. It is noteworthy that the cabinet had no control over 68% of the State's budget; the rest being under the Shah's direct control. We had to work with just 32% of the budget, which was too low to do anything with. The prime minister asked every department to bring down their budget by 20%. 20% of 32% was not a significant amount. At the same time, the military spending increased and eliminated all savings. I concede that we didn't have the correct perception of what was happening in the country, and we didn't take steps in time to prevent those events, but I believe that the Amouzegar cabinet had a much greater resolve to stand and fight than its successors. As soon as we saw the earliest signs of serious unrest in Esfahan (early summer 1978,) martial law was declared over there. But it was not martial law like we witnessed afterwards when soldiers stood by idly in the streets and people put wreaths around their necks or carnations into their rifle barrels. We took action and within twenty-four hours it was over. We managed to restore order in Tabriz (autumn 1977) by necessary administrative actions and arresting those instigators who were not able to escape and start somewhere else. Azarbayjan stayed calm to the last days of the Shah's regime. What I mean is that when the government felt the danger, it fought back successfully. What brought down our cabinet was the fire at cinema Rex in Abadan. Of course, at the time, most people, including those who today say the Amouzegar's cabinet came for "specific" missions, insisted that the fire was the work of the Savak, the government, and the Shah. It was against all sense to claim that the government would burn 400—500 people to death, but nobody was ready to listen to reason. Later on, it was proved that all was done by religious edict (not specifically the cinema in Abadan.). Well before that they had destroyed the only cinema in Qom and in the course of several months, 30 to 40 cinemas suffered serious acts of sabotage. Only the Rex cinema was blamed on the government. Anyway, the government could not survive that blow. In my opinion, the resignation of the cabinet was wrong at that juncture. It is a fact that the unrest started at that time. However there was no revolutionary momentum during 1977 or early 1978. What was happening at the time, as I was following it day by day, was mobile groups of a few dozen attacked banks and bars and wine shops in different cities and moved to other targets. Iran's forces of law and order were totally unprepared for such tactics. The Iranian Armed Forces had been strengthened considerably, but we did not have a riot police. The police force responsible for keeping order in the cities consisted of policemen who earned a mere $160 per month! And you can imagine how a policeman could make a living with that amount.

Iran's security forces were not prepared because the country was not supposed to confront such a situation. In fact, Iran was the "Island of Stability" and tranquility. It was progressing, becoming the second Japan. It was about to become the 5th industrial power of the world (of

course, I do not believe in those claims; we had too many shortcomings)
No one could imagine at the time that we would have street unrest and
fifty saboteurs around causing trouble from say Roodsar to Zanjan.
Unfortunately, the forces of law and order did not have the means
to prevent such incidents unless the Army intervened with all of its
strength, which at the time was clearly unnecessary. We did that, as I
mentioned earlier, in Esfahan when there was real danger. The army
reacted quickly and without much violence all was over.

**JAAM-E-JAM: Mr. Homayoun, many people believe that America
had a leading role in the events that took place in Iran and that
the superpowers had a major role in this issue. They believe that
the superpowers are the ones who must give the green light or red
light. What is your opinion about this issue?**

Homayoun: I think the people who think this way are mistaking power
politics with street crossings. The superpowers have limited authority
and options, and if it were really up to them to change things by
pressing red and green buttons, then the world would have been in
greater trouble. Fortunately it is not the case. The superpowers have
so many difficulties in their own domains that it is hard to imagine
they have this kind of power in powerful and populous lands further
away. If you look at Britain, you see that they for decades have been
unable to solve problems in Northern Ireland.

Despite this, we still regard England as controlling everything in
Iran. Or take a look at America: you will see that in Central America,
which is actually in their "backyard", America is weak and is going
to lose the entire area, but there is nothing this superpower can do.
1800 American soldiers were sent to Beirut. Two of these soldiers were
killed. There was serious commotion all over the country, demanding

the withdrawal of the soldiers to the United States. They didn't care about Lebanon and American policy in the Middle East. I am convinced that if a few American advisors are killed in El Salvador, the same thing will happen there too. Superpowers are stuck with such problems! Look at Russia, it is drowned in Afghanistan and does not know what to do about Poland.

We, in order not to assume our responsibility or doing something, in order not to fight, blame the superpowers. Naturally, if we wait for the green light, we will not take part in any action because it is not up to us to change our destiny. This defeatist attitude is doomed to failure. That's why I insist that the issues concerning revolution to be explored in detail so that we would not have to rely on God's will. Fully studied and explained so that we come out of this fatalistic attitude. All our culture and literature is filled with submission to god's will, with the wisdom of not trying and waiting for the providence, to the extent that our greatest lyrical poet belittles wealth and power that is earned by enterprise; only if it comes with no effort it is considered worthy. Now we have added the Anglo-American providence to God's will, rendering ourselves as mere pawns.

Just imagine the psychological state of a nation that imposes slavery and captivity on itself, relinquishes its own autonomy and waits for others to show it red or green lights. I would like to ask those making these claims, the following questions: which foreign power called you to the streets for demonstrations? Which foreign power told you to watch Khomeini's face on the moon and look for his beard among the pages of the Koran? These acts were done by people themselves. Now those millions of men could claim that they were given the green light. If so, they themselves are to blame. The car or the person going through green light is responsible. If nobody passes through the green light, nothing will happen. There are innumerable memories, films, pictures and witnesses of ladies and gentlemen who took part in demonstrations, and meetings and did their best for the revolution's success. In this very city during 1978-79 how many meetings did you attend where every one was talking of the Islamic Republic and "He should go, no matter who would come (meaning the Shah). When the political atmosphere is so poisonous with hatred and animosity towards a person and regime, what green light is needed to start the revolution. Take Turkey, for example. Do you think that if the entire world would encourage people to start a revolution and all B.B.C is devoted to broadcasts in Turkish. Do you think they could persuade the Turkish people to go to the streets and demonstrate? Would they follow the instructions of the B.B.C? No way! The Turks care about their own national interests not what US or Britain wish. There is so much talk about a green (Islamic) belt the Americans put around Soviet Union to prevent those Moslem societies from falling to communism. Turkey too has common border with the Soviet Union and is a Moslem country. So why has there been no Islamic revolution and no Islamic government in Turkey? In Turkey, extremist Moslems are put in jail instead of being revered? The Turks stand by their own national interest. I hope Iranians once and for all take responsibility for their own actions, both personal and national; show their will and belief in themselves—otherwise the future of our country will be even worse than it had been before!

JAAM-E-JAM: Mr. Homayoun, let's talk about the role of the Shah. In one of the interviews that we had, one of the ministers in the cabinets of Amir Abbas Hoveida and Jamshid Amouzegar said that the Shah did not interfere in the affairs of the country. He helped them as an advisor—only when the ministers had problems and needed some advice. What is your opinion about that?

Homayoun: As far as my work as a journalist or the minister of Information and Tourism is concerned, sadly I cannot agree with this view. When I worked at Ayandegan, I was called many times by the Minister of Information and informed about the Shah's dissatisfaction with what was published in the paper. In 1969, I was ordered not to go to my office for 5 weeks. I returned to work after mediation. Mr. Javad Mansur was the then Minister of Information and is a witness that the Shah—I was dismissed from my paper for complaining about the names of the streets and squares in Mashad, too many of them in the name of the royal family, sometimes doubly. I also had shown the inappropriateness of questioning the propriety of calling many items in the so-called charter of the Shah and People Revolution, as they were administrative measures. A few years later another of my colleagues caused The Shah's wrath that he was completely forced out of the company and the paper. During my time at the ministry, our problem with the press or rather their problem with us, usually started from the highest authority. His Majesty's discontent with the Press came to me through the prime minister and relayed through the hierarchy to the "culprit" in the journal concerned. That claim is not at all correct and I would like to mention a few examples. The Charter of the Shah and People Revolution which included nineteen articles was announced by the Shah himself with no input from government departments even though they covered the most important aspects of policy making, defining all priorities and strategies. No ministry had any hand in their formulation. They all were to implement the programs. During those years, the Iranian Parliament approved the cabinet's bills not because of the Prime Minister or Ministers' recommendations, but because they had been approved by the shah. Usually the bills went through without any significant change.

The Kish Island Development, a project that up to the time of my appointment was costing 16 billion Rials, had no official connection to any governmental department. It was a pet project of the former minister of royal Court. Hoveida, who had become the Court minister, suggested that our ministry purchase the project. We were not very enthusiastic and The National Oil Company paid the price and Iran Air agreed to supervise the project. I mention these instances not for exonerating the cabinet. Anyone working for the government of Iran during the last 25 years knows that it was a very concentrated system and even second and third degree decisions were made by the highest authority. By emphasizing these points I want to draw attention to the lessons of those years. If we want to build a new Iran, we should not let (and I emphasize on this point) the Shah become involved with executive affairs. We should not let him be a leader or the commander of the country, the decision maker. We should let the king be a king, a Constitutional monarch. Mohammad Reza Shah is dead and I will be the same sooner or later. We will all die, but that country will remain; and it should be better governed; better than the past. Otherwise it will have to face the same disasters in different forms.

JAAM-E-JAM: After your removal from the government, you were imprisoned by the Shah's order. What was the charge? Why were some of the former cabinet ministers imprisoned by the Shah's regime? What occurred to you in prison? For how long were you imprisoned? How did you succeed to escape while some others stayed in prison and were eventually hanged?

Homayoun: One of the biggest mistakes made by Mohammad Reza, was the mass arrest of former high officials and ministers of his own government. The list of these prisoners was prepared by general Moghaddam, the chief of Savak who used the occasion also to settle some personal and political scores, as did some other influential people who added to the list. The list included Hoveida, the former prime minister and court minister, some nine former ministers, a former police commander, the former head of Savak and altogether more than 30 officials. These arrests were part of the policy of the numerous concessions given by successive cabinets after us to the opposition against the Shah's regime. But this foolhardy did not bring any goodwill towards the Shah. On the contrary the revolutionaries came to the conclusion that the Shah's regime was getting weaker and was nearing its end, as it is throwing parts of its own body to hungry wolves and whetting their appetite. Another consequence was that all other high officials became fearful for their lives and lost any confidence in the Shah. They started to be more and more concerned for their own security. Some of them escaped from Iran using various pretexts. Some of those who stayed tried to cooperate with the opposition to the Shah's regime. One of them was Tehran's serving mayor. He presented his resignation to Khomeini, who at that time, was not in power. The arrests only speeded up the end of the Shah's regime. I was charged for attacking Khomeini by publishing an article in Etelaat Newspaper. Many things could be said about this article, and now is the best time to talk about it. The article was an answer to Khomeini's cassettes sent to Iran. After Mostafa, the son of Khomeini, died, there were rumors that he was killed by the Savak. I am sure it is not true. I think he had gastric problems and may be he had eaten too much. Anyway it had nothing to do with Savak, but his death was used by Khomeini and his followers to attack Shah with unprecedented harshness. One Ayatollah Rowhani went as far as announcing from a mosque at Qom that the Shah is dethroned. It was in 1977 while the Shah was still in Iran. These made the Shah very angry.

It should be noted that the Shah was very sensitive about what was said about him or his country. Even when a newspaper in say, Gabon, wrote something against Iran, the ministry of Information would immediately be ordered to prepare an answer or the ministry of Court would be ordered to write an article and publish it in the newspapers. Our advice to ignore such stuff was of no avail. Anyway, after what Khomeini had sent and Rowhani's statement, the Shah ordered Hoveida to prepare an answer to them. Hoveida had a press bureau at the Prime Minister Office and had transferred it to the Ministry of Court. A nondescript piece was written by someone (I know the man, but as he may be in Iran. I prefer not to mention his name.) The Shah found it too weak and ordered a stronger tone to be prepared. The new version attacked Khomeini, his Indian ancestry and his record of opposing reforms. It was brought to me while I was in Restakhiz Party Convention, too busy with party affairs, So I gave the envelope, without opening it, to a reporter of Etelaat who was passing by. It would have been better if I had opened the envelope even though Hoveida had called me the day before about the Shah's order to get what will be sent published in a newspaper as soon as possible. As minister, I should have opened that envelope and read the article. I should have guessed that such an article might have dangerous consequences. But even if I had read it, I most probably would not have paid too much attention to it. At that time, the winter of 1977, I did not take Mullas seriously and did not believe them to be able to take over Iran. The editor of Etelaat called me and warned that publishing the article would cause trouble for the paper in Qom. I told him he knew who is behind the article and it has to appear in the paper and Etelaat had enjoyed the Shah's regime's largess for 50 years and it was time to do some sacrifice. They called the prime minister and he after knowing the origin of the article told them to carry it on. Other important newspapers published it afterwards. After our resignation, Etelaat, to clear its name, published a scathing article and put the whole blame on me. They went as far as falsely claiming that I had threatened to take over their premises. This claim that was irrational because we were not able to run the publishing house. It was the time everybody wanted to endear him/herself with the revolutionaries. I did not react out of deference to the Shah and the Court Minister.

JAAM-E-JAM: In the circumstances that that letter was published causing the unrest, you, as the then cabinet minister, could have prevented its publication—the letter that caused unrest and you didn't and you answered that you didn't know. Bur, later on, when you found out that it was ordered by the Shah, why didn't you resign?

Homayoun: As I have mentioned earlier, I should have opened the envelope and read the letter, but I didn't. I have also told you that even if I had read the letter, I still might not have considered it as significant. I did not see it as any thing important because there was no unrest at the time. Now we are talking about an article causing unrest. In 1977, in December 1977, we had a country that we thought was one of the more stable countries in the world. Who could imagine that an article might start a serious unrest, and an unrest lead to revolution? Unrest could be quelled; every day there is unrest somewhere in the world. Take Chile. It has been mired in street demonstrations and bloody clashes for the past 6 months. More people have lost their lives there than during the revolutionary period in Iran, and nothing has happened. It is because the government is standing fast and fights. I am not talking about the rights and wrongs of the Chilean situation. The point is that the regime in Chile has not been overthrown by unrest. This is true for with Zia-Ol-Hagh (in Pakistan,) with Egypt, etc. Of course today, with the benefit of hindsight, we may say that the article was ill advised. But at the time, at the most it could be said that the article would lead to some local disturbances. It is true that I didn't read the article before passing it to the Etelaat reporter. I took the envelope with the yellow seal of the ministry of Court and gave the typed pages to him. This was negligence on my part, but it was not a matter of resigning my post, since I knew well before that it is the Shah's wish. If at that time I knew what I know today, your point would have been right. I should have resisted and resigned if necessary. But like the Shah, I could not envisage what happened during the next year. Now going back to your question, when the article against me appeared, it became the talk of the town. I became the chief culprit and responsible for all disturbances; even though apart from the incident in Qom, other demonstrations and disturbances had more to do with local circumstances and mishandling by responsible authorities. In Tabriz, for instance, the mourning gathering for the 6 victims of Qom turned to serious disturbances due to a decision to close down the mosque in which the mourners were to hold prayers. In Qom itself, however, every thing went smoothly.

When the Shah started his policy of appeasement and surrender and started to put his loyalists into prison as a concession to revolutionary forces, I was a clear candidate. I had remained silent and actually accepted all accusations. I did not want to weaken the Shah. Even today if I were in the same situation I would have done the same, but this is another story. Our prison was in Jamshidabad, the Iranian military police garrison. In prison we were treated with a mixture of deference to our status and the limitations of ordinary prisoners. I have no complaints about that. I learned a lot in prison, including the state of armed forces that was the first priority for the Shah. During that time some 600 soldiers and NCOs had deserted from Jamshidabad, which was too many. There was no heating oil or gasoline for military vehicles. Our Army (the 5th non-nuclear army in the world as it was claimed) was lacking fuel reserves for short-term use, let alone a strategic reserve for the time of war. The morale of the army was low as

I could see from that vantage point. The army was humiliated, enduring six months of inaction in the streets. It was a broken force at the end. Those who are condemning the final declaration of non-intervention by the armed forces (February 12, 1978) should understand that the army at that stage could do nothing.

JAAM-E-JAM: Mr. Darioush Homayoun, may I repeat a part of the question I asked you last week? Please let us know regarding your imprisonment and how you managed to escape.

Homayoun: We were in prison for about 3½ months during which we heard many times that we were going to be executed by the Shah's regime, the same regime we had served. It must be mentioned that Mohammad Reza Shah, despite being under pressure by his military and civilian advisers, never issued the order for our execution. I know that almost any plan presented to the Shah at the time for managing the crisis, included our trial and execution. On February 11th, the day of Revolution, we heard from radio that the Army has declared its neutrality. It was like being between the devil and the deep blue sea. Anything happening was going to be against us. We were just waiting for our destiny. At about 3:30, a large crowd gathered around the compound. The gate was open: a white banner was hanging over it proudly proclaiming 'Jamshidabad Islamic Garrison." There were speeches. We were watching them from the window and also informed by some of our prison guards about what was happening. The commander of the garrison welcoming them said: "we are brothers." Some in the crowd started embracing soldiers to take their arms. An officer led them to the museum and they seized what was there and shooting started which continued for some 3 hours. A number of soldiers were wounded and Dr. Sheikh-ol-Islam Zadeh, a former minister of public health, attended them, thus forsaking the opportunity to escape. Many grenades exploded. The crowd that was trying to takeover the garrison was from leftist groups that had successfully invaded most of army garrisons in the capital. Some of them were shooting from apartments facing our prison and our rooms sustained a few hits. Meanwhile, many prison guards had disappeared and the internal doors of the vast prison were wide open. A soldier appeared and informed us that the attackers want the prisoners free. As the Iranian military police headquarter had at the time 600-700 Iranian military men among its prisoners, many of them had joined the revolutionaries. We took the chance and ran out of the prison while the shooting still continued and the compound was full of people. I had put on my reading glasses and had grown a beard (from the first day I had the feeling that I should grow a beard. It probably had a role in saving me. Mine was a known face.) On the way out, I heard someone asking if Hoveida was there and another told him that he was not. A few minutes later, we were free and out of prison. Two or three of us either stayed in their cells or would otherwise be recognized and captured. One gave himself up to a leading Mullah in the hope of joining the new government! And two were arrested in their houses. All of them were executed. The rest of us survived. I stayed in Tehran for 15 months, changing hiding places. The sun did not shine on me, so to speak, but it was an excellent opportunity for reading and contemplating. After the hostage taking at US embassy I lost any hope for the overthrow of the new regime in Iran. I was waiting for the opening of the schools and Universities and the start of mass protests by thousands who felt betrayed and deceived by the Mullahs. The hostage crisis changed that attitude and they renewed their allegiance to Khomeini. It was then that I decided to get out of Iran and after two attempts and a possibly fatal collision with revolutionary guards I finally managed to reach Turkey and then Europe through Kurdistan.

All these years I have heard many comments about the anti-Khomeini article and its role in the revolution. It is ironic that I am known to many people not for the many things I have done in life, but for one that I really did not do. My answer to those simplistic claims has been that if a revolution could start by a single article why they do not write a hundred and get rid of the Mullahs! It is true that it was a spark; but it fell into a haystack. If not for hay, there could not be a fire. The extraordinary importance attached to that article should not blind us to the fact that all conditions for a revolution were in place. More important were decisions and policies of the successive cabinets in dealing with the revolutionary situation. Giving concession after concession, and giving in at every juncture; imprisoning loyalists and giving free hand to opponents and enemies and even obeying their orders—I know that Beheshti (Ayatollah, and the mastermind of the Islamic Revolution) did give instructions to government agencies and especially Savak and they did as he wished. There has been no revolution in the world enjoying so much cooperation by the regime that was to be overthrown. In no revolution has the country been so easily presented to the revolutionaries. The attack on Khomeini (even though well-founded) was a mistake; but there were innumerable occasions after that to save the country and at every step there were only mistakes.

JAAM-E-JAM: Mr. Homayoun, Besides the uprising following the publishing of that letter in the newspaper to which you pointed out, it was said that the salaries and allowances paid by [public] offices to the Mullahs were cut at the time of Dr. Jamshid Amouzegar, and their earnings from charity organizations were cut following the Shah's orders. They believe that it was one of the reasons for the uprising leading to the revolution. What is your opinion?

Homayoun: No. It was not cut following the Shah's orders. It was a general policy. As I mentioned earlier, at the start of our cabinet all government agencies were ordered to reduce their expenses by 20% in order to balance the budget and fight inflation. The prime minister's office and the Endowments Agency were the two main sources of bribing many Mullahs and as a result, part of their allowances was cut. However, several other government departments continued giving money to their Mullahs who were known as Court clerics and had no standing and influence. These clerics continued to receive money from the Court ministry, Savak, and the vast endowments of the 8th Shiite Imam under the Shah's guardianship. They did not have a role in the revolution. The revolution was led by Mullahs who were financed by Libya and could pay their religious students two to three times more than others.

JAAM-E-JAM: Mr. Homayoun, we are interested in your opinion regarding the late Shah, the monarchy, the Constitutional Law of 1906 as well as any other government or Constitutional Law.

Homayoun: Mohammad Reza Shah has an outstanding place in the history of Iran because of his work for the Iranian people. Also, he was the first king overthrown by the people. It is a bitter fate for a king who spent his entire life serving his country. He made many mistakes that are recorded in history but he also did a lot of good work for Iran that will also be recorded in history. His personality was somewhat a combination of Reza Shah and Ahmad Shah, and even Nasser-Eddin Shah. This was a strange and complex combination. His destiny was tragic because if the people who plunged themselves into this revolution had just waited for 2 or 3 years, there would not have been any need for such madness. The Shah's regime was in the course of a fundamental change, both from personal point of view and policies and priorities.

In my opinion, monarchy is the most suitable regime for Iran. For me, monarchy is not a matter of sentiment; I think of it as a political necessity. In my opinion, the monarchy is a political necessity because it is beneficial for Iran. There is nothing in my blood binding me to any form of government. I look at the country's situation and its history and the characteristics of this nation, and come to the conclusion that monarchy in its newer form, as a constitutional monarchy is the best solution for the problems of continuity and the role of government in Iran. Here, I would like to say something about the Constitution of 1906. Actually there is not such a thing. The Constitution everybody is talking about and was in force, to different degrees until 1979 and many exiles want to go back to, was approved in 1907 and is a faulty document full of contradictions. The 1906 document has 51 clauses all about the rights and workings of the parliament and the administration's obligations towards the Parliament. Under the 1907 Constitution many of the progressive policies and reforms of the two Pahlavis, including women's rights, would have been impossible. Under that document all sorts of discrimination was going on: against women, against non-Moslems, non Shiites; the laws of the land should have been approved by a group of five top ayatollahs (that was ignored from the start.) If we want popular sovereignty we should separate Mosque and State. The constitution of 1907 was good for the time, now we need a constitution and a monarchy fully in democratic tradition.

JAAM-E-JAM: Mr. Homayoun, many people believe that readers of your book entitled *Yesterday and Tomorrow* provide a different interpretation than this. Would you please tell us about your book and its contents?

Homayoun: They probably have not read the book. It is to be expected. Most of Iranians make unfounded judgment. Anybody reading the book will find out that in the early pages I have used Reza Shah I about the founder of the dynasty, showing that I hope for a Reza Shah II. In this book, I tried to explain the situation of Iran as it really was and the way I saw it, without interfering my own feelings, without complaining and whining, without slogans. I wrote about what I had witnessed from the inside of the Shah's regime. In the third chapter of the book, I tried to present a plan for the future of Iran. It is not only an administrative and political plan. It is a plan for national consensus. The book has come under attack for criticizing Iran's development strategy. I heard people say many times: "How could someone who was a minister himself, criticize?" Well, first of all, one should not be deprived of the right to express his views even if he has been a minister. Second (this point is very important), what I have written in the first chapter, are the same views, of course with a different tone and wording, during 10 years of Ayandegan. There were many at the time who thought that I can write like that due to my special ties. There is nothing fundamentally different in that section of the book from my positions in the past. But even if I had not expressed such views before, now I have the right and duty to talk about what I think is right. If we could not learn these basic values from these free lands we are living in, when would be the time?

Ahmad Madani

Commander of the Navy and Governor of Khuzestan after the revolution

Ahmad Madani

February 21, 1982

JAAM-E-JAM: There are different opinions about you: opponents and proponents. But the most important issue is regarding your collaboration with the Islamic Republic of Iran, and then your separation from this regime, i.e. the Islamic Republic which has been in fact very controversial. What is your view regarding the future of Iran?

Ahmad Madani: I send my regards to the nation of Iran, and I thank you for your kindness for this interview. First, what ought to be done in this political struggle, is to overthrow the government of Iran, and then to determine a replacement. Due to the collaborations of the current ruling enemies, all of the foundations of the country have disintegrated. This government is a government of demagoguery armed with the weapon of religion.

I think that in order to root out this regime, i.e. the Islamic Republic, a comprehensive struggle is required. And, this goal cannot be reached by the political activities of a single political entity, but rather it is necessary that all the political forces forge a coalition. But this coalition must be formed according to evaluation [of the forces]. Prior to the victory of the revolution, it was said "the Shah must leave; at any cost". Therefore, in the struggle of the revolution, it had negative consequences and the extremists and the non-independent left consolidated their power.

Now, there is a lesson that has been learned from the mistakes of the past. Therefore, I do not say: Khomeini and his regime must go—at any cost. Rather, I state: Khomeini must leave on the condition that if he leaves, then it would be to our advantage. In the case that Khomeini and his regime would be gone at a cost that would result in the death of thousands of thousands, and homelessness of the people, and a country which is more ruined, and lack of security, and more killings, then people would not obtain anything but a civil war and disintegration [of the country]. And to prevent this, the coalition members have to accept the people and also know what the people inside the country wish and search for, and prepare for it, in order to not face the resistance of the people, and to definitely have the people on their side. Otherwise, it would be very difficult to achieve victory in [the overthrow] of the current ruling enemies.

JAAM-E-JAM: Do you believe in referendum?

Madani: Definitely. In my latest letter entitled "Our Way", I have proposed the comprehensive future government. Of course, I have stated that it is a proposal. I have comprehensively stated this issue, and said: the future government of Iran must be determined by the nation.

We state our own way, we put forth our plans to be proposals. But it is the people that approve it. However, this proposal can not be implemented immediately.

In the said letter, I said that we consider three stages for this. A stage of overthrow, in which all the forces collaborate and each force according to its own [capabilities]. The second stage, from the stage of overthrow until the extraordinary situation so that there would be security and calm in the country and the people could vote in an informed manner. People everywhere in the world have knowledge, there are disasters which cause lack of knowledge temporarily, and when the leaders provided guidance, and informed the people in an unbiased way, and surrendered to the opinion and votes of the nation.

I think that this would not be a problem and that the people could vote in an informed manner. And everywhere in the world, we have seen examples of this. There were people who were living under colonialism for years and they were no longer able to have knowledge, but there came nationalist leaders and informed the people. The people awakened, and decided. In the third world, we see the example of India which really has a valuable democracy.

JAAM-E-JAM: I have a question regarding you and other oppositional figures against the Islamic Republic. As far as we remember, all oppositional figures in Iran had followed the path of the late Mossadegh. Currently, each and every oppositional figure against the Islamic Republic is pursuing and continuing in a separate path for their political activities. What is the reason for the divergence of paths considering that you could have a more positive impact for the future of Iran and the liberation

of Iran if you pursue your political activities under an umbrella organization?

Madani: I have to make one point clear. The followers of the path of Mossadegh, almost all of them, do not have the discipline that they should have in the context of a Front. Mossadegh established the Front. Front is different than a political party. As long as Dr. Mossadegh was there as a political figure, and his unequivocal leadership, there was no issue and there was no discord, and the National Front of Iran—with all the groups consisting it—continued in its path. Later, the leadership was gone, because the parameters of the Front was not demarcated, we saw that it lost its parameters, and now it is interesting that we see that [political organizations] from the non-independent left to the non-independent right, to the supporters of a republic, to supporters of the Monarchy, they all consider themselves to be followers of Mossadegh's path. This has caused a problem, and for this reason we have proposed that a council [be established] comprised of the leaders of the National Front of Iran, both inside and outside the country. Inside the country, the matter can not be pursued, those outside the country [should] now determine the parameters of the Front and the path so that it has discipline and as a result there would not appear so much conflict among the followers of Mossadegh.

One of the reasons that we now see that some have distanced themselves from others is [due] to the lack of the demarcation of the parameters. It is natural, there is coordination in the support of Iran, everyone wants the liberation of Iran. This is the reason why I think that there would not be a problem in [forging] a coalition.

The movement for the overthrow has two dimensions. The coalition movement of different forces—temporarily—to achieve a common [cause?] and the united movement, which is foundational, and goal oriented—and both movements can exist, and there is no problem. Whoever is a supporter of Iran and the nation of Iran could participate.

JAAM-E-JAM: There are many questions in the minds of Iranians far from the homeland regarding your political activities. Many of these individuals have this question in mind: what was your intention for collaborating with the current regime in Iran, i.e. the Islamic Republic, in various governmental positions, including the Commander of the Navy, the Governor of Khuzistan, and the Minister of Defense? Is it because you did not succeed in becoming president, that you left the arena, and you left Iran? Or essentially was it the case that while you were collaborating with the current regime, i.e. the Islamic Republic, you became informed of the nature of the regime, i.e. the Islamic Republic, and this led you to leave and commence oppositional activities against the regime, i.e. the Islamic Republic, from outside the country?

Madani: This is an interesting question. All of your questions are interesting. There were many political figures who were in Iran at that time until the last days that I was in Iran, and they know about my interviews and the objections that I stated to the regime, i.e. the Islamic Republic, that my confrontation with the regime, i.e. the Islamic Republic, was not because of loosing careers.

I want to state here that prior to the victory of the revolution, I was among those who believed in and still believe in the revolution. The revolution had another path, and the inheritors of the revolution have another path. In the first days and the first months of the revolution when these anti-Iranians—meaning the inheritors of the revolution, meaning the current ruling enemies—had not yet revealed their anti-Iranian dimension, they collaborated with the revolutionaries

In the first days, I accepted the burden of the ministry of national defense, the navy, the Arya Navigation, and it was not easy to accept to be in those political positions in that era. However, when we saw that slowly these inheritors of the revolution, from any organizations, presented the opposite of what they had originally said, and took a stance against the nation, I severely confronted them.

This not my claim here. Look at the media of the country, at that time, and the statistics, and the documents that are available. I had interviews there, what I said, my confrontations, they are all the bases of my claims today. And, from the moments that I found that these people are against the nation, I severely confronted them. And, regarding my political positions, I myself resigned.

I myself resigned from the Ministry of Defense. I myself resigned from the position of the Governor of Khuzistan. I myself resigned from the Navy. I myself resigned from the Arya Navigation. After the presidential elections—in which the nation pursued efforts to determine for whom to cast their vote—which I do not want to state—and later when they insisted that I accept the position of Prime Minister, and I absolutely refrained because the anti-Iranian nature of the regime, i.e. the Islamic Republic, was by then completely clear.

JAAM-E-JAM: Mr. Madani, I believe that there is an ultimate question that has been set forth by many people, and the press have written about you, or in fact have written against you, and it is on the minds of many people, and it is regarding Khuzistan and the order which you gave to kill an innocent group of people, and the

order which you gave to exile Shabir Khaghani, and many other times that you have instituted violence against the people. These are what are stated regarding you. Of course, the intention is not to try you in the court of the people, and that you reject the accusations and obtain immunity. However, these are what are said regarding you. Of course, in the future, history will render judgment. But, it is not bad that you give our audience explanations.

Madani: I want to state an introduction, then I will talk about the issue of the beginning of the occurrence of the revolution of the people in Iran. There was more or less insecurity everywhere in the country during the first two months of the revolution when I was the National Defense Minister of Iran, and also the Commander of the Navy, and also the Director of the Arya Navigations, and also the director of the board. I worked on these matters, and concurrently I worked on the issues that I knew. Slowly I preferred to resign from national defense and to only conduct the Navy and Arya Navigations, so that I could organize it better and to establish a new force.

Immediately following my resignation from national defense, Mr. Bazargan insisted that I accept the position of Governor of Khuzistan. Khuzistan was a region in which there was much riots, and until then—two months after the revolution—it did not have a governor; any one to whom it was proposed to accept the governorship of Khuzistan, did not accept. Well, there were riots and anxiety, and there was a heavy responsibility. Although I knew that it was a burden, I accepted it because I considered it to be a national and Iranian duty.

I went to Khuzistan. Now, it is interesting that in seven riots in the region, and with all of those riots, insecurity, and lack of calm, I have to say that with the efforts of the nationalist people of Khuzistan, and I want to add the know-how and determination, and with the discipline that I had—without praise about myself—in any case, I was able to—with the least casualties, keep the map of Khuzistan as part of the map of Iran. Meaning that in seven riots and ten months of my governorship in a province of approximately four million individuals and with all the conspiracies that the foreigners had for its separation, the total casualties of Khuzistan is 49 individuals from which fourteen of them were from the forces, and 35 individuals from the opposing forces.

Now, this figure of 49, I have seen it reaching four hundred thousand individuals. I have seen it reaching seven hundred thousand individuals. I have seen it reaching 48 thousand individuals. And I have to say that if I were not there in the region, the killings if Khuzistan would have reached thousands of individuals and Khuzistan had continued to be under instability.

In the battle of this situation, of course there were persons that I had to temporarily send afar from the region so that they would not be in the region. Including Mr. Asheikh Taher Aal Shabir who was the most powerful clergy of the region; he is naive, he had become the tool of others and I saw it best that he temporarily not be in the region because there was insecurity and [inaudible] it was possible that the situation would have been worse.

I temporarily send him far from the region. And, I want to tell you so that you know that to go to war—as they now say—against the clergy is not easy. It was a [inaudible] measure, but I tried to preserve all of his positions; but he not be in the region.

Menashe Amir

Middle East Affairs Analyst; Chief Editor of Israel Foreign Ministry Website in Persian; Ex Head of Persian Services of the Voice of Israel.

Menashe Amir

Date of Broadcast: October 21, 1984

JAAM-E-JAM: Today we are interviewing Mr. Menashe Amir, an expert on Iran and on Middle Eastern affairs. Mr. Amir has always done his utmost to encourage Iranian culture and Iranian studies and to publicize his native country, which he left many years ago. As an expert and commentator on issues concerning Iran, Mr. Amir has been interviewed often on radio and television, including CNN. His views and opinions have reached many people through the radio and TV programs of the Israel Broadcasting Authority. He was recently appointed Director of the Persian Broadcasting Services of the Voice of Israel.

Mr. Amir, since you, like many other Iranians, love your country and are concerned about the problems in Iran, could you please give us some possible causes leading up to the events that have taken place in Iran.

Menashe Amir: The revolution in Iran was obviously caused by a number of internal and external factors that have been the topic of many discussions and the subject of many books. One of the causes leading up to the revolution was the Shah's campaign to weaken the Mullahs. This was not acceptable to some groups in Iran. The rapid implementation of the Shah's plans to pave the road for Iran to reach the "Great Civilization" increased dissatisfaction and fomented the uprising. The silencing of political rivals and the lack of political growth drove the Iranian people in different directions. Unfortunately, in this sort of atmosphere, the Shah's grandiose plans for Iranian development were not appreciated by the people. And in addition the Shah did not have the best of advisers.

Regarding the external factors, it can be said that the Shah's attempt to develop Iran into the world's fifth superpower was a cause for concern among many countries in the region, including the Arab states, as well as some countries outside the region. All these factors together led up to something that should not have happened.

JAAM-E-JAM: Considering the fact that Saddam initiated the war, how do you interpret the Iran-Iraq war?

Menashe Amir: It is true that [at first] Saddam attacked Iran, and in the same pattern that Israel did during the Six Day War (1967): he attacked six Iranian military airports simultaneously. He also invaded Qasr—E-Shirin and entered Iranian territory.

But it was Khomeini's arrival [in Iran] and his provocations in Iraq that were the main motives for Saddam's attack on Iran. We should be aware that Iraq is a country with three major ethnic and religious groups: the Kurds, the Shiite Arabs, and the Sunni Arabs. Saddam and his socialist Baath party wanted to run Iraq along socialism and nationalism lines in order to unite these three ethnic groups. As Khomeini's strength in Iran grew, he (Khomeini) claimed that because the majority of Iraq's population was Shiite, the regime there [in Iraq] should be a religious one and the Shiites should hold power. This would be tantamount to putting an end to Saddam's Baath rule in Iraq, with the risk of dividing Iraq into two or three separate states, Shiite, Sunni, and Kurdish. This was one of the main reasons that Saddam attacked Iran, in order to protect it before it became too late to overthrow Khomeini's regime.

Of course there were other reasons as well, such as realizing Iraq's dream of becoming a regional superpower (which goes back 2,000 years) and of controlling the Persian Gulf and the Straits of Hormuz and of conquering the three large islands of "Big Tomb," "Little Tomb" and Abu Mussa. And there were other reasons for Saddam's attack on Iran as well, such as Saddam's desire to seize the Khouzestan resources.

JAAM-E-JAM: In your opinion, what will the war lead to?

Menashe Amir: As I mentioned earlier, this is not a war between two nations or two countries, this is a war between two ideologies, i.e., Khomeini's ideology of government based on fundamentalism, and Saddam's ideology of government based on nationalism and socialism. It is also a war between two personalities: Saddam, who is extremely ambitious and, as I mentioned, wants to rule the region, and Khomeini, who is not content with a revolution limited to Iran but, since he sees himself as the leader of the oppressed people of the world, would like to spread his revolution to other countries. His intention was to invade Iraq, which is home to the largest number of Shiites outside Iran. He also meant to overthrow the Wahhabi government in Saudi Arabia and the royal family of Saud in order to control Mecca and Medina. Then, in his irrational way of thinking, he intended to invade Jerusalem and seize control over the holy places of Islam from Mashhad to Jerusalem, establishing a Shiite empire in the region. Thus so long as Khomeini is alive, and so long as Saddam Hussein is in power, and so long as internal and external factors make it possible, this war will continue without an end in sight.

JAAM-E-JAM: Since the price of oil and oil production has come down to a minimum, what is your opinion regarding the present economic unrest in Iran?

Menashe Amir: Iran's oil sales have decreased significantly, but the country can still pay for the war and maintain a sufficient supply of oil for domestic consumption. So long as Iraq cannot make it completely impossible for Iran to export oil, the Khomeini regime will be able to pay for the war.

Obviously, cost of weapons bought by the Islamic Republic is constantly on the rise. With each day that goes by, the price of domestic necessities and consumer goods goes up. Inflation and the current economic crisis are clearly among the factors provoking the discontent felt by the Iranian people which, in turn, can lead to uprising and the regime's, the Islamic Republic's, overthrow.

JAAM-E-JAM: Many people believe that the superpowers supported Khomeini. They think England has helped him survive. What is your opinion?

Menashe Amir: I believe that domestic elements were more important than external ones in bringing about the revolution.

Obviously, however, external factors played a significant role as well. You mentioned England, but I believe that the revolution in Iran took place because of the United States' misguided policy towards Iran and the region as a whole. I think America is to blame for the Shah's fall. In my opinion America has made at least two major mistakes in its policy. The first mistake was in 1963, when Kennedy was president. The Americans created the impression that the Iranian regime, i.e. the Shah's regime, was so corrupt that it would soon topple and Iran would fall into the hands of the communists. So Kennedy pressured the Shah to begin a revolution "from the top" and in this way save Iran from the danger of communism. It was the implementation of a series of stages of the White Revolution that brought about Khomeini's rise and culminated with his famous speech at the Fayziyeh School in Qom.

[The second mistake took place] some time later, when [Jimmy] Carter was elected to the American presidency. Being unfamiliar with the situation and the political and social reality of Iran, he embarked on a policy that proved to be disastrous, insisting on a measure of political freedom for [the people of] Iran. Together with other factors, this extreme pressure on the Shah eventually lost him control of the country and ended his rule in Iran.

JAAM-E-JAM: How do you foresee the future of Iran?

Menashe Amir: Obviously, as an Iranian sympathetic to Iran, I am optimistic about its future. Even though the present regime seems strong, it is in fact weak and will be overthrown, because it is basically incompatible with the nature and traditions of Iran.

It is very important for Iranians to rely on themselves rather than on foreign elements. They may get help from foreign elements, but they should not rely on them. They should remain confident and cooperate with one another. I have no doubt that they will ultimately succeed.

JAAM-E-JAM: Thank you very much, Mr. Amir, and to our viewers, good-bye.

Shahin Fatemi

Secretary-General, Iran Liberation Front; Chair & Professor, International Business Administration, the American University of Paris

Shahin Fatemi

March 24 & April 14, 1985

JAAM-E-JAM: Dear viewers, today we find it essential to have a short discussion regarding the Constitutional Monarchy Councils due to their importance on the current political atmosphere. The first stage of elections of the Councils is said to end this week and that the final votes will be cast next week. There is no doubt that JAAM-E-JAM Television, as a responsible and committed media source, will have an analytical discussion about the elections. It must be noted that no one from JAAM-E-JAM and its staff—including the president and producer, writers of news, and others—has participated nor will they participate in the elections, and JAAM-E-JAM and its staff will continue to play the role of a responsible media provider and observer of political issues.

We sincerely hope that people will be elected from among individuals who have good names, are truly committed, and are informed of political issues.

The second issue is regarding the 24 hour stay of Dr. Shahin Fatemi, the Secretary-General of Iran Liberation Front, in Los Angeles and in this short stop he had a visit and dialogue with us which we will broadcast in two segments.

JAAM-E-JAM: Mr. Fatemi, you are a political figure, and undoubtedly your trip to this land has a political aspect and related to the activities of the political struggle. May I ask why you have come to Los Angeles during the heat of political campaign especially the elections of the Councils?

Shahin Fatemi: Well, if I had known the political atmosphere would be so hot, I would probably not have come now. The only heat I see here is the hot weather, which is pleasant after the cold winter in Europe. The purpose of my trip, which had been postponed for a long time, is related to the book I have written about the economy of Iran. This book is about to be published and I am in contact with the university regarding its publication. The main purpose of traveling to Los Angles was specifically due to Mr. Bibiyan's invitation to participate in a dialogue with JAAM-E-JAM Television which I had promised him and that's why I am in this part of the here [America] and staying here for just 24 hours.

JAAM-E-JAM: Dr. Fatemi, considering the intensification of the war crisis and the bombardment of Iranian cities in the Iran-Iraq war, what is your view regarding this war and its consequences?

Fatemi: The events occurring in the recent days makes every Iranian worried to the extent that it is inexpressible. This is a catastrophe that we never experienced. The bombardments of the cities of Iran, especially Isfahan—not because I was born in Isfahan—but when it is stated that Isfahan has been bombarded, it reminds me of the city's historical monuments; it is our national capital.

The thousands of innocent compatriots who lose their life daily. This war, I have said it many times, is the consequence of the revolution. This inauspicious revolution caused us many damages and this war, the Iran-Iraq war, is the direct result of that revolution in Iran, meaning that had that situation not occurred and the Imperial Iranian military had not been weakened such, the Shah's regime had not been disintegrated, Iraq would never had dared to invade Iranian soil. And those who caused this revolution, the responsibility of this war is theirs.

I consider Iraq to be the invader, and I believe that regarding the war that it is the sole issue which, if necessary, every Iranian—despite all the opposition that she has with Khomeini—to defend the homeland, must fight Iraq. The issues which we have with Khomeini concerns us. We do not need Sadam Hussein to overthrow Khomeini. And now I believe that as long as these two dictators, Khomeini in Iran and Saddam in Iraq, are there, the solution to this war will be very difficult to reach, and it is possible that it would result in a much wider conflict in the region. We hope that this would not occur, but unfortunately, the [war] is progressing in that direction.

JAAM-E-JAM: Don't you think that the real movement must be launched inside the country? Would you please tell us what you have accomplished inside the country thus far? Don't you think

that it is becoming too late, and if the people do not receive you, what would occur? Had you implemented the right strategy, at this time, considering the crisis in Iran? It would have been the best time to overthrow the regime, i.e. the Islamic Republic.

Fatemi: The method that you stated: the fundamental struggle is inside or outside—this division is artificial. There is no [division regarding] the inside or outside. The struggle of the Iranian nation is monolithic. Inside there are possibilities and what can be done is very limited; outside, there are many many more possibilities.

What is our responsibility is not that we say the real struggle is inside or outside [of Iran]. Our responsibility is to organize this struggle. That is, to carry out what is possible outside, to the best manner, and what must be carried out inside, be related to outside. Those who are inside, the largest expectation that they have from us is to convey their pleading for justice to the world, because you know they do not permit any foreign journalist to enter Iran now. The same is true for Albania and China. You know better than I do regarding the news; if one does not hear any news, one believes that there is no news, and because there are no journalists who are permitted to go to Iran. If we do not reflect the news that we obtain regarding Iran, the world would believe that that the nation of Iran has endorsed Khomeini and has accepted this regime, i.e. the Islamic Republic. We ought not to permit this image in any way to take shape in the world. And, regarding the issue had we implemented the right strategy we would have reached our [goal] sooner, I have stated before, it is really not possible to answer regarding this issue that easily. The time to overthrow the regime, i.e. the Islamic Republic, has always existed. This regime, i.e. the Islamic Republic—what the western commentators who say that this regime has been relatively stabilized, they do not understand at all. This is impossible. In a country where there is a sea of blood dividing the people from this regime, reconciliation is never possible. There is no family who is not in mourning. Believe me, throughout history, perhaps no one has killed Muslims to the extent that Khomeini has.

This man who entered the country in the name of Islam has killed Muslims more than anyone else. From the Crusades until now, from the rise of Islam until today, I do not know of anyone in history who has killed Muslims so much, and in the name of Islam.

Well, such regime, i.e. the Islamic Republic, could never reach a reconciliation with the nation of Iran, nor would the nation of Iran forgive this regime. This is one reason. The second reason is that this regime, i.e. the Islamic Republic, is antihistory, meaning this regime is at war with what is modernization, progress, and today's world; and it will never triumph in such a war. Therefore, it could not provide stability for this regime.

What it has created is a political irreconciliation, and invasion with violence where the people are in bondage and kept under the threat of arms. It is similar to a steam boiler that could explode any minute. You are right in saying that considering the regime, i.e. the Islamic Republic, is at war and due to the deadlock of the regime, now, it is best to act now. But the liberation of Iran has one pre-condition. I believe that that is for those who want to get rid of Khomeini, for the region be stable, and liberate Iran, the first thing to be done is to be united under the flag of the Constitutional Monarchy. Regarding this matter, I would explain during subsequent questions why I believe the liberation of Iran is only possible via constitutional monarchy.

JAAM-E-JAM: You have had a main role in proposing the issue of the Constitutional Councils. Would you please state what role do these Councils play in the future of the people especially the people inside the country specifically in the formation of serious struggles both now and in the future?

Fatemi: Regarding the Councils, if by proposing the councils you mean that we, that is, "Iran va Jahan" in every opportunity and other interviews have introduced and addressed the issue, it is accurate. However, the initiative of the proposal of the issue of the Councils is from the King himself. And when in the message of the Ninth of Aban [October 31] in the previous year, the King proposed this plan, there was opportunity for others to express their opinions, and from the beginning, I personally and the Iran Liberation Front, the political office, the Iran Liberation Front, Dr. Amini the leader of Iran Liberation Front, all supported this proposal. It is a proposal that is timely, it was necessary that they be established here. It has a great impact on the struggles outside the country and inside the country. Because, one of the problems which we have always faced was the conflict and the division among us Iranians. The Constitutional Councils will be a center for the convergence of those who believe in the rule of law and a constitutional monarchy. And this will bring together the disparate forces—whether inside or outside the country—for the liberation of Iran. This is a measure that perhaps should have been initiated earlier, but the pre-conditioned had not been met, and now that it is formed, and the speed with which it has progressed in the last few months, has created much hope inside the country.

The organization in which I engage in political activities, that is, the Iran Liberation Front, which you know is comprised of nearly fifty pro-monarchy organizations, believes in the restoration of the regime of Constitutional Monarchy in Iran. And it does not mean that we are opposed to the opinions of other individuals who consider other types of regime for the future of Iran. By no means.

We believe that we could reach the aim sooner in Iran in this way, and regarding this issue, we have always been prepared and are prepared to debate and discuss with individuals who consider other ways, and to show them that this is the way of return to Iran. However, regarding—you can be sure that there do not exist any other way except Constitutional Monarchy in Iran.

When I personally chose this way, the late Shah had not left the country yet. I had an audience with the Shah four times in the Niavaran Palace and in the presence of the Shah and I pleaded that he not leave Iran. At the time when the political elite thought that the departure of the Shah from Iran would propel the country towards calm and stability, I—who myself had neither a political position in Iran, nor wanted a political position—had an audience with the Shah four times on different occasions. And I tried, to the extent that an Iranian could have an impact, to plead with the Shah to not listen to these words. And today I also state to you that had the Shah not left Iran, today you and I would have been talking in Tehran, not in Los Angeles.

Abdul Azim Valian

Minister of Land Reform (1967-1974); Governor of Khorasan (1970's) in the Shah's regime.

Abdulazim Valian

Interview with Abdul-Azim Valian
At the Washington, D.C. Demonstration
Broadcast Date: August 4, 1985

JAAM-E-JAM: It was at this Washington D.C. demonstration that JAAM-E-JAM's correspondent interviewed Mr. Valian.

JAAM-E-JAM: Among the participants of the demonstration of July 29, 1985 in front of the Congress, I see Dr. Valian, the former Minister of Land Reform. Mr. Valian, what is your view regarding today's demonstration? And your view regarding the recent political movements and political struggle?

Abdulazim Valian: I believe that today's demonstration of some of our compatriots represents the reality that the people have reached the conclusion that they have to be politically active for the liberation of the country, and that this movement ought to be in the direction of solidarity. And, today, as you see, approximately seven thousand people have gathered here. Of course, I regret to say that a larger number of people could have gathered here, but comparing the number of people who have attended to the number of people who have had gathered here in the past years, the number of today's participants is much higher. This is hopeful. It is certain that in order to return to our country, we have to be united and have solidarity. I state that now is not the time that this person or that person fight each other regarding small differences of opinion whence the pursuing of it is not here, it is inside our country. Instead of bringing people closer together, they cause divergence. Hopefully, when we return to our country, there are many statements that I have to state. There are many statements that the oppositional leaders against the Islamic Republic or those who consider themselves to be oppositional leaders against the Islamic Republic and they are all correct. Were you present at the gathering commemorating the fifth anniversary of the death of the late Shah of Iran, last night? The king whom they did not appreciate, and we have now reached this situation. The people gathered in the streets and said: "He must go, and the Ibn-I Muljam must come." And God sent Ibn-I Muljam.

JAAM-E-JAM: Do you watch JAAM-E-JAM Television's programs in Washington, D.C.?

Valian: Regularly.

JAAM-E-JAM: What is your view regarding JAAM-E-JAM's programs?

Valian: I believe that it is a very very interesting program. Especially, you have been determined in this belief that without accepting responsibility for the views expressed by the participants, you broadcast the opinions of all people, and for this reason I respect and I hope that you will always preserve, and at your side, I wish you continued success.

Abdul-Azim Valian

January 19, 1986

JAAM-E-JAM: Dr. Abdol-Azim Valian, the Minister of Agriculture, Cooperatives and Rural Affairs who conducted the final stages of the Land Reform, died in Washington following a heart attack.
Recently, JAAM-E-JAM Television had an exclusive interview with Mr. Valian at the Washington D.C. demonstration.

Our condolences to his family. We will broadcast parts of the last interview of Mr. Valian, former minister of the Shah's regime.

Valian: I am clearly stating that this is not the right time for people to argue about trivial differences, which must be dealt with inside our country, and not here, that instead of trying to unite people, they alienate them from one another. In the future, these differences of opinion can be solved inside Iran.

There are many statements to be said, but I will express them when we return to our country. There are many statements that the leaders of the opposition to the Islamic Republic—or those who present themselves as leaders of opposition against the Islamic Republic and they are right in doing so—should state. I am telling you all of them are right. I am just requesting to put these differences aside in order to resolve them inside of Iran. What is good for all of us is to have solidarity in order to return to our country. The fact is that our nation wants a king to be "The Shadow of God" and we saw the results. In the beginning, His Majesty Mohammad Reza Pahlavi was the best example of the Constitutional Monarch in the world, but people wanted him to rule in addition to being a constitutional king. Those authorities and administrations—in order to escape responsibility—called him "Our Commander". Well, this Commander accomplished many tasks, didn't he?

Now His Majesty, Reza Pahlavi the Second, will return to Iran as a Constitutional Monarch and he himself wants to be a Constitutional Monarch, but you will see that the Iranian people would insist that he govern.

I did not leave Iran just so that I stay alive. I came here to be able to answer the kind of questions you are asking.

JAAM-E-JAM: Mr. Valian, you held the position of the Governor General of Khorassan and at the same time you were the Nayeb-o-Tolieh. Would you please comment on the renovation of the areas surrounding the Haram?

Valian: What we accomplished was done according to the "Law of Development".

Every year, 7 Million pilgrims visited the Haram and its surroundings, including [people like] your sister, my mother and your mother. Along the way to the Haram, they would hear at least 300 times the answers to questions such as: "Would you like to be a sigheh (temporary marriage)?"

There were many houses and smugglers' places there. The City Council approved that this area should be purified. We cleaned the area around the Haram of Imam Reza. We paid the money to them. If you ask people of Mashhad, they all support me. I know a cabinet minister in the Shah's regime who told me: "After the 28th of Mordad, this regime, i.e. the Shah's regime, is illegal," I reply to their arguments thus: "Why did you stay until the last day and in government positions of authority and later you stayed in order to receive a position of authority by Khomeini?"

I am responsible for what I have done. Those who said it was not possible to speak openly, I swear on the Koran that they were lying. They are dishonest. In fact, they didn't want to speak. And what happened in the end? In the old regime, i.e. the Shah's regime, I stated my opinions.

I was responsible in the field of the Land Reform, and I had worked for 52 months in Khorassan. I am ready to explain what I have done in order to explain the nature of my work. This question is still the same: if we were not good, why do they regret the days that are gone?

Broadcast Date: January 26, 1986

JAAM-E-JAM: Abdol-Azim Valian was the minister, Minister in charge of the Ghods-i-Razavi, the executive in charge of the Land Reform Plan during the Shah's regime, the Minister of Agriculture and the Minister of Cooperatives and Rural Affairs, and Land Reform in the Shah's regime, and in the last years of the old regime, i.e. the Shah's regime, he was the governor of Khorasan for a period of four and a half years.

Before the Islamic Revolution, Valian was imprisoned along with a group of cabinet Ministers. On the day of the Revolution, while hospitalized in a military hospital in Iran, he succeeded to escape from the Revolutionary Guards of the Islamic Republic in Iran and arrived in the United States a few months later.

In the last six years, Valian did not appear in any political scene, but he did take part in the demonstration which was staged in Washington D.C. and openly appeared in public and it was at this demonstration that he had his first and last interviews with JAAM-E-JAM Television.

Valian: Since I took steps against these people, it is natural for them to turn hostile against me. In the Land Reform Plan, we obtained the land from the landowners and divide it according to the law. As the minister, the responsibility regarding this issue was mine. It is clear that these landowners who did not approve of the Land Reform, turned against me. The Mullahs had many interests in the form of estates bequeathed to them.

In order not to cause discrimination among the farmers, we included the bequeathed lands to the Land Reform Plan, otherwise the farmers who had newly owned bequeathed lands would not be able to enjoy the benefits of the land because these benefits had to go to the Mullahs.

Well, The Mullahs condemn me for this reason but they have not yet caught me.

What has been stated by some that not all the Mullahs are bad people, is accurate. In no society can you reach the conclusion that they are all good or all bad. Anyway, if what I have done is considered to be a sin, I take the responsibility for it. I have come out of Iran not just to stay alive, but to live a life that will enable me to provide good answers for the kinds of questions you ask.

Kourosh Aryamanesh (Reza Mazluman)

Professor of Criminology, Tehran University Law School (in the Shah's regime); Deputy Minister of Education in the Shah's regime. Reza Mazluman (Kourosh Aryamanesh) was assassinated in Paris in 1996.

Reza Mazlouman (Kourosh Aryamanesh)

Broadcast: September 21 and 28, 1986

JAAM-E-JAM: Dear viewers, in the arena of battle with the current regime of Iran, i.e. the Islamic Republic, the role of the branch of Neghab is unforgettable. Neghab believes in the restoration of monarchy as a system of government in Iran. It initiated a nationalistic movement in Iran and since Dr. Kourosh Aryamanesh (Reza Mazlouman), while residing in Iran was one of the organization's key players, we have conducted an interview with him in Paris.

Reza Mazlouman, a professor of criminology at Tehran University Law School, and Deputy Minister of Education in the Shah's regime, is the author of 11 books in the field of criminology and social disorders. He served as a member of the executive board

of the Scientific Society of the university as well as Chairman of the Society of Criminology.

In 1972, he authored the book entitled "Femicide under the Ban of Law" which led to the uprising of some religious people against him, but he was not afraid. Dr. Mazlouman believes that the truth ought to be said, and he therefore authored seven books overseas. He opposed Khomeini since Khomeini's arrival in Iran, and established "The Society for the Defense of the University Faculty and Students' Rights and Honor." After underground struggles under the title of "The Organization of Iran Patriots" and after the defeat of the "Uprising of the 18th of Tir," he had to leave Iran. He has been living outside Iran for six years and is currently directing the National Movement of Iranian University Faculty and Students.

Manouchehr Bibiyan: You have changed your name.

Kourosh Aryamanesh: When I am able to dress the beautiful and proud name of Iranian why should I assume the borrowed foreign name. The name of Reza might be good for the Arabs. The last name of Mazlouman for the same reason. My father has determined it for me. Now that I have reached the period of awareness, I can choose the name of Kourosh and the [last name of] Aryamanesh for myself, which in my view both of them are beautiful and Persian. The name of my daughter is Mahtab. A Persian ought to speak and write Persian, and know all of Iran's civilization and culture. The reason for the fall of our country in my view was nothing but one [reason]: meaning that we did not know ourselves to know who we are, and as a result, in any case, we are facing such circumstances these days. Others came and fed us their absurdities

Manouchehr Bibiyan: In your view, as one of the leaders of Neghab Organization or Nojeh, what was the reason that these organizations were revealed inside Iran?

Aryamanesh: In response to your question, I should mention that there exist several issues, which of course, unfortunately, perhaps each person knows aspects of it, but history will shed light on the issue. However, what I can talk about as a criticism of ourselves is that we, first and foremost assumed that the enemy is weak, and secondly we assumed ourselves to be very strong. We entered the struggle without realizing that we faced a cruel enemy with no mercy toward anybody.

The second issue which exists, and unfortunately, I have to admit is that we did not have information regarding the lack of informed persons who had entered the struggle. The lack of being informed from this perspective I state: we—none of us—were previously involved in a struggle in this manner against a system in the manner of Akhund system. For this reason, to an extent we assumed ourselves to be strong to an extent more than what was possible. And, with the lack of information which unfortunately we had regarding the power of the enemy, this uprising which was in the prospect of continuing in a very positive way, it was revealed prior to being implemented.

After leaving the country, I heard through my contacts-although I can not confirm it—that unfortunately foreign elements did not agree with the uprising of the Iranian people against Khomeini at any cost. They say that—although I have no reason at all regarding this issue—that, in any case, they were involved in discovering and in reporting it to Khomeini and Bani Sadr.

Manouchehr Bibiyan: When these organizations were discovered, how many members of the Organization were killed, meaning Shahid? Was it revealed by the people who were themselves members of the groups, or whether there were people in your organization who were elements of the Islamic Republic and the agents of the regime, i.e. the Islamic Republic?

Aryamanesh: Regarding Shahid, I should, if you would permit, make a correction. I think that we must utilize the word Janbakhteh regarding Iranians. Shahid is an unsuitable name for us, for me as an Iranian it is unsuitable and it is an Akhund word that has come into existence gradually in Iran, and Shahid is entirely wrong. We ought to definitely say the Janbazan of Iran; those who lost their lives for Iran we must say Janbakhtegan.

But, regarding the number of persons who lost their lives for Iran and for their goal, to the extent that I remember, approximately 250 individuals and from this figure there were 149 Iranian pilots and officers who were executed, but all of them I believe created a legend with their courage, all of them. Because at that time I myself was followed. And despite the fact that ultimately a number had to leave Iran, I remained in Iran in order to organize these groups and remained until the 11th of Shahrivar. Five people from my own group were executed, which unfortunately I have to say after I left Iran, three of the groups were discovered. But because I connected all of the groups to myself, and they [the Islamic Republic] could not find any clue, and this was announced in the court of Akhundism that Reyshahri expressed this issue that: "we did not find any clue regarding that individual", and as I said these are the numbers, but they did not give the figures regarding those who died under torture in the prisons. In any case, perhaps later it would be more clear that [how many] were killed under torture.

This is the figure according to the names of those who were executed and written in the newspapers. Whether there were other people who were killed, which I can not confirm this issue exactly, but there are many rumors. As I said, in any case, because I was an academic, I had not participated in struggles in this system. My job was to go to class and teach and I went forward, but because my homeland was in danger, I entered the arena of struggle like a soldier, and we established underground organizations.

In any case, it is evident that I also encountered my mistakes in this system of my own struggle, because I did not have information to the extent that I ought to have had. The Iranian officers and others in these various organizations, more or less, encountered similar mistakes.

More than any other, the mistake which we all had was that we announced [this uprising] to everyone. Because we assumed that we would surely win, and this caused to some extent, our defeat. In any case, as I said, we lost a battle, there is no problem, and we must continue the war and we have never lost the war, and as long as we are alive, Khomeini and Akhundism will never be victorious in Iran.

Manouchehr Bibiyan: In these seven years, the Iranian opposition leaders against the Islamic Republic, have they been able to develop roots inside Iran? Or this opposition to the Islamic Republic outside the country have been expressing slogans? With the existence of many media, has the opposition against the Islamic Republic or the national oppositional leaders against the Islamic Republic, or others who claim to be opposition leaders against the Islamic Republic, do you think that they have a strong base inside the country?

Aryamanesh: In response to your question, I should say that the base that you refer to is of two types. One of them is a popular base that whether the people of Iran agree with [inaudible] outside the country or not. The second [type] there is an issue of a [political] force for the overthrow of the Islamic Republic. I ought to say that I do not agree [in any way] with the method of operation of the opposition against the Islamic Republic outside the country. The operation of the opposition forces against the Islamic Republic outside the country—to an extent, not to a small extent but all of the political dimension of the issue, and they say, this person should also be [among our group], that person also, we should have him [in our group], and we should have that person also, and in my view this totality becomes a combination of a collection, which—would not in any way reach us to an appropriate result. Ten percent of [our efforts], or more, I should say, of the power that they are utilizing outside the country, had they directed it towards inside the country, and therefore we could have established forces for the overthrow of the regime, i.e. the Islamic Republic, in its real meaning, inside the country, we would have reached appropriate results much sooner.

Outside the country, there are persons who are engaged in struggle, and their existence is valued. However, I do not believe at any cost that the persons who are outside the country ought to converge. If we all convene, what could we do? In contrast, if we have ten people inside Iran—who can mobilize the people, we would be able to accomplish many tasks inside Iran. Unfortunately, this mistake exists. And, another point, which the university colleagues, and others, came here and were in contact with us, is that they say that the people who are outside the country think about prior to 1357 [1979]. They do not at all think about the changes that have occurred inside the country, and therefore as has been said while inside the country there is another issue.

What we are announcing here currently—and I have many times written about it—is that unfortunately, because we do not pay attention to changes in the society of Iran, we talk about other issues. We ought to understand what the people of Iran want, and really adapt our own movement based on the thoughts of the people of Iran, and create the movement—inside Iran.

Inside Iran, we ought to create the force for the overthrow of the regime, i.e. the Islamic Republic. And it is this force for the overthrow, which should it proceed, that the people of Iran—they have suffered so much from the oppression and injustice of this system that they—would immediately, I believe, follow that force for the overthrow, and they would accomplish the task.

Unfortunately, all of the elements of the spark exist for the explosion; only the issue of the spark itself is at issue that ought to exist and that spark must be accomplished by that force for the overthrow, which ought to be formed inside the country.

More or less, the opposition to the Islamic Republic has announced that "we have the requisite forces inside the country"—and regarding this issue, what they say is not inaccurate. There does exist [such political force], however, announcing this—which has occurred inside Iran many times—in my view, it makes the system of the Islamic Republic and the regime, i.e. the Islamic Republic, aware, and keeps the people again—to an extent—in the hope that in any case "perhaps we could not accomplish it soon," which later might cause disappointment and hopelessness. Some time ago, one of the individuals had stated that in that specific month, March / April, events would occur in Iran. This is either true or false. If it is true, the fact of saying it is not necessary at all, and to make the regime, i.e. the Islamic Republic, aware that whether in the month of March or April they search, and in any way, find the roots of it. If it is false, why should we state such statements and cause disappointment by the people, because we then see that there is nothing occurring. In my view, these are wrong.

We ought to know the system exactly and deeply which is very oppressive and horrible, really, it does not have mercy toward anyone, and secondly, we have to perform our tasks in a very exact manner. The important issue is that this system of struggle which I talked about is wrong because a regime in Iran under the name of Akhund and Akhundism has come to power in Iran with the force of pressure and oppression, as the regime, i.e. the Islamic Republic, has remained in power with pressure, and injustice, and we have no choice but to remove it from power with force. These systems of struggle—to publish newspapers and announcements, and to ask that that Ayatolllah or this Hojat al-Islam be invited—and these people were also the founders of the destruction of Iran—this type of operation is nothing but deteriorating ourselves in front of the nation of Iran. We ought to speak from the standpoint of power and powerfully and truly concentrate all of our forces inside the country.

Manouchehr Bibiyan: Is your collaboration with Dr. Ganji a political collaboration?

Aryamanesh: Dr. Ganji, in any case, there is no need that I introduce him: he is without doubt a patriotic man and he has utilized all of his efforts—during the entire time that I have been involved—to expand his activities, and to change it from the way it has been in the past few years. But I state that I as the coordinator of academics and the colleagues who had been inside and outside the country with roots of struggle also inside Iran, I state that I collaborate with all the nationalist forces and whoever truly enters the struggle for the overthrow, against Khomeini and his group, to truly join the struggle, we also assist him/her. And we will collaborate with Dr. Ganji anytime he asks us to collaborate regarding his activities and we could collaborate with him just as we collaborate with all the other forces of struggle.

Manouchehr Bibiyan: We know that you are severely against Islam—or we have heard, and this is known in your writings and talks. Do you think that in Iran where 40 million Iranians live and the majority of the people in Iran believe that they can see Khomeini in the moon, and the majority of the people in Iran have extreme religious beliefs—there are people that still when they want to get up they place their hand on the ground and say Ya Ali [in the name of Ali]—and they always ask for religious assistance from the Imamzadehs, have the Iranian opposition leaders against the Islamic Republic and the persons who want to liberate Iran, do you think that your goal will reach results?

Aryamanesh: There are several questions in your question. Meaning there are several answers to your question, and I believe that it is several questions in one question. First, I state that what I just referred to: changes in thoughts and idea which have occurred in Iran during the past seven years, because we are far from the processes inside Iran, we have disregarded them. And, truly, the nation of Iran is not the same nation of seven years ago. If they place their hand on the ground to rise and say Ya Ali and rises from the ground, this is an issue of habit, and we must not consider it as thoughts and beliefs. There are many things that are possible that they say because it comes from one's childhood but they are not beliefs. As we see now that a large number of people are changing their names and changing their ways, and changing their beliefs.

And at one point in time, any person, in any case, has accepted a religion due to the reason that he/she has been born into a family which had that religion. But, after a period of time, when he/she knows himself/herself, and gains total awareness, it is at that point that he/she must find his/her own way. I believe that religion ought to be separated from politics, and these two elements must not be combined in any way. In the future of Iran, any person shall be free to have any religion that he/she wants, and no one could bother him/her. It is only religion mixed in politics which is wrong and ought to be defeated with all force.

But what you stated, the issue of Islam, see I speak from the perspective of my specialty. In criminology, we never deal with the issue of the criminal to always condemn the criminal, rather we think about the factors that created crime. We say that it is the factors that turn a healthy and righteous person into a bad person. And until there is no struggle against those factors, never could a society eliminate crime in society. Even though the criminal is killed, because since the day human beings have been created and the world has been created, criminals have been executed, but criminals still exist. Because we do not proceed to see the reason that criminals have been created.

During these seven years, we have had a religion that is different from the religion which ruled our society. I don't want to go to the roots of it because in this short time, one could not talk about it. The religion that existed inside Iran was a religion under the title of Islam, but a hundred percent Iranian because we had entered the arena with good words, good thoughts, and good deeds, and we stated this issue everywhere.

We state [in our literature]: "do not bother an ant which is carrying seed; the ant has life and is living life, a sweet and happy life."

We state: [in our literature]: "do one's utmost to be kind to people, breaking hearts is not an art." These are in our literature, culture, and history.

But, what has happened that they stone the Iranian woman on the 11th Tir 1359, they cut hand, they cut feet. The reason is that we implemented the old Arab culture—in the manner it had existed before—in Iran, and we threw away those beautiful Iranian foundations. We must truly know the roots of disorders to be able to struggle against them.

The roots of disorder are not the Akhunds; it is what factors create Akhunds. We must root out the factors which advance Akhundism and illiteracy in this society. We respect the customs that teach humanity, and fairness, and stand against barbarism.

If one assumes that the religion of Islam is truly a religion of kindness and humanity, I would accept it also. However, if we accept that it is not this way, well, we must think about it. I think that Khomeini and the Mullahs who have reached the Marjae Taghlid since the time that they were students of Islamic seminaries, and today they are Grand Ayatollahs, know Islam better than all Iranians inside and outside the country. Khomeini had said many times that "who says True Islam? have we implemented false Islam?" If what is occurring inside Iran is compatible with this Islam, then all Iranians ought to be opposed to it. If it is not compatible, then they ought to reflect on this issue with reason and logic. And, none of these Ayatollahs have said that what Khomeini has done is contrary to Islamic instructions. Even Ayatollah Khoei who is outside the country, and is not threatened by any danger.

Therefore, Iranians who are engaged in struggle and our hearts beat for our country and we love our country, we ought to say the truth as it is. The truth is bitter, it is painful, but it ought to be said. I give a very brief example. Our job ought to be like the job of a physician. When a physician faces his/her patient, the patient in no way likes the physician because he/she gives him/her bitter medicine, but the physician performs his/her job in a correct manner: he/she wants to remove the illness. We, had the intellectuals of society had known the truth and reality of society in Iran in the Shah's regime and had placed it at the disposal of society, and the ruling regimes in the past in Iran had also permitted it, I think that we would not have faced such a disaster today.

Akhunds did not provide the right guidance to people and what they say it not compatible with today's world. And we, the intellectuals and the academics of society went to work, taught and left without having contact with the people and without seeing how the people were being poisoned and these promoters of religion were imposing their ideas to the people, and this false language was taking root in their minds. Therefore, I say as Voltaire said: truth ought to be said, know that you may lose your life but always state the truth. Because if we don't have the opportunity to save society, at least our children will have the requisite peace.

Manouchehr Bibiyan: There are many stories about Nojeh, but what I want to ask you, and if you want it to be broadcast we will broadcast it, and if you don't want it to be broadcast—as with hundreds of other interview segments that we have and now it is not the time to broadcast them. It is this: was Mr. Shapour Bakhtiar—at the time that it appears that you collaborated with him—informed about the day and hour of the Nojeh Operation?

Aryamanesh: I ought to state this issue to you that the Organization of University Academics which engaged in underground activities under the cover of Iranian Nationalists with different titles [such as] Jaam-e-Jam, Kave-ye Ahangar, etc., we issued different announcements, it was an organization which operated side by side with the Neghab Organization. Similar to other organizations, I was in contact with but I absolutely was not involved in the content of what this organization or group—in any case the persons outside the country or those persons who are outside the country who were involved in [the content]. From the beginning when I was engaged in the political struggle, my contact inside Iran was [inaudible] who had come from Oveisi, therefore, in this organization, at the same time that I was in contact with the Neghab Organization, we engaged in our own political struggles.

Without doubt, as far as I am informed, Dr. Bakhtiar was also in Iran but as I stated the roots of this information, the information regarding that an uprising is in process, is not that simple so that I could now comment on it because I truly do not have the necessary information. I can only say that as far as I have information, we proceeded with some generosity in the movement, and this was wrong: we considered the enemy to be weak, and we considered ourselves very strong.

Manouchehr Bibiyan: What is your message for the viewers of JAAM-E-JAM Television?

Aryamanesh: My message to all those who truly think about Iran and are patriots are two: 1) let us refrain from differences, accusations, and refrain from imposing our thoughts to others, and all of us to walk on the path of one direction, and 2) also, keep our distance from the system and way that groups and individuals are in the possible process of transforming to the way of Akhundism again. Because, essentially, this is not the duty of Iranian patriots.

We ought to conduct our political activities and struggle on the basis of Iranian Nationalism. Outside the country, I have seen that a group of individuals state hat religion ought to be attacked via religion, Akhund ought to be attacked by Akhundism. These statements and activities, unfortunately, were stated and conducted during the Constitutional Revolution also. They involved a group of Akhunds and the result of the Constitutionalism was what we saw in the Constitution. The Constitution has absolutely changed. The real Iranian Nationalism has been excluded. With the articles that have been created in the document, the Constitution has ruined Iranian Nationalism. We ought to consider this time that if we succeed to remove the Akhunds from power in the country, to [prevent] other Akhunds with different faces from entering the arena of politics.

Everyone will be free to conduct any political activity in any attire, but in no case in that attire to be able to enter religion into the arena of politics. Even if an Akhund should want to remain and conduct political activities, he is free also. But he has no right to conduct these political activities in the context of religion, because religion is personal and ought to remain personal. I believe, my suggestion is that, my request is that everyone conduct political activities in the way of Iranian Nationalism. Iranian Nationalism is what the people would accept. Do not rely on issues that are outside the boundaries of our power and outside the boundaries of our knowledge and awareness. If I, to any extent, want to support religion, in any case, it would not be to the extent that Akhund is informed of it. Therefore, I would [inaudible] create others' suffering and would destroy my own value. Therefore, the best method of struggle to suppress these people, whom the people of Iran extremely support now, is to [inaudible] [defend] the Iranian flag, Iranian territory, and Iranian Nationalism.

I say good-bye to all esteemed and dear viewers of JAAM-E-JAM and thank the dear friends, JAAM-E-JAM, who have assumed great troubles in enlightening the truth and have really embarked on this path with fearlessness.

Manouchehr Bibiyan: Good Thoughts, Good Words, Good Deeds is response to hundreds of books.

Aryamanesh: Exactly

JAAM-E-JAM Television's Round Table Discussion
with
Ahmad Madani

Participants and interviewers:

Manouchehr Bibiyan, Farhang Farahi, Manouk Khodabakhshian, Manouchehr Omidvar

June 27, 1988

Manouchehr Omidvar, JAAM-E-JAM: Mr. Madani, the Iran of today is facing a critical point. Do you, as one of the oppositional leaders against the Islamic Republic, have an implementable plan for the liberation of Iran? I am not referring to a philosophical plan, meaning that you would have groups, or cells, a determined date, [rather] an implementable plan for the overthrow of the regime, i.e. the Islamic Republic, or change in Iran? Or you have not started this work yet?

Madani: If I have [a] plan, I, in my belief, assume that I betray the nation of Iran or to keep them hopeful in the issues and while I don't have any ideas. This was a betrayal to the expectations of the nation and entire nation that if we don't have solutions at least not be an obstacle to the nation of Iran. At least if we are not useful, I don't' want to be—I, to my extent, am on the side of other moderate Iranian nationalists. These moderate Iranian nationalists that I say are in the government positions, in the foundations of the revolution, in the clerics, are everywhere—they are not all bad people. Many of them are good people. They are located everywhere; they are outside, they are inside [the country].

On their side—which is not necessary that its appearance have, as they say, be open, rather it is a step that has to reach results. And perhaps some day we could answer the question which you have asked me to the nation that on that day when you asked me and today I present to the nation of Iran the results of these efforts in my small share.

Farhang Farahi, JAAM-E-JAM: General, when you began your correspondence with some of the statesmen and clerics of Iran, it was the first days or months that Iraq had attacked Iran, and had placed Khuzistan under its control and influence, and the regime of the republic, i.e. the Islamic Republic, was in fear. On that day, they, i.e. the Islamic Republic, needed an authoritarian military man, a military commander, and someone with knowledge, and for this reason my impression is that it was at that time that they referred to you, and they pursued a flexible policy vis-à-vis you and they were also faced with responses. When were your correspondences cut off, or you felt that you no longer—as statesmen who are the preservers of rights of Iranians—could collaborate with them?

Madani: Since the beginning when I came out of Iran, I started these correspondences, because I was not a stranger to them. We were together for many years, and I pointed out to them what our goal had been, what was our plan, what agreement we had with each other before the revolution, and in what direction we wanted to go, and why did you separate. And I have always believed that there is an impact in stating which does not exist in not stating.

For this purpose, I used to write, and I wrote with respect because this was communication, it was dialogue, it was discussion, I wanted the [correspondence] to reach them, and I wanted them to read the plans. I essentially never insult. I observed the etiquette that I had to observe, and I now observe in the correspondence that I have with the authorities inside [the country].

Until a few years ago—which you know of this issue, they referred to me and wanted me to become Prime Minister and Commander in Chief. I did not want any pre-conditions. I said that "I don't want any pre-conditions or political positions; I might accept to be a servant of an elementary school in Kerman also, but let's see in that limit of being a servant would I have authority? Very well. You say, I am most willing to come inside [the country]. I have to perform my duty; I have to be inside at this critical situation. Most willingly, but I can not come inside and be ruined, become a tool [of your policy]. I have discussions about principles with you. I would have discussions if you grant absolute authority considering the rights of this nation of Iran, to end the Iran-Iraq war, most willingly. If you grant authority [in order that] the rule of law be established in Iran and security, so that anyone with any religion and belonging to any sect—only rule [of law] would govern—could come to Iran and I would say: 'It does not concern us what is your religion. It does not concern us what sect you belong to; we want know-how and Iran-friendship from you, we are not concerned about anything else, and be certain that we tell the truth and we don't lie.' Would you permit me to establish these [principles] in order to begin reconstruction [of the country]? And, begin the second phase of the revolution, the reconstruction, [then] I will come with all my existence. If not, you want me to come and continue the direction of your policies? I don't accept this trap."

Manouk Khodabakhshian, JAAM-E-JAM: If Dr. Madani goes inside Iran and with the collaboration of factors in the regime, i.e. the Islamic Republic, ends the war, and later as Prime Minister, do you think that he would want to create a continuity for this regime,

i.e. the Islamic Republic? Would it not be a negative political record for Admiral Madani who has come and has become the successor of individuals such as Khameneie and Rafsanjani who are not acceptable from the perspective of the people?

Madani: I state to you that it would not be for the continuation of this regime, i.e. the Islamic Republic. As I said: because they did not want to accept my pre-conditions, I did not accept their direction either. Therefore, it is not the continuation of this regime, i.e. the Islamic Republic. It is the return of this regime, i.e. the Islamic Republic, from the situation of extremism, destruction, and creating problems to the second phase of the revolution: meaning popular sovereignty, meaning reconstruction, meaning flexibility, meaning replacing extremism with faith, and such issues.

Manouk Khodabakhshian, JAAM-E-JAM: This is a philosophical and ideological view. What would be the regime's structure, organization, and system?

Madani: I state to you that if I assume that in the existing situation we want to launch radical changes in Iran, that we want to make 180-degree changes in Iran, and to transfer this regime, i.e. the Islamic Republic, [from its current situation] to another regime, I must state that it is imaginative.

Farhang Farahi, JAAM-E-JAM: Do you believe in calm transfer of power?

Madani: Yes, at least the evaluation which I have made in the current situation [is that] because the issues of today are different from those of tomorrow; it is different from the issues of six months later. In the current situation I believe that if we assume that [we] could make radical changes in Iran, it is imaginative.

Manouchehr Omidvar, JAAM-E-JAM: General, some of the people of Iran believe that all of the changes that have occurred in Iran are due to foreign influence. Meaning that the simple thinking exists to the extent that they forced the Shah from Iran, they brought Khomeini and that they themselves have to take Khomeini and bring another person. I do not consider foreign forces to ever have such capabilities. Personally, because we see that the biggest superpower in the world is still involved in a country of two and half million such as the country of Nicaragua, is busy with Cuba, and could not even influence its surroundings as it would like. Or, in Afghanistan. I want to ask you to what extent do you consider that the foreign forces have power, and what do you consider their role to be in the future changes of Iran?

Madani: Today's world is connected but with its own limit and degree—not outside its limit and degree. In each main change and transformation, we find change in its own roots. If it is a revolution; I don't say coup d'etat—coup d'etat might occur repeatedly, it does not have background either. It requires collaboration. It is another type. I am not referring to that—I am talking about revolution. Revolution requires background, similar to water that suddenly does not become 100 degrees.

This starts from a [certain] degree, and slowly reached 100 degrees. When I [consider] the record—without I having a protest as a, or having an oppressive view, not at all—but the record of the previous regime, i.e. the Shah's regime, after the coup d'etat of the 28th of Mordad [1953] until the day that the revolution occurred, [if] we [re]view this twenty-five years, we have our own answers. And the people who were in Iran on that day and were in the government or were in the region of the country and they subtracted and added everything, they themselves predicted that [Iran] was going toward [the direction] of revolution.

This regime, i.e. the Shah's regime, was in the [direction] of changes inside [the country]. I must state that the current regime, i.e. the Islamic Republic, is a reflection of yesterday's regime, i.e. the Shah's regime. The existing regime, i.e. the Islamic Republic, is the creation of the old regime, i.e. the Shah's regime. I ought to say this. But this point must also be considered that in every revolution at the crossing, also would be situated in the direction of activities of outside the borders.

Manouchehr Bibiyan: Recently, the American government announced that it has made financial assistance to some Iranian opposition leaders against the Islamic Republic including you. How did you spend this fund? And did you make any commitment in exchange of receiving this fund?

Madani: I state to you that when I exited from Iran in September 1980 I stated my plans to Iran, I talked to the world, it was reflected from the media, and I said that without conditions if persons are willing to help us, we accept the help.

From the United states, there was help in 1980-1981, beginning of 1981, an amount that I don't exactly know now but almost 1 million, 1 million and almost 200-300 thousand dollars that I myself was not the receiver, I used to give it to my office but the list of expenses I myself issued at that time. And financial help was given to—some who perhaps in the future I will give the list to the nation—almost a thousand persons, more or less outside and inside.

The day they referred to me and they asked about my plans, I said that my plans would only be given to the nation of Iran and no one else.

And, later it occurred that—I want to say this bluntly—one of them said that the President of the United States wants to have information regarding our plans. I said that the President of the United States for me his value is less than a Kermani construction worker. The people who want explanations from me and can supervise my plans are the nation of Iran and no one else.

My stubbornness was continued to an extent that The New York Times and The Washington Post—as you have read and I don't want to repeat it here—said that he [the President of the United States] wanted to continue his way independently, and because he did not want to compromise with anyone, we cut off our relations and from 1981 the relations was cut off.

Farhang Farahi, JAAM-E-JAM: General, in your meetings with American authorities, have you received approval for your moderate paths?

Madani: I say to you that it is not necessary that the United States give us approval. The nation of Iran must give me approval. The nation of Iran has given approval to my moderate way, but the world has to know what we are doing; the world must know that we have a moderate way. The world must know that hostage taking would not be replaced by hostage taking. The world must know that the violator of the rights of a society doesn't want to be replaced as the violator of the rights of a society. The world must know that we don't want to create religious fascism or political fascism.

We believe in international law; we believe in the rights of the society. We believe in the principles of popular sovereignty, but now also if without pre-conditions those in the world want to help me, I announce that I accept without pre-conditions.

The Death of Khomeini

Manouchehr Bibiyan's Interviews with Amir Taheri, Reza Pahlavi, Shapour Bakhtiar, and Daryoush Homayoun

Interviews conducted via telephone a few hours after Khomeini's death

Broadcast Date: June 4, 1989

Manouchehr Bibiyan: Mr. Taheri, Manouchehr Bibiyan speaking from JAAM-E-JAM Television. Permit me to discuss the death of Ayatollah Khomeini that occurred in the few hours ago in Iran. Who was Khomeini? And what would be the consequences of the death of Khomeini in the future of Iran?

Amir Taheri: First, permit me to describe his biography for the viewers.

Mr. Khomeini was born on November 9, 1902 in the small city of Khomein or the province of Khomein that is located in the 320 kilometers south-western Tehran. His family had spent some time in India and also in the Najaf Ashraf. He began his theological education from childhood and later he was a student of Ayatollah Haeiri in Qom and with the collaboration of Ayatollah Haaeri, they organized and established the seminary of Qom.

Mr. Khomeini was not interested in politics until after WWII when he published a book against Kasravi, the renowned Iranian writer and intellectual, and he issued a death threat against Kasravi; of course later he [Kasravi] was assassinated. After that, he [Khomeini] was collaborating with Ayatollah Boroujerdi, and he tried to be elected to Congress for a time. But, Ayatollah Boroujerdi was against this undertaking, and ultimately the process of the Shah's White Revolution occurred, and Mr. Khomeini became the leader of the opposition of the Shah's Land Reform and Women's Rights which was granted. And in the riots which occurred in Tehran, Qom, and other cities, his name became recognized as the leader of the opponents of the Shah and the Shah's reforms.

Later, he was exiled to Turkey, and there after some time he decided to transfer to Najaf Ashraf in Iraq, and there he was in exile for fifteen years. From there, of course, as you know, when the revolutionary situation emerged in Iran, Mr. Khomeini went to France, and he lived near Paris for a period of four and a half months, and he organized the Islamic Revolution from there. In returning to Iran, of course, after ten days he succeeded to overthrow the Administration of the last Prime Minister of the Shah, that is Shapour Bakhtiar, and to create his own Islamic government.

In the ten years of the Islamic government of Mr. Khomeini many major events occurred in Iran—in which the Iran-Iraq was is at the zenith of these events—and also the many executions that occurred and also hundreds of thousands of points which has existed in this regime, i.e. the Islamic Republic, that when we calculate, we see that for every hour of the government of Mr. Khomeini, ten Iranians have been killed. Meaning, in the past ten years, more than 1,600,000 Iranians in war, in the various attacks, killed in executions, and also nearly three million and a half Iranians are outside the country in exile, and four and a half million Iranians inside the country who are among the war refugees, and more than 6 million Iranians who are at working age are now unemployed. Millions of Iranians, particularly girls and women, are deprived of education, and one can not find almost any family in Iran who has not suffered from the government of Mr. Khomeini.

The death of Mr. Khomeini has occurred at a time when Iran is facing four large crises. The first crisis is regarding his successor because the formula which they were supposed to find for the successor of the Velayat-i-Faghih (Governance of the Jurist) has not been found yet, and consequently who would assume the role and duty of Velayat-i-Faghih—and his responsibilities which has been predicted regarding his position in the Constitution of the Islamic Republic.

The second crisis that will continue is the issue of the Iran-Iraq negotiation. Iraq continues to have occupied parts of Iran. The negotiations between the two sides have stopped, and without Khomeini—who could, in any way, direct the negotiations towards one direction or another direction—it appears that it would be difficult to continue the negotiations.

The third crisis that Iran is facing is regarding Iran's relations with the outside world due to the issue of Salman Rushdi. This relations became deteriorated and now without a strong politician at the head of the Islamic Republic's government, the solution appears difficult.

The fourth crisis is that the leaders of this regime, i.e. the Islamic Republic, have not yet managed to agree on a single economic policy to begin economic growth. You know that there are expected big economic problems that in any case would endanger the security and stability of the regime, i.e. the Islamic Republic, and in these issues also the absence of Khomeini would certainly be a factor.

Manouchehr Bibiyan: Dear viewers, now, we are communicating via a direct line with Reza Pahlavi. Bibiyan speaking from JAAM-E-JAM Television. With thanks for your speaking with JAAM-E-JAM Television, would you express your view regarding post-Khomeini Iran?

Reza Pahlavi: The most important issue that would occur is that with the death of Khomeini, the Islamic Republic has ceased to exist in the way of the meaning or connotation of "the Islamic Republic", and also in the way that we knew it in these ten years. The last people who at the time Khomeini was living—were in the process of government due to the stance of Khomeini himself—now they no longer have that stance on religion, and many clerics who from the first day of [the Islamic Republic] were opposed to Khomeini, now they can express their views much more openly.

In the previous situation until Khomeini was in power, they did not have the possibilities of the current situation, and also many elements lower level of hierarchy of the authentic clerics and higher level clerics were not in a situation who could directly oppose Khomeini. Now that Khomeini is no longer on the scene, there would open a new political scene in the politics of Iran. And in the vacuum that is created this politics would no longer permit the current leaders in the levels of government to have—from the stance of religion they could no longer have the smallest significance and legitimacy among the people. And, the majority of the people who most likely take their orders from reliable and higher-ranking religious sources—rather than the current people—would certainly pay more attention to the words of those leaders.

Therefore, I think that not only our compatriots inside Iran and outside Iran ought to ever more intensify their efforts in the goal that we have which is the liberation of our country and the restoration of national sovereignty. But, in particular, I believe that the Iranian clerics in the current situation must play their role in one of the most vital era of the history of our country. And, with the removal of the last individual who could—from that stance of religion—impose his views on the nation of Iran or via government, and with the creation of this vacuum, can fill this vacuum and create a new political scene.

In the current situation, therefore, our first step in this new chapter that is opened, after the era of Khomeini, is conducting ever more communication regarding the current issues of the country, strengthening the spirit of our compatriots inside the country. And, as you know, I have many times referred to the significance of the solidarity of all the Iranian nationalist forces, which I believe is [towards] the principal and ultimate goal. And it is natural that my first expectation from my compatriots, particularly from the compatriots outside the country, is in the direction of supporting their compatriots inside Iran because they have much more freedom and possibility for movement and struggle against Khomeini—at least now that Khomeini does not exist. But I want to say that against the remnants of those who exist now in the government of Iran. And, they ought to be forging the lines of their struggle, and in a vast solidarity at the national level which must replace the current government of Iran, i.e. the Islamic Republic, and ultimately end with the ultimate victory of the nation of Iran.

Manouchehr Bibiyan: Dr. Bakhtiar, Bibiyan speaking from JAAM-E-JAM Television. Please explain your views to our compatriots regarding Iran after Khomeini.

Shapour Bakhtiar: The ruins that Khomeini delivers to an oppressed nation with his death, and unfortunately the government which he implemented in Iran during ten years, has caused Iran to be in the current economic and social situation, etc.

Now that this man has died, I don't suppose that [even] ten percent of the nation of Iran be sad regarding this loss. And I believe that the majority of the nation of Iran have temporary calm until the next decisions occur due to this death, which God-willing the hope of all of us is that the government that must come to power in Iran absolutely not be a government of the Mullahs. This is the opinion of the National Resistance Movement of Iran and I personally regarding this issue. We struggle against any type of government by the Akhunds. However, what would result, it is too early to know exactly the issues that would be declared regarding foreign and domestic policy and the forces which would stand against each other. I don't suppose that any of these Akhunds would be able to have Khomeini's domination over the groups the numbers of which is very, very few.

Manouchehr Bibiyan: My next question is what is the plan of the Iranian opposition against the Islamic Republic after the death of Khomeini?

Shapour Bakhtiar: The plan of the opposition against the Islamic Republic, in my opinion, if it is authentic, it does not have pre and post [Khomeini]. We have been struggling for ten years. We began the struggle for democracy, for nationalism, and a progressive Iran, and now with the removal of this man, of course, there would be more hopefulness. However, the Iranian opposition against the Islamic Republic that would want to in any way collaborate with the persons who have spilled the blood of so many people would be rejected by us.

Manouchehr Bibiyan: Mr. Daryoush Homayoun, Bibiyan speaking from JAAM-E-JAM Television, and I want to ask questions that

are naturally regarding the death of Khomeini. My first question is how do you describe the Iran of after Khomeini?

Daryoush Homayoun; The Iran of after Khomeini, similar to Iran during Khomeini's era, is a hell of disorder, chaos, and ruin. However, to a higher degree perhaps.

Khomeini has died in a situation where the entire regime of the Islamic Republic is involved in the struggle for power, and is in the process of determining the future political regime of Iran. Changes in the Constitution, the issue of leadership, the issue of who would replace Khomeini in this regime, i.e. the Islamic Republic, the issue of concentration of executive power by one or two officials, the issue of the judiciary—all of these are issues about which the leaders of the Islamic Republic are struggling. In addition to intense personal and political rivalries that only Khomeini could moderate.

In the absence of Khomeini, the claimants to power would struggle against each other with more freedom of action, and if the regime, i.e. the Islamic Republic, was faced with instability in the era of Khomeini. Today, after Khomeini, certainly it is facing much more instability, and even threatening its existence. But we ought not to forget the vital role of Khomeini in maintaining the Islamic regime in Iran and the regime of Velayat-i-Faghih [Mandate of the Jurist].

Khomeini had a unique position in this regime, i.e. the Islamic Republic, and without him, no one could bring about and maintain this collection of chaos under a united regime.

It could be stated with confidence that the hope of the overthrow of the Islamic regime in Iran is more optimistic and closer to reality after the death of Khomeini. As long as Khomeini was alive, the possibility of overthrowing this regime, i.e. the Islamic Republic, was much less.

After Khomeini, all the possibilities exist to bring about fundamental changes in the situation of Iran. In addition, Khomeini died at a time when he has no following among the current generation or the next generations of Iran. Khomeini has died in defeat: he has been defeated by Iraq, he has been defeated in the domestic issues of Iran, he has been defeated in the international arena, and even in Velayat-i-Faghih [Mandate of the Jurist]—who was himself the originator—he was forced to modify and announce that the country can not be run by religious laws.

In all of these circumstances, Khomeini, the possibility that in the future they idolize and make myths about him, he ruined this in his own era. A person who is defeated while living, in the future after his/her death it would be difficult to place him/her in the issues of hero or myth. The death of Khomeini, for the nation of Iran, from all perspectives, today in particular, is a good occasion, and it is proper that we announce this day as the day of national joy.

Manouchehr Bibiyan: A few minutes ago, we contacted Ms. Pari Sekandari in Paris, and she announced that the Iranian military has been mobilized and is in an alert stance. What is your information regarding this issue?

Daryoush Homayoun: I don't have much information regarding this issue. I only heard that a political group which is headquartered in Iraq, which has been supported by Iraq for years, has converged its people from various places in the world and they possibly are considering to concentrate [their forces] on the border of Iraq and utilizing the death of Khomeini to again initiate an operation. If the Iranian military has announced that it is in an alert stance, it is due to the same reason: to block the possible invasion of this group to the bordering areas of Iran. But essentially in the situations when a leader in the circumstances of Khomeini dies in a country, the announcement of readiness by the Iranian military forces is very natural.

Sir Anthony Parsons

The last British Ambassador to Iran in the Shah's regime; In the 1960's he was Ambassador and had many political missions in Khartum, Oman, Ankara, Cairo, Baghdad, and ultimately Tehran.

Manouchehr Bibiyan's Interview with Sir Anthony Parsons

Location of the Interview: Ashburton, England at Parsons' Residence

Air Date: October 29, 1989

Manouchehr Bibiyan: For a period of five years, you served as Britain's Ambassador to Iran, and for five years you were consulted by the late Shah. What is your opinion and interpretation of the late Shah? Do you consider him a dictator, a distinguished statesman, or an indecisive individual?

Parsons: I did see a great deal of the Shah during those five years. I think that the Shah had some of the qualities of all the descriptions that you have given. He was dictatorial—there is no doubt about it—in the way he ran the country. He also was, I think, a considerable statesman, particularly in the foreign affairs field. One of his troubles perhaps was that he was more interested in foreign policy than he was in domestic policy and gave it much more attention—certainly in the last few years of his reign. There is no doubt that as somebody to do business with on foreign policy, he was very impressive. He knew all his subjects very well. He had a very clear idea of where he wanted Iran to go, what Iran's policy should be towards the rest of the world. And, he made a very strong impression certainly on all the Western and Eastern cabinet ministers and heads of governments who used to come and visit him, and also on me. But when the difficult time came, in the last year, in the year of the revolution from '78 to '79, he certainly showed himself as somebody who found it extremely difficult to make strong decisions. He was trying—and I think this does him great credit—right up to the very end to find a political rather than a military solution to the revolution. He was searching amongst all the political establishment of Iran to find somebody who could run the country and bring down the revolutionary temperature which rose from the beginning of 1978. But he certainly did find decisions extremely hard to make at that stage. But before that, until 1978, he appeared to all those who knew him and had to deal with him, like myself, to be very decisive.

Manouchehr Bibiyan: In his book, *Answer to History*, the Shah states that during Iran's crisis, William Sullivan, the United States' Ambassador to Iran, constantly encouraged him to leave Iran. What was your advice or suggestion to the Shah?

Parsons: Well, certainly the idea of leaving Iran—the Shah leaving Iran—was never in our minds, and I don't think that it was in the American Ambassador's mind either, until perhaps the very last days when it was pretty clear to all of us that the regime, i.e. the Shah's regime, was on the point of collapse. My advice to the Shah throughout the period of the revolution, which I gave on a purely personal basis as somebody who had been in his country for some time, was that he must find a political solution of some kind, that a solution to military repression would not work. And, particularly after October 1978, when the whole country just about went on strike, it became very clear to me that there was no military solution to the problem and that the appointment of a military government in Iran would probably signal the end of the regime, i.e. the Shah's regime. So, my advice, again for what it was worth and presented entirely personally, was that he must continue to try to find a political solution to the problem. But certainly I never suggested that he [the Shah] should leave the country.

Manouchehr Bibiyan: A group of Iranians, especially those on the left, attribute Reza Shah's rise to power to the British. What is your opinion regarding this issue?

Parsons: Yes, I know that there is a lot of popular folklore in Iran that Britain was behind Reza Shah's coming to power. An examination of the documents at the time, which are now of course all public, and an examination of the diaries of the people who were concerned with that period of Iranian history proves that this was not the case. The British authorities in Iran in 1920 had considerable respect for Reza Khan, as he was then, as the Commander of the Persian Cossacks, and he was holding them together as a very effective officer. But it was certainly never a part of any British plan that he should become Shah. I think that this is part of a lot of folklore in Iran, which sees the hands of the British behind all events in your country.

Manouchehr Bibiyan: The Pahlavi regime continued for more than half of a century. Do you consider the Reza Shah and Mohammad Reza Shah's period as a progressive era for Iran?

Parsons: In many senses of the word, yes. When the Pahlavi regime came to power, Iran was isolated from the mainstream of economic and social development going on in the rest of the world for many years. And it was economically very underdeveloped, a very underdeveloped country. By the time the Shah fell, Iran was certainly one of the most industrialized countries in the whole region. It had a modern system of communications, great social changes taking place—perhaps too rapidly and too fundamental. But there is no comparison as it were between Iran of the 1920's and Iran of the 1970's. By the 1970's when the oil prices went up, Iran was very close to an economic breakthrough out of being a developing country into being a developed country. So, in that sense, in the broad social and economic sense, yes, it certainly was a progressive era, no doubt about that.

Manouchehr Bibiyan: With regard to your extended residence in Iran, you are definitely informed of this public opinion that nearly every political event that occurred in Iran in the past was interpreted by Iranians as acts of British influence in Iran. For example, during the past hundred years, the Iranian people have regarded the religious elements as Britain's Fifth Column in Iran. How has this thinking been founded among the nation of Iran regarding Britain? And, what has really been the role of your country in Iran in the course of this century?

Parsons: Well, I think it is very natural that it developed. I mean, after all, there is no question about it that for the best part of more than a century that Britain and, of course, Tsarist Russia were the two principal foreign powers dominating Iran. And, there is no question about it equally that Britain did interfere in Iranian internal affairs throughout the nineteenth century and well into the twentieth century. I think the tragedy is that the Iranian people continued to believe this long after it ceased to be true. I mean, I know that an awful lot of Iranian people still believe this to this day, even as regards the revolution of 1978-1979. But the actual fact is, the truth is, that after 1951, after the nationalization of the Anglo-Iranian Oil Company, and then the resumption of relations with Britain in 1954, successive British governments were absolutely determined to have a normal relationship with Iran and to get rid of this business of the past. To have no more to do with Iranian internal affairs than any embassy does in any country, let us say France or Germany. I mean, as I have said, to really normalize relations with Iran. And this was the objective of the whole streams of ambassadors, of the last of them being myself. The trouble was that, as I discovered at the time of the revolution, that although we had normalized relations on our side, that the Iranian people as a whole did not regard this as having happened from their side, and that they still believed that the British hand was behind all the events even of the revolution, and totally wrongly. That is the truth, whatever Iranian people may believe.

Manouchehr Bibiyan: Did you have any diplomatic missions to Iran at the time of premier Mossadegh?

Parsons: At the time of Mossadegh we had an embassy there until 1952 when Iran broke diplomatic relations with us, and our embassy didn't return until 1954 as far as I can remember after Mossadegh's fall.

Manouchehr Bibiyan: Were you not personally residing in Iran at that time?

Parsons: Myself, no. During that period, I was in the embassy in Baghdad, which I have no doubt arises great suspicion on the part of a number of people in Iran.

Manouchehr Bibiyan: Do you foresee any chance for the Iranian opposition leaders against the Islamic Republic abroad to return to power?

Parsons: Well, this is an impossible question to answer. And I think to some extent I may be a prisoner of my own past in that my last experience of Iran was the revolution and in the light of what I saw during the revolution, I find it very difficult, myself, to imagine any of the external Iranian opposition parties against the Islamic Republic regaining power in Iran. Apart from that, Iran has had eight years of extremely bloody and damaging war from 1980 to 1988. And it would seem to me that it would be very difficult for the people of Iran to accept somebody in power who had not shared this experience of theirs over the past ten years and particularly the experience of eight years of warfare. I would be very surprised if any of the Iranian opposition groups against the Islamic Republic—the external Iranian opposition groups against the Islamic Republic—regain power. But of course, I have been wrong about Iran many times and I could be wrong again.

Manouchehr Bibiyan: Mohammad Reza Shah was a friend of the West including the United States and Britain. However, after he left Iran and became ill, none of his friends were willing to allow him to enter their countries. Why?

Parsons: Well, I think its something of which many of us can very well feel ashamed. As you rightly say, he was a close friend of Britain and he was a close friend of America, and indeed [of] other countries in the West. And we didn't accept him. I think the only person who comes really a hundred percent well out of the events following the Shah's departure from the country is the late President Sadat of Egypt. The problem really was this and I speak quite honestly on it: after the events of 1953, our feeling was in Britain that if we accepted the Shah in our country, that there would be immediate retaliation against whatever was left of British presence in Iran, out of genuine fear that there was going to be some attempt to restore the Shah to the country, as happened in 1953. I was personally convinced from early 1979 onwards, from March 1979 onwards, that if the retaliation would take the form of the seizure of the British Embassy and the holding hostages of the staff, and it was really that consideration in mind that we were reluctant to have the Shah in our country. He never in fact asked to come to Britain, but that was the thought behind our attitude at the time. I mean, we weren't proud of it, but we had our own people in Iran to think of.

Manouchehr Bibiyan: Would you describe one of your interesting memories regarding your residence in Iran that you would like to tell our viewers?

Parsons: Well, I can say that it was as a whole over the five years, it was undoubtedly the most interesting diplomatic experience that I had. I arrived in the country [at] the beginning of 1974, just after the oil prices had been tripled at the OPEC meeting in December 1973. So, I was there to see this enormous economic boom and all the flood of economic activity that went on in the mid 1970's. That was fascinating. A unique experience. I was then there, of course, to see the whole thing collapse. And to me, to be in Iran from 1978 to 1979 was rather like being British Ambassador in Paris in 1789 or British Ambassador to St. Petersburg in 1917. I mean, I lived through one of the most dramatic and important revolutions of modern times. And, in between that, of course, my wife and I, my family, we did have an extremely enjoyable time. I mean, Iran is a large and extremely beautiful country with many fascinating things to see. We traveled everywhere in the country. We saw a great deal of it. The whole thing is an experience which I wouldn't have missed for anything. It's one of the reasons I wrote a book about it after I left the country.

Manouchehr Bibiyan: Would you like to make any other comments or give any messages?

Parsons: I think the only message I have for the Iranian people is this: that I appreciate the extent to which Iran has suffered over the past ten years, the loss of life, the damage to property, the prevention of economic development that has resulted from the war. And I very sincerely hope that Iran will now be able to settle down, rebuild the country and produce a better economic and social future for all its people. Thank you.

Marvin Zonis

Professor, University of Chicago; consultant to the various administrations, United States; former Director, Center for Middle Eastern Studies, University of Chicago; and American Institute of Iranian Studies (president, 1969-1971).

Marvin Zonis

Date of the Interview: June 6, 1991

Location: JAAM-E-JAM Studio

Habib Momayez/ JAAM-E-JAM: Mr. Manouchehr Bibiyan, the producer and President of JAAM-E-JAM Television Network, and I have put together certain questions pertinent to the themes outlined in your book. In 1976 you and I were participants in a symposium at Persepolis, where many of your distinguished colleagues, experts on Iranian Affairs, were also present. The topic of discussion was Iran: Past, Present, and Future. No one at that conference warned of any recognizable, pertinent, objective revolutionary conditions. Fifteen years later this is indeed the contention of your book that the Pahlavi regime was not overthrown

because of the overwhelming strength of the Iranian opposition against the Shah's regime, but because of the failure of the Shah to exercise effective political power and control which was at his disposal. What occurred was a *Majestic Failure*[14]. This is the title of your book. Could you elaborate on that please?

Marvin Zonis: When I began to try to understand the Iranian Revolution, the thing that really struck me more than anything else was that it was amazing that the Shah lost, and that the revolutionaries won. I couldn't really understand how it could be the case when the Shah had the army, the police, the money, the government, and the support of foreign powers. He had all these assets that any ruler could have. The revolutionaries had nothing. How could he have lost power?

And, as I began to think of the revolution in those terms, the answer that I came up with was that he lost power because he didn't exercise the instruments of control which he had in a very effective manner. So, I saw the revolution as a failure of his leadership, rather than as the brilliance of the revolutionaries.

JAAM-E-JAM: As you have stated in your book, the fall of the Shah had great international consequences, some, of course, catastrophic. Had he remained in power, would the world have been any safer?

Zonis: You see, I think what is amazing is that the fall of the Shah, I believe, was one of the most important events of the twentieth century. I really am not exaggerating when I say that. I don't think that it is the

---

[14] Marvin Zonis, *Majestic Failure: the Fall of the Shah* (Chicago: University of Chicago Press, 1991).

most important event of the twentieth century, but it certainly must be ranked as one of the three or four most important events. And, if we look at the region of the world, the Persian Gulf, since the rise of the clerics, since the fall of the Shah, it is easy to see why I believe that. Because the significant international events that have occurred since the fall of the Shah would not have occurred had he remained in power.

For example, the first thing that happened was, of course, the clerics and their allies seizing the American embassy and taking prisoner fifty-two American diplomats, which led to disastrous consequences both for Iran and also for the United States, and the region. After that, the Soviets invaded Afghanistan. They would never have invaded Afghanistan had there been a powerful Shah on the throne with the Imperial Iranian Armed Forces, and the support of the United States behind them. They would never have dared offended Iran or the Shah through that invasion.

Of course, after that was the Iran and Iraq war which was one of the great tragedies of Iranian history. Had the Shah been on the throne, there would have been no invasion of Iran. There would not have been hundreds of thousands of Iranians dead.

Most recently, of course, there is the Iraqi invasion of Kuwait which again would never have occurred because Saddam would never have challenged the power of the Shah who brought stability to the Persian Gulf. So, no matter where you look in that part of the world, which is, of course, crucial to all of us because we depend on the oil that comes from the Gulf, we find the same story: that the Shah of Iran was a great regional stabilizer, and when he fell from power, the stability of the Gulf went with him.

JAAM-E-JAM: The Shah was portrayed by the western media, particularly during the 1970's, as a ruthless dictator. In your book, he appears neither as very gutsy and ruthless, nor as much of a dictator. Is this a fair assessment?

Zonis: You know, it is a wonderful thing that I have, of course, thought myself. Everybody in the United States thought he was such a tough, strong, ruthless, hard, and tough leader. And, there are some wonderful stories around that are examples of that. One of them is the last U.S. Ambassador—as he is called Ambassador Sullivan—who was, of course, the American Ambassador to the Philippines, and gets a call to come to Washington. And, he flies to Washington from the Philippines, and he sits down with the Secretary of State, Cyrus Vance—the Secretary of State for President Carter. And, Cyrus Vance says: "Ambassador Sullivan, we have a new job for you. We want you to go to Iran". And, Sullivan is amazed, and he says: "What do you mean you want me to go to Iran. I have never been in the Middle East in my life. All of my diplomatic service for the United States has been in East Asia, in the Far East, in the Philippines, in Cambodia. In all those countries. In Laos. I don't know anything about Iran." And he says: "That's all right. What you know is how to deal with ruthless and tough political leaders. So, we are going to send you because you are a great expert on dealing with tough guys."

Everybody in the American government thought this was true. Of course, once I started to do my research, what I found was quite to the contrary. There was an outside Shah. The outside Shah was the guy that we all know: with the sashes, and the medals, the uniform. Looked like a tough guy, right? But, underneath that outside surface was a guy who, I think, was struggling to generate the energy and the psychic strength to allow him to be the Shah. I think it really wasn't a job that was easy for him to do. It was not easy for this guy to be Shah because, I think, his own character structure was really quite quiet, passive, and not at all ruthless.

JAAM-E-JAM: Well, of course, your book is a psycho-political, a psycho-biographical portrayal of the Shah. You talk of the Shah as having had a dual personality. What were those personalities?

Zonis: Well, you know, I try to capture that if I can go back to this book. I don't know if you can see it. But, on the cover you see I have two faces of the Shah. And, one is this sort of public figure that we all know-the Shah as the ruthless dictator, the tough guy, the tyrant. But, behind him there was always this sort of worrisome, fearful, younger boy whom I think never grew up into this guy. And, the two sides of the Shah, I would say, were the tough guy which he thought he had to be in order to be Shah. I think the Shah always felt that the Iranian people wanted their ruler to be a kind of tough, hard, bitten man so he tried to be that in this kind of picture. But, behind him was this worried fellow who, remember, had a very traumatic childhood.

There are some wonderful stories in this book about what it was like for the Shah to be the son of Reza Shah, I'll never forget one of the things I learned from one of my informants—one of the people I interviewed. It was about how when Mohammad Reza was two years old, his father decided to take another wife, and he didn't inform Taj-al-Mulook—when she became, as we called her later. But Reza Shah didn't inform his wife, the mother of the Shah, of Mohammad Reza Shah, that he was going to marry another woman. And, she threw him out of the house, and they were screaming at each other, and they no longer had a relationship. Well, he grew up; Mohammad Reza Shah grew up in a house in which there was tremendous tension and rage between his mother and father. And, his father, of course, was so powerful, and it was very fearsome to have a father like Reza Shah.

JAAM-E-JAM: Your book identifies several psychological pillars on which the Shah depended. When those pillars disappeared, he was paralyzed. He lost the revolution. What were those pillars?

Zonis: Well, I have to tell you Mr. Momayez, I am impressed that you have read the book because you obviously have these things down, and thank you for paying such attention to it. It is exactly the argument of the book. The argument of the book is: "How did this young, worried, fearful, [and] frightened young man do his job as Shah?" And the answer that I have come up with is: there are really four things that he used to give him strength.

The first was, of course, other people and he became almost bonded to those other people. He established a very close relationship, I think, with three people. He was more close to those three people than any other three people in the world, and they were, of course, the gentleman that he brought back from Switzerland when he was first a student there, who was the son of the groundskeeper at the Le Rosy secondary school. And, he was someone who lived in Iran when they returned from Switzerland all the way until 1960 when he died. And, so, that relationship with Ernest Peron was extremely important to the Shah—a very close personal relationship.

The second person was, of course, Asadollah Alam. The Shah was very closely connected to Alam from both of their childhoods up until Alam's death from leukemia in 1977.

And, the third person was, of course, Princess Ashraf, his twin. Now, here is a person who was his twin. And, I think, he delivered [inaudible], and she was always, of course, much stronger, tougher, harder than was the Shah.

So, I think, there were these three people that he got a lot of strength from.

The second pillar of his psychological pillar, I think, was his belief that he was divinely protected. The Shah used to talk about this a lot in his speeches. And, people thought that he was doing this for political reasons: to convince the Iranian people that, for example, he was a good Muslim or that he had a relationship with God, and therefore the Iranian people should support him. Well, he may have done it for that reason, but I am absolutely convinced that he genuinely believed that the Lord had selected him to do some special divine work. It goes back—and many people will remember this—to the time when the Shah as a young boy was threatened with a number of life threatening illnesses. He had diphtheria, he had typhoid, he had a number of illnesses which in Iran in those days were enough to kill people. And, yet, he didn't die. And, he had dreamed that Ali, Mohammad the Prophet, the Lord himself, came to him in those dreams, and protected him from his illnesses, and saved his life. He took that to mean that they had selected, the Lord had selected him rather for special work. That was the second pillar.

The third pillar was, of course, his belief that the Iranian people loved him. And, what was so amazing about that was how he continued to believe that even when the evidence was clear that they loved him less than they loved other people. And, I remember, for example, how sophisticated the Iranian people were in communicating the fact that they didn't love him so much. In the early 1970's, I remember going to a concert of the Tehran Philharmonic in Tehran. The Shah was there with his family, and they came into the royal box, and everybody stood up and applauded. But, it was rather polite applause. It wasn't very widely enthusiastic. Everybody sat down, and then the conductor of the orchestra came in, and everybody cheered more enthusiastically for the conductor of the orchestra than they cheered for the Shah. So, it was a way of communicating that the Shah wasn't so popular after all, but the orchestra conductor was more popular than the Shah, in some sense. So, it was a way in which the Iranian people knew how to communicate.

Politically, it was acceptable to Savak because they couldn't criticize anybody cheering a conductor. Everybody does that in every concert. But the point is even though there was that evidence, the Shah didn't see it. Again, he believed that he was loved by the Iranian people, and he thought that their love was so important that it gave him strength. That was the third thing.

The fourth thing that gave him strength was his relationship with the United States. This was a very important point because the Shah was deeply embroiled psychologically with the eight American presidents that he knew personally. First he met Franklin Roosevelt who came to Tehran in 1943 for the Tehran Conference. And, the Shah met every single president from Franklin Roosevelt through Jimmy Carter. In fact, when we remember that extraordinary event when Jimmy Carter came to Tehran for the last New Year's Eve in the palace and toasted the Shah as "Iran as an island of stability in the Middle East", however absurd that quote now looks retrospectively, the fact is that these American presidents were—it would be an exaggeration to say they were fathers for the Shah, but they were—very powerful people in the Shah's mind.

And, he said as long as the Americans support me, nobody can touch me. All through the revolution, he was telling people: "Don't worry, the Americans are behind me, I can't lose the revolution." Well, and of course, it was unfortunate that he thought that, but it indicates how important the Americans were to him.

So, those were the four pillars. It was his association with other Iranians, belief in divine protection, the support of the Iranian people, and the support of the United States. And those four things allowed him to be Shah, which he would not have otherwise been able to do.

JAAM-E-JAM: A question about the future. It is popular these days to talk of New World Order. Certainly, the present regime in Iran, i.e. the Islamic Republic, does not belong in this World Order. Do you see much of hope for this regime, i.e. the Islamic Republic?

Zonis: It is a very difficult problem that this regime, i.e. the Islamic Republic, is in. I think it's very tragic. The most obvious reason is because people like yourself, Dr. Momayez, and people like Mr. Bibiyan and JAAM-E-JAM Television who could be providing for the development of Iran, whose talents could be used for developing and improving the conditions of Iranian society are instead using their talents and their brains to develop American society. It's a great strength of American society is that it brings people from all over the world, puts them to work in this country, and uses them to strengthen America. Unfortunately, Iran is not benefiting.

The second problem is that these clerics—the regime in Iran, i.e. the Islamic Republic—is fundamentally hostile to the basic forces of modernization. And, unless these clerics can be brought under control and forced back into the mosques, I think there is very little chance of the Iranian society developing economically and becoming a country which was as strong as it was economically, politically and militarily in the last years of the Shah's regime.

The fact of the matter is that these clerics have unleashed very primitive forces in Iranian society. I think that, for example, the population of Iran is fifty-five million people. The economy, however, is smaller than it was in 1978. We have twenty-three million more people and a smaller economy. So, on a per capita basis, Iran is becoming an impoverished, backward country. It's very rapidly beginning to look like Pakistan and Bangladesh. This was a country that was developing, that was on the verge of becoming a European country. And now it is on the verge of becoming a South Asian backward country so I am very pessimistic. One ray of hope is certainly that Mr. Rafsanjani realizes that if he doesn't turn the economy of Iran around, the consequence will be that the clerics will be thrown out in another violent revolution. So, if he does allow in western capital economic development, if he does allow the Iranian people to participate in their own well being, there is some hope. In the meantime, things are very bad, and as we all know, the civil liberties, the human rights of the Iranian people are regularly violated by this regime, i.e. the Islamic Republic.

In concluding the interview, Manouchehr Bibiyan asked Marvin Zonis the following question:

Manouchehr Bibiyan: There are millions of Iranian people who are now wandering all over the world as a result of the Iranian

Revolution and the most important role that they consider regarding their own status as wanderers is the issue of Huyser. You yourself have written in your book that the role of Huyser in Iran was mysterious and it was not known what his role was.

Zonis: Yes.

Manouchehr Bibiyan: Iranians believe that the visits of Huyser to Iran caused the fall of the Imperial Iranian military. I want to know your view regarding this issue.

Zonis: My sense of it is not entirely clear. My own sense is probably that what happened was that in the waning days of the Shah's regime, I suppose Brzezinski must have said to himself: "We can't let this go; there must be some way to keep this man in power. Let's send a fellow with close ties with the Imperial Iranian military and with close ties to the Shah" because Huyser had worked with the Shah. "Let's send him to Tehran and see what he can do". And, I really think that he was sent with a view toward seeing whether there was an option, for example, to use the Imperial Iranian military to keep the Shah in power. I think that there wasn't one decision which had already been made, and they gave Huyser orders to go to Iran and stage a military coup or a military crackdown. But, my own sense is that they said to him: "Go out there and look at the range of alternatives that are available for preserving the Shah in power" because, of course, that was the goal of Brzezinski, and that was the goal of President Carter. I think what happened was that Huyser got there, and when he met everyday with the senior generals of the Shah's military, he came to the conclusion that it was simply out of the question to stage a military coup to keep the Shah in power because the Iranian generals on whom he would have to rely were not willing, or able, or committed to having a coup or using the Imperial Iranian military, using the Imperial Iranian Armed Forces, to stay in power. It was very late in the game. And you remember that one of the reasons they were not in favor was because Khomeini had declared that the Iranian military could not be used to kill Iranian people. And, I think the Iranian military, indeed, would have disintegrated very quickly if it had started to really try to use force to keep the Shah in power and I think some generals believed that. Other generals, I think, didn't have the competence, didn't have the will, didn't have the strength to command troops to take action. And, finally, of course, we now know that there must have been some generals who had gone over and made their peace with the revolution. The main point that I am making is that I think Huyser realized that the Imperial Iranian military was not a stable base on which to take action to preserve the Shah, and I think when he came to that realization, he left. And, when he left, the end was very near.

Moshe Katsav

The Iranian-born President, the State of Israel (2000-2007); Deputy Prime Minister; Minister of Labor; Minister of Transportation; Minister of Tourism; Knesset Member

Manouchehr Bibiyan's interview with Moshe Katsav

Place of interview: Los Angeles, JAAM-E-JAM TV Studio
Date of interview: January and February 1993
Manouchehr Bibiyan: Mr. Qassab, welcome to the JAAM-E-JAM Studio. We call you Mr. Qassab, but I know that in Israel they call you Mr. Katsav. I am glad to have you at the JAAM-E-JAM Studios. I remember that we had an interview in Israel about 7 years ago and the interview we held in your office was of great interest to our compatriots, especially due to your Iranian origin. The words you said in Persian attracted their attention. I hope that even though it is difficult for you, we would be able to communicate in Persian.

Moshe Katsav: I am not fluent in Persian, but I hope we can communicate in Persian. Yes.

Manouchehr Bibiyan: Thank you, Mr. Katsav. At the beginning of this interview, would you please let us know when and where you were born and the time you left for Israel? Please tell us a little about yourself.

Katsav: Thank you. I am very glad to be at the JAAM-E-JAM TV Studios to talk to you. I was born in Yazd, a city in Iran. When I was 2 years old, we moved to Tehran where my father used to work at the Kourosh School. Three years later, my father, mother, sister and I immigrated to Israel (1951). Since then, we have been living in the city of Kiriyat Malachi, where I was later elected as Mayor.

Manouchehr Bibiyan: I guess you were 24 at the time.

Katsav: Yes. I was a 24-year-old student when I was elected as Mayor of the city I immigrated to from Iran. Obviously, I am a friend of Iran and I love that country. I love the Iranian people, Iranian music and Iranian culture. Receiving Persian books, Iranian newspapers and Iranian music is the best present in the world for my parents. Iranians living in Israel are close to one another. I love Iran very much.

Manouchehr Bibiyan: Would you like to go to your country of origin where you were born and see it again?

Katsav: I would very much like to travel to Iran for a visit. Since 1951, when we left Iran I have been there twice, but not in Yazd. I left Yazd at the age of 2. I do not remember Tehran very well, but I do remember the Kourosh School very well. I would very much like to travel to Iran again and visit Yazd. I really wish to go there. I would very much like to go there.

Manouchehr Bibiyan: So do I, as do many other Iranians. May I ask you some other questions?

Katsav: Yes please.

Manouchehr Bibiyan: As you have noted many times, Iranians have played an important role in Israeli politics and economy since Israel's Independence. You are the first Jewish person born in Iran serving as a minister in the Israeli government. At present, you are a candidate for leadership of the Likud Party and you have the chance of being the Prime Minister of Israel. What message do you have for Iranians?

Katsav: I have been a member of Israeli Parliament for 15 years as well as a Minister in Israeli cabinets for 8 years serving as the Minister of Labor and Minister of Transportation. I am on very friendly terms with Iranians living in Israel. I am sure it is very important for Iranians to have someone of Iranian origin serve as Prime Minister of Israel. Two weeks ago in Holon, a little boy of nearly 11-12 [years of age] came to me and said: "I am Iranian too." I realized that this boy was very proud of being an Iranian. I am sure that the little boy heard about me in school, in the street or through the newspapers, his parents, or his friends. Coming to me and saying that he was Iranian showed that he was proud of being an Iranian. I am very proud to hear a little boy make such a statement.

Manouchehr Bibiyan: Mr. Katsav, do you have a special plan for the expansion of Iranian culture in Israel?

Katsav: Yes, we do, but not very much. I know that it is necessary and it is very important for people of Iranian origin living in Israel. You know that Israel and her neighbors are not on friendly terms. Arabs still see us as their enemies. We would very much like to make peace with them. If there is peace, we will be able to enjoy more of the Iranian music and Iranian culture. Israeli TV programs are currently transmitted in both Hebrew and Arabic to neighboring Arab countries.

Manouchehr Bibiyan: Mr. Katsav, will peace negotiations continue the way they do today if you are elected prime minister?

Katsav: There is no doubt that a person born in Iran is more familiar with the mentality of [people in] the Middle East. This person would know how to negotiate with the Arabs. They are better able to understand one another and [in this way] it will be easier to achieve peace. Up until now, people born in the Middle East had no problems with the Arabs. I hope that we will be able to bring peace not just for this reason, even though this is a good reason in itself.

Manouchehr Bibiyan: It will be a source of pride for Iranians if you are the Prime Minister of Israel. My question is: who are your opponents in this election campaign?

Katsav: There are four candidates for the Likud party leadership. One of them is Beni Begin (the son of the late Menachem Begin), the second is David Levi, former Foreign Minister and Prime Minister's deputy, the third is Bibi Netanyahu, former Israeli Ambassador to the United Nations, and I am the fourth one. We have a good relationship with each other and we are friends. I hope that this relationship will continue in the future too. I believe that most Israelis would like the prime minister to be from the Likud Party again. I think that Israelis are not pleased with the Labor Party. After the elections, we would have to re-establish the Likud party so that we can be in power again.

Manouchehr Bibiyan: Mr. Katsav, what does it mean for the Middle East if an Iranian is elected as prime minister of Israel?

Katsav: First of all, I believe that the way of the Likud Party is the best way to achieve peace in the Middle East. I am positive that our way is better. I believe that a person born in Iran is better able to make peace between Israel and Arabs. If I am elected prime minister, then with God's help, I will be able to promote this matter.

Peace between Israel and the Arabs is a very important issue today. We have been fighting each other for 46 years and there was too much bloodshed. I would like to make a new start. We would like to start rebuilding Israel.

Manouchehr Bibiyan: Mr. Katsav, even though you are a member of the Likud Party, you are on good terms with the Labor Party. Is it possible that a new Likud Party would be created during your term in office?

Katsav: I think that at present, the Likud Party itself is turning into a new party following Menachem Begin and Yitzhak Shamir who were in charge of the party prior to Israel's independence (1948). Now in 1993, we, the son of Manachem Begin, Bibi Netanyahu, David Levi and I are young and our goal is not to change the ideas of the Likud Party because the Likud is going to renew itself. I do not know what is going to happen in the Middle East in the next 10 or 20 years, but I am sure that a new Likud Party will be established.

Manouchehr Bibiyan: I want to ask a question and I don't know whether anyone has asked you this question or not. But it is an important question which I have to ask you. During the Iranian

Revolution, the Likud Party was an active political party in Israel and even Prime Minister Begin was a member of the Likud. I would like to know whether you knew at the time that a revolution might occur in Iran. Could you foresee what was going to happen in Iran? Could you foresee that there was going to be a revolution in Iran? Did you think that if a new regime would come to power in Iran and the monarchy no longer exist in Iran, and a republic would be established—an Islamic republic or other type of republic—whether the relationship between Iran and Israel would remain the same or not?

Katsav: No, we did not know. We did not know that such an event would take place in Iran. We knew that the Shah was in a very difficult situation. We knew that many Iranians went to the streets [to demonstrate] against the Shah. Of course we lost a lot due to the lack of friendly relations between Iran and Israel. I remember the time when I talked to the Ambassador of Iran in Israel, Dr. Mortezaie, two to three weeks before the Revolution. I asked him: "Will the Khomeini Regime win? What will happen to the relationship between Israel and Iran?"

He answered: "In the coming 10-20 years, Iran will not have a good relationship with Israel, but after that, it will realize that Israel is the only country in the Middle East which can be to Iran's advantage. It is to Iran's advantage to be on good terms with Israel." I do not know whether Iran has understood that. Iran is very isolated. Today's world is a world of cooperation. Countries help each other and cooperate with one another. Iran cannot live alone while the entire world is against this country. Iran may learn a lesson from Iraq that wanted to live alone. Iraq is now isolated and no one is willing to cooperate with it. Even Arab countries abandoned their relationship with Iraq. This is a good lesson for Iran. This country would be better off changing its policy and going in a different direction, i.e. to be on better terms with the world. Israel is part of this world as well. Our duty and responsibility is to promise Israelis, Iranians and all nations around the world that we are ready to help them have better lives. I am not sure that Iran is ready to make this kind of promise.

Manouchehr Bibiyan: Mr. Katsav, if you would become the prime minister of Israel while Iran's policy remains unchanged, what will your policy be towards the Islamic Republic of Iran?

Katsav: We do not want to [inaudible] in their affairs. Iran must decide which way to follow. We would obviously prefer that Iran has a better relationship with the world—with America, Europe and Israel, but this decision should be made by the Iranian regime, and not by us, America or Europe. Iranians should change their policy. They should start a new way.

Manouchehr Bibiyan: In your interview with the Persian Service of the Voice of Israel, you said: "Dear Iranian brothers, if I am the Prime Minister of Israel, I will appoint several young Iranians in the cabinet. I am asking your help in reaching this goal." Would you please explain your goal more clearly?

Katsav: Democracy in Israel is very powerful. Young Iranians are not involved in politics. They are shy and strict, and I do not know the other reasons. I am not pleased to be the only Iranian in the Israeli Parliament, but I hope to be able to be the leader of one of the largest parties (Likud).

I entered politics at an early age. I was a mayor, but today I will be able to work with other candidates [such as] David Levi, Beni Begin (son of Menachem Begin) and the ambassador of Israel in—

Manouchehr Bibiyan: United States.

Katsav: Bibi Netanyahu. Every one of us would like to be the head of the Likud [party]. This would show that Israel is a democratic country. I have immigrated with my parents to Israel in 1951, but I reached a position which enables me to run for the Likud leadership. But, of course, I await and wish that more Iranians would be involved in politics. Of course, I will help them. I am certain that the Jews of Iran could contribute to Israel's government, to the State of Israel.

Manouchehr Bibiyan: Thank you very much Mr. Katsav for giving us your time and for coming to JAAM-E-JAM Studios for this discussion. I believe that today's interview will impress many people. I know that you are staying in Los Angeles for only 20 hours, but you let us ask the questions that perhaps the people would have liked to ask you and you have perhaps given convincing answers.

Katsav: I hope that next time I will come to your studios as the Likud leader.

Manouchehr Bibiyan: We will be very glad to see Iranians with esteemed high position everywhere around the world. It will make us very proud. Thank you very much.

Katsav: Thank you.

Manouchehr Bibiyan's Interview with Moshe Katsav

Date of the Interview: November 16, 1996

Manouchehr Bibiyan: Welcome to Los Angeles Mr. Katsav. My first question is regarding the Oslo Agreements. In the 1993 and 1995 Oslo Agreements between Yasser Arafat and the Labor Party, what issues were agreed to which were opposed by the Likud Party and you and your colleagues who are the top leaders of the Likud Party?

Moshe Katsav: First, I want to apologize for not being able to speak Persian very well. Permit me to respond in English. But, I will begin my response in Persian.

Manouchehr Bibiyan: Thank you.

Katsav: We have never been opposed to peace. We, the Likud Party, made peace with Egypt—the largest Arab country—for the first time.

Now, I will respond in English. Yes, it is right. We opposed the agreements Oslo A and Oslo B because we believed that those two agreements could not reach us to real and permanent peace. We believe in peace and in Israel there is no difference between the political parties about this important historical goal—to reach peace. The question is which is the best way to reach real and permanent peace? And about the way, there are some differences between the Likud and the Labor Party. We are a democratic country. We decided and announced many times that we honor and respect all the commitments—the international commitments of the previous government—of the

Labor government. So, because we must continue and respect the international commitments of the previous government, we have the intention and we are very determined to continue the way of making peace—the better way. And, I believe that in this better way, we could reach real and permanent peace in the Middle East.

Manouchehr Bibiyan: You talked about many issues facing the Likud Party after its rise to power, with the exception of Jerusalem. Yasser Arafat, in some of his interviews and speeches, talks about Jerusalem. They consider Jerusalem as belonging to Palestinians. However, since the formation of the Likud government, you have not talked about the issue of Jerusalem and its future. Do the Oslo Agreements discuss the issue of Jerusalem?

Katsav: The Palestinians, the Egyptians, the Arab world, the White House, all of them claim to raise the question of Jerusalem many times, and to discuss and negotiate about this issue. When we came to Camp David, Prime Minister Menachem Begin said to President Anwar Sadat and President Carter, very dramatically but very determined that Jerusalem is not an issue to discuss. And, you see, we have a peace treaty with Egypt without including Jerusalem as a part of it. Regarding the Madrid Convention, President George Bush and the Arab world—including Syria—they said: we will not come to the Madrid Convention if Jerusalem will not be an issue on the agenda. Israeli Prime Minister, Yitzhak Shamir, said very dramatically but very determined: "Jerusalem is not an issue, it will not be an issue on the agenda." And, you see, the conference in Madrid was held without Jerusalem as an issue to discuss on the agenda. But, unfortunately, under the Oslo Agreement, the previous Israeli government has agreed that Jerusalem will be an issue, and the Arabs, the Palestinians, they have the right to raise this issue on the agenda. So, we have the intention to start to talk with the Arabs and the Palestinians about the final solution between us and them. And, according to Oslo, they have the intention to raise this issue of Jerusalem. So, we are very determined. The Labor Party, the Likud Party, ninety-five percent of the Israeli population believe that Jerusalem should remain united, and Jerusalem could not be divided, and Jerusalem should remain under Israeli sovereignty and Jewish sovereignty.

Manouchehr Bibiyan: Another question, which I would like to ask, is regarding the Islamic Republic of Iran. The Islamic Republic has always been severely opposed to the Arab-Israeli Peace Process. In negotiating peace with the Arabs, do the two sides—Israel and the Arabs—share a common policy toward the Islamic Republic? Or do you have separate policies?

Katsav: We have no conflict with Iran. Not with the Iranian people and not with the country itself. We admire, we love the Iranian background and history. Unfortunately, the rulers in Iran are against Israel. And, when they became the rulers in Iran, they became extreme in their hostility toward the Israeli people and Israeli government. So, we believe and we want to cooperate with the Iranians. But they reject. On the contrary, they try to isolate Israel. But, now, Iran itself is isolated in the international community. So, we do not have any deals with the Iranians. Not because of us. And, I hope that they will change their policy, and that they will become some day—very soon and in the very short run—an equal partner in the international community. Since the revolution in Iran, Iran is very isolated and the international community has boycotted Iran. It is not good for Iran itself, it is not good for the Iranians, and it is not good for the rulers in Iran. And, I deeply hope that there will be positive change in their Iranian policy.

Manouchehr Bibiyan: Are you optimistic about the future of peace? What problems do you presently have with Arabs regarding peace?

Katsav: Of course we desire peace. Everyone in Israel, all the parties in Israel, desire to reach real peace, permanent peace, peace with security for the Israelis and for the State of Israel. But, since the recognition of the PLO, terrorist activities have increased dramatically. We never had such a big number of terrorist activities in Israel as it started since the recognition of the PLO by the Israeli government in September 1993. The Palestinian Authority does not fulfill its commitments toward Israel. They do not respect and honor their commitments toward the Israeli government. And, our expectation is that the Palestinians will take responsibility and will not use the Jewish morality, the Israeli morality for political purpose. I hope that the Palestinians will understand that it is really a historical opportunity to reach real and permanent peace with all the meaning. They cannot on one hand talk peace and on the other hand to give a hand to terrorist activities. They must stop totally any kind of terrorist activity. And we are not in the Wild West, as it was in American history: if you do not accept my position, I will shoot you and kill you. We are in the process of making peace in spite of all the difficulties, all the differences. We must arrive to the compromise without using guns for achieving goals.

Manouchehr Bibiyan: After the Likud Party came to power, bombing in the buses and centers with large populations in Israel decreased visibly. And, the tone of the Israeli officials—the Prime Minister and Cabinet Ministers—became moderate toward the Islamic Republic. Has there been a direct or indirect negotiation with Iran, which has resulted in the decrease in terrorist activities?

Katsav: I don't blame the Labor Party for the increase of terrorist activities. You mentioned very terrible terrorist activity at the beginning of the year in Tel Aviv and Jerusalem, when the previous government in Israel was in power. I blame only the terrorists; I blame only the Arab leaders—our enemy. So, I hope that the situation, the calm, which was started since the last election, will continue and will be continued. And I hope that they will not be able or will not try to start new terrorist activities. It is not related to Iran. Iran tries to cooperate with the terrorists in the Middle East and give them all their backing. And I know very well that from the South of Lebanon, Iran is very active and involved in terrorist activity. But, Iran itself could some day suffer from this negative initiative. And, unfortunately, we have no cooperation with the Iranians. And, I hope that the Iranians will change their policy toward Israel and give us the possibility to deal with the Iranian rulers.

Manouchehr Bibiyan: Please answer this question in Persian. What occurred in the exhibition in London which took place a few days ago? Was your visit to the Iranian booth at this exhibition a coincidence or was it pre-planned?

Katsav: I, myself, do not know what the issue was. But, I went over to Iran's booth, which was close to Israel's booth at this exhibition in London. I talked to them. They knew that I was Deputy Prime Minister and Cabinet Minister. They were happy to talk to me. I invited them to come over to Israel's booth. They came. We talked and said that God willing, one day Israel and Iran will resume relations, so that they can come to Israel and that we can go to Iran. We opened the map. They gave me An'aam, I gave them An'aam.

Manouchehr Bibiyan: They gave you cadeau [gift], and you gave them cadeau.

Katsav: Yes. We hope that one day we can see each other in both Israel and Tehran.

Manouchehr Bibiyan: How did you know where exactly the city of Yazd is on the map? I have heard that you immediately pointed to the city of Yazd on the map.

Katsav: [Laughter] I knew. I am not illiterate. I opened the map and I knew Bidiook [in Hebrew]

Manouchehr Bibiyan: Bidioook: Daghighan [exactly]

Katsav: Exactly where the heart of Yazd is.

Manouchehr Bibiyan: For the Iranian community, would you discuss the issue of the discovery and reconstruction of the tunnel in the neighborhood of the Western Wall, which caused controversy. Is it true that the Solomon Rooms are in the area of this tunnel, and that the Palestinians, who are in possession of the Al Aqsa Mosque which is located on the Western Wall, have made an opening and have descended in the tunnel and have taken possession of the Solomon Rooms? An Israeli newspaper has reported that eight months before the Labor Government's term in office ended, the Labor Government knew about this issue and that when you and your colleagues came to power, you also knew about this issue but you kept silent and did not talk about it. Is this true?

Katsav: The Palestinians, the Wagf in Jerusalem, they knew very well, in the last three years, about the work in the tunnel. They visited there and they saw the plan. And, they never said anything about the discovering of the Western Wall. The Western Wall belongs to the Jews. I hope that the Palestinians, the Muslims, have no claims about the Western Wall. Our holy temple was destroyed almost two thousand years ago. And, we have only this piece of the wall from the holy temple. So, if it was so difficult for the Palestinians, why in the last three years they never said anything about the work in the tunnel. I will tell you why. Because they knew at that time very well that there is not any danger to Al Aqsa. It has nothing to do with the Muslim monument in Jerusalem. And, the direction of the Western Wall is quite opposite to the direction of the Al Aqsa Mosque. It is correct, it was a best package deal, which the previous government gave to the Muslims and to the Palestinians, i.e. the possibility to pray on the Solomon Rooms on the condition that we will be able to open the way for more visitors to come to see the Western Wall in the tunnel. I must say that the complete Western Wall and the part of the Western Wall in the tunnel is significant; it is magnificent. It is unbelievable. One stone weighs more than five hundred tons. How did the Jews bring these heavy stones, two thousand years ago, to put it and to build the Western Wall? It is unbelievable, and I have no answer. In any case, each year almost 70,000 people visit the Western Wall in the tunnel. And by opening the tunnel, we give the possibility to 400,000 visitors, each year, to come to see the glory of the Western Wall in the tunnel. We had not any political purpose by opening the tunnel. We just wanted to give the chance to more visitors to enjoy this historical monument. And, of course, it is not regarding to any conflict between Jews and Arabs.

Manouchehr Bibiyan: What price are you willing to pay for peace? As they say in Hebrew: Zot Omeret Eizo Mekhir?

Katsav: Peace is good for all sides. It is good for the Arabs; it is good for the Israelis. Bloodshed is bad for all sides. It is very bad for the Arabs; it is very bad for the Israelis. And, of course, we are ready to pay a very high price to reach real peace and permanent peace. And, we hope that we could arrive to the compromise with the Palestinians. We have some ideas and we raise those ideas on the table, not by the media.

Manouchehr Bibiyan: If it is possible, please respond to this question in Persian. What message do you have for Iranians?

Katsav: You leave me no choice but to speak in Persian. I am very happy to be here and to talk to you. I have been in the United States for almost a week. Every time I can see the Jews, I can see the Iranians, of course, it makes me happy. It is very important to me that we stay close together with Iranians, and be close. I thank you very much for giving me time to talk to you. I send my greetings to all Iranians living in the United States.

Manouchehr Bibiyan: Dear viewers. In Israel, the Iranian Jews say to Mr. Katsav in Hebrew: "Geyim Bekha", "We are proud of you". And, it was about the same time last year when I was in Israel and Mr. Katsav kindly invited me for his birthday celebration. There, 400 top Israeli officials, including the Cabinet Ministers of both the Likud and the Labor Party, the Joint Chief of Staff, and other top officials who are friends of Mr. Katsav, were present. And, Mr. Netanyahu was there, and I had the honor to talk to him briefly. Of course, he invited me to go to the Knesset, the Israeli Parliament, on Tuesday of that week which unfortunately I could not to go to the Knesset that day. That night, I realized how much Mr. Katsav is respected by even the Labor Party and other political parties in Israel. But, what was surprising to me was that for the first time, I saw that the hotel was surrounded with the Israeli military forces. I think the reason for this was that it was a short time before that

that Yitzhak Rabin was assassinated, and for this reason they were cautious to prevent other unforeseen events. In any case, with thanks to Mr. Katsav for this interview, including his responses in Persian. Until the near future, when we talk again.

Katsav: Thank you Mr. Bibiyan.

Abul Hassan Banisadr

The first President of the Islamic Republic

Abulhassan Banisadr

Manouchehr Bibiyan's Interview with Abulhassan Banisadr

Date of the Interview: 23 June 1999

Manouchehr Bibiyan: Prior to the revolution, it appears that the National Iranian Oil Company was engaged in conducting negotiations to participate in projects and exploitations of the North Sea petroleum, and perhaps those negotiations resulted in contracts. Do you have any information regarding this issue, and if you do, what are the facts? And what happened to Iran's share? Does Iran still have a share in those projects?

Bani Sadr: The National Iranian Oil Company in the Shah's regime invested in the petroleum of the North Sea. But, after the Khordad 1360 (1982), that is, the coup d'etat against me, among the issues which have remained suspicious until today, it is this [Iran's investment in the] petroleum of the North Sea. On one occasion, [Premier] Bazargan asked: "what happened to the North petroleum? What happened to Iran's share of the petroleum of the North?" And, we also raised the issue abroad several times, and there is still silence [on this issue]. In any case, the information which I have is this. Silence. What really happened to it I do not know.

Manouchehr Bibiyan: You are saying that after the revolution, regarding the petroleum of the North Sea, which refers to the petroleum of the North Sea and Iran's share in the British sector of the North Sea, there was no longer—

Banisadr: Yes. Yes, the petroleum of the North Sea.

Manouchehr Bibiyan: Yes. And after the revolution there was no longer any official agenda to discuss this issue?

Banisadr: They did not even answer the questions which were raised on this issue of what happened to that oil? Did they transfer it to the British? Did they sell it? Did they buy it? There is silence.

Manouchehr Bibiyan: Do you have any other comments on this subject? Because this issue—

Banisadr: Any other comment requires accurate information, and I do not have it.

Manouchehr Bibiyan: You do not have?

Banisadr: The extent of my information is what I told you.

Manouchehr Bibiyan: When Khomeini came to Iran, was Khomeini determined to assume total authority and power, or

did the persons who were in his entourage create this political situation or circumstances for him to assume this totalitarian position in Iran?

Bani Sadr: The latter is accurate. Now, we are not saying that he was not interested in power. He had a tendency to seek power. However, when he arrived in Iran, he did not see the possibility in himself or the [political] environment to advance this totalitarianism. These tools were provided for him and he used these tools. First, a preamble to the constitution was provided which was based on public sovereignty. In fact, the Velayati-Fagih [Governance of the Jurist] was not a part of it. The hostage-taking issue occurred, the Pasdaran [Revolutionary Guards] was established, the revolutionary court was established, the [revolutionary] committees were created, [and] the tools of power were established. Later, the hostage-taking also provided the necessary internal and external circumstances. The Majlis-e-Khebragan [Assembly of Experts] also encouraged the Governance of the Jurist. This was supposed to—and Mr. Khomeini turned the Governance of the Jurist into a Totalitarian Governance.

Manouchehr Bibiyan: The last question that I want to ask you is what came to my mind regarding the Imperial Iranian military. In the process of the revolution, the Shah's military declared its neutrality, or it surrendered. Therefore, who is responsible for the execution of the Shah's military officials and leaders?

Bani Sadr: At that time, from the time Mr. Khomeni was in Paris, the late Forouhar came and brought a message from the leaders of the Shah's military. According to what he said, from the Shah's military leaders. And, I told Mr. Khomeini, and he wrote a letter, a long letter which we gave to Mr. Forouhar. And, when we descended from the aircraft, Mr. Forouhar left earlier than we did because he wanted to give the letter to the Shah's military leaders. And after that, after the [occurrence] of the revolution, as he did with other promises that he had made, he did not fulfill them. He also arrested many of those helpless people and killed them, and Mr. Khalkhali said that he killed them upon the orders of Khomeini. I don't believe that he killed them all upon the orders of Khomeini, because Khomeini did not act; he reacted.

Manouchehr Bibiyan: Thank you Mr. Bani Sadr for this interview and with your permission, we will publish this interview in our forthcoming book.

Bani Sadr: Very well. Thank you.

Manouchehr Bibiyan's Interview with Moshe Katsav

Date of Broadcast: January 2005
Location of the Interview: the Presidential Palace

Manouchehr Bibiyan: I would like to ask a question and it's up to you to decide whether or not to answer it. My question is about Iran's nuclear capabilities. According to different sources, Iran would be able to develop nuclear bomb in the future. If Iran develops nuclear bomb and long-range missile capable of reaching Europe, does Israel view itself as being in danger?

Moshe Katsav: I hope that Iran will not be able to develop nuclear weapons. Iran does not have any need for nuclear weapons. No enemy threatens the existence or security of Iran to justify the development of nuclear weapons.

Iran does not need long-range missiles. Iran suffers from tough economic and social conditions, and is better off investing its resources in developing the country rather than destructive weapons. Instead of investing its resources in destruction, it would be better off investing in improving the lives of poor people.

Israel has no conflict with Iran. There is no conflict of interests between Israel and Iran. We do not have a common border with Iran. Jewish people have lived in Iran for 2,500 years. There is no conflict either between Judaism and Islam. Islam came about only 1,430 years ago, and we respect Islam. The Arab nation and the Jewish nation have the same father. If Iran would try to hurt us, we will defend ourselves. Our scientists are among the leaders in the world, and with God's help, we will be able to defend ourselves as much as necessary in case we need to. I would like to stress that we have no intention to have a war against Iran.

Manouchehr Bibiyan: Thank you very much.

Moshe Katsav: Thank you too. Please give my best wishes to everybody.

Index

About the Author

This intriguing book by Manouchehr Bibiyan, producer and president of Los Angeles based JAAM-E-JAM Television Network, is a rare political document and a credible historical primary source on the history of modern Iran.

Based on the many interviews of Mr. Manouchehr Bibiyan and his staff with Iranian public figures over the years, *Secrets of the Iranian Revolution* is a unique and rare glimpse behind the scenes of one of the most turbulent modern revolutions.

Mr. Manouchehr Bibiyan, the producer and president of JAAM-E-JAM Television Network, continues to be a prominent, influential, active and permanent presence in the arenas of music, culture and politics as he has for the more than fifty-three years in Iran and the United States. He was born on November 22, 1933 in Tehran. After completing high school and higher education in Tehran and Tel Aviv, he soon contributed to the field of Journalism. Prior to the Iranian Revolution, Manouchehr Bibiyan was Iran's biggest producer of Iranian music and for twenty-five years (1954-1979), he produced eighty percent of Iran's music.

During the Shah's regime, Iran's national radio and television produced about ten percent of Iran's music. Therefore, throughout this period it primarily broadcast the music produced by Manouchehr Bibiyan's music company, Apollon. As President of Apollon Music Company, he introduced the most successful and celebrated Iranian singers to the Iranian public. With the cooperation of young and talented songwriters and composers, Mr. Bibiyan introduced pop and jazz to Iranians, revolutionizing Iran's music industry.

During the Iranian Revolution and with the likelihood of the imminent establishment of an Islamic republic, Manouchehr Bibiyan left Iran and established residency in Los Angeles. In 1980, he founded Pars Video in order to preserve Iranian music, language and culture outside Iran. A year later, in 1981, in response to historic necessity, he founded JAAM-E-JAM Television. This medium was a bridge between the displaced Iranians in their first few years of exile and a link to the larger community in America.

Within a few short years, JAAM-E-JAM Television was broadcasting its programs nationwide, and currently it broadcasts worldwide via satellite. In addition to broadcasting news reports, political commentaries, theatrical plays, modern music and informative and educational programs, JAAM-E-JAM Television broadcasts a program entitled *Tribun-e-Azaad* (Open Forum), consisting of interviews conducted by the author, Manouchehr Bibiyan, and his staff with world leaders and political figures. *Open Forum* became a medium for recording, preserving and presenting the secrets of history. Both Iranian and world statespersons participated in the forum.

For the first time in history, Iranian statespersons from the old regime of the Shah narrated the historical events and revealed the secrets of the causes and consequences of the Iranian Revolution for the hundreds of thousands of viewers of JAAM-E-JAM Television.

These interviews and discussions were recorded on video, and the text of these fascinating and insightful interviews is now presented in this volume as an oral history and a significant primary source on the modern history of Iran and the Iranian Revolution of 1978-1979.

LaVergne, TN USA
21 October 2010
201706LV00002B/128/P